The Betrayal of Charity

The Betrayal of Charity
The Sins that Sabotage Divine Love

MATTHEW LEVERING

BAYLOR UNIVERSITY PRESS

Cover Design by Natalya Balnova
Cover Art: Betrayal of Christ, 1308-11, Duccio di Buoninsegna,
(c.1278-1318) / Museo dell'Opera del Duomo, Siena, Italy / The
Bridgeman Art Library International

Library of Congress Cataloging-in-Publication Data

Levering, Matthew, 1971-
  The betrayal of charity : the sins that sabotage divine love / Matthew
Levering.
      p. cm.
  Includes bibliographical references (p.   ) and index.
  ISBN 978-1-60258-356-6 (pbk. : alk. paper)
  1. Charity. 2. Sin--Christianity. 3. Thomas, Aquinas, Saint, 1225?-
1274. 4. Love--Religious aspects--Catholic Church. I. Title.
  BV4639.L448 2011
  241'.677--dc22
                                    2010052544

Printed in the United States of America on acid-free paper with a
minimum of 30% pcw recycled content.

To
Joy Levering

Contents

Acknowledgments

This book focuses on the sins against charity, but it arose from the generosity and kindness of many wonderful friends. Michael Root, whom I have been privileged to call my friend since we enjoyed a good Italian dinner together in Naples (Florida) some years ago, and Jim Buckley, a friend from the Evangelicals and Catholics Together group in New York, invited me to speak at the June 2009 conference of the Center for Catholic and Evangelical Theology. That presentation developed into chapter 5. Greg Reichberg invited me to co-organize a conference on the Catholic theology of just war. This conference took place in July 2009 and was lots of fun, largely because of Greg's organizational skill. Working with him was a real delight; may God make it possible again soon. My participation in that conference resulted in the essay that forms chapter 7. As I was preparing these two essays, it became clear to me that an exciting research project on the sins against charity might be possible. Following the path charted by St. Thomas Aquinas in the *Summa Theologiae*, I began to write other chapters with this goal in mind.

Kevin Thornton, who shepherded my *Christ and the Catholic Priesthood: Ecclesial Hierarchy and the Pattern of the Trinity* through Hillenbrand Books, invited me to deliver a lecture to the Liturgical

Institute at Mundelein Seminary in April 2009. At the instigation of David Fagerberg, part of this lecture was published as "Liturgical Mediation: Help or Hindrance to the Unity of the People of God?" (*Assembly: A Journal of Liturgical Theology* 35 [2009]: 50–54). The full, revised version became chapter 6. Through the kind auspices of Scott Hahn, I published "Charity and Empire: Is Trinitarian Mono- theism Violent?" (*Letter & Spirit* 5 [2009]: 155–71). Chapter 1 is a revised version of this article. Many thanks to Kevin, David, and Scott for their ongoing friendship. Other chapters benefited from insights of the students who took my spring 2009 course on charity, includ- ing John Froula, Jared Kuebler, Chad Raith, and David Tamisea.

I wish also to thank Romanus Cessario, O.P., under whom I stud- ied the theological virtues as a graduate student in the late 1990s. Carey Newman of Baylor University Press took this manuscript in hand in a simply extraordinary manner. For his encouragement, and for that of the two anonymous readers, I am deeply grateful. Alan Mostrom, a gifted doctoral student in theology at the University of Dayton, compiled the bibliography. I have too many other debts to mention here, but let me particularly thank Reinhard Hütter, Jared Staudt, and Tim Gray for their friendship in editing *Nova et Vetera*; Thomas Joseph White, Andrew Hofer, Bernhard Blankenhorn, and Richard Schenk for their Dominican encouragement; Hans Boersma and David Novak for the privilege of working together on ecumeni- cal and Jewish-Christian dialogue, respectively; and all who have phoned and visited my family and me during our adjustment to Dayton.

My gratitude for such friends and benefactors is all the deeper given that the experience of abandonment is all too common in this world. To know the sins against charity requires knowing charity. Thus the charity of my parents, brother, and in-laws continues to inspire me. I owe special thanks to my mother for reading and dis- cussing portions of this book in relationship to her own work.

I dedicate this book to my beloved Joy Levering. Beloved wife, dear companion in good times and bad, faithful and wise friend, trea- sured mother of our children, "Set me as a seal upon your heart, as a seal upon your arm" (Song 8:6). May God the Father, Son, and Holy Spirit be praised now and forever.

Introduction

In chapter 13 of his First Letter to the Corinthians, the Apostle
Paul famously praises charity as never-ending and as greater even
than faith and hope. As the biblical scholar Richard Hays observes,
however, Paul actually devotes most of his attention to charity's
opposites. Hays shows that "the weight of Paul's interest falls upon
the eight negative items in the list, most of which correspond
closely to the behavior of the Corinthians as described elsewhere
in the letter."[1] Why are the sins against charity so prominent in
Paul's exposition? The answer has been well expressed by William
Cavanaugh, adapting the opening line of Jean-Jacques Rousseau's
The Social Contract: "Humankind was created for communion, but
is everywhere divided."[2]

Hays goes on to say that "Paul's poetic depiction of love's character is aimed at calling the members of the Corinthian community out of schism and into unity with each other."[3] Read properly,
therefore, 1 Corinthians 13 is the very opposite of "all sweetly sen-
timental notions of love"; instead it sets forth "a rigorous vision of
love that rejoices in the truth and bears all suffering in the name
of Jesus Christ."[4] As Paul makes clear, we can learn what love
requires only by facing the consequences of our lack of love.

Nonetheless, Hays does not think that charity has enough heft to serve as one of the unifying themes of New Testament ethics. Instead, he chooses the themes of community, cross, and new creation. Because the word "love" rarely appears in Mark, Acts, Hebrews, and Revelation, Hays suggests that "a synthesis of the New Testament's message based on the theme of love drives these texts to the periphery of the canon."[5] These texts lack the word "love," but they teach about the cross, which is what love means. Hays is on guard against the contemporary correlation of "love" with "inclusiveness."

If the word "love" lacks the heft that it once had, can its meaning be recovered so that Jesus' commandment "that you love one another as I have loved you" (John 15:12[6]) reclaims its proper centrality? Pope Benedict XVI's recent encyclical *Deus Caritas Est* is a recent attempt to reclaim the centrality of love. With an eye to sins against charity, he emphasizes the unity and reconciliation that love brings: "Love is 'divine' because it comes from God and unites us to God; through this unifying process it makes us a 'we' which transcends our divisions and makes us one, until in the end God is 'all in all' (1 Cor 15:28)."[7] This emphasis on unity appears in Jesus' promise that the one who loves him will be loved not only by the Son, but also by the Father and the Holy Spirit, so that "we will come to him and make our home with him" (John 14:23).

The present book likewise attempts to reclaim the centrality of love for moral theology and indeed for all areas of theology. For this effort I am particularly indebted to St. Thomas Aquinas, who places charity at the center of his *Summa Theologiae*. Aquinas explains that charity is the friendship that arises when the triune God, who is infinite love, "communicates his happiness to us."[8] Aquinas fills out the concrete meaning of love by examining its effects: interior joy and peace, exterior mercy, beneficence, almsgiving, and fraternal correction. Like Paul, Aquinas' discussion of charity in the *Summa Theologiae* also attends carefully to its opposites, among which Aquinas includes hatred, sloth, envy, discord, contention, schism, war, strife, sedition, and scandal.

Although in contemporary theology the sins against charity have not received attention as a group, nonetheless each of them has a prominent role within specific contemporary discussions. As we will see, hatred comes up in recent critiques of monotheism by such scholars as Regina Schwartz, Laurel Schneider, and Harold Bloom; the problems associated with sloth are raised by Timothy Jackson's effort to dissociate Christian charity from belief in life after death; envy plays a major role in American understandings of self-reliance, informed by Ralph Waldo Emerson; ecclesial discord and contention form the subplot of John O'Malley's presentation of the Second Vatican Council's breakthroughs; Walter Brueggemann and others critique liturgical hierarchy as a masked power play that foments schism; the theology of John Howard Yoder aims to help Christians embody an alternative to war, strife, and sedition; and René Girard's theology of the cross hinges on his interpretation of scandal.

Profoundly influential in their respective domains, these discussions are also widely separated, so that their leading figures rarely interact with each other. A close look at each discussion, however, shows that controversy over the nature of charity (and thus of the sins against charity) drives the discussions. This is not surprising since contemporary theology operates within a highly divided cultural context that hungers for love, joy, and peace without consensus on where to find them. By engaging such diverse discussions in a relatively brief fashion, the book's chapters on the sins against charity may appear disjointed to those who fail to perceive the unifying purpose. But in accord with Alasdair MacIntyre's warning against conceiving morality as "a distinct and largely autonomous category of thought and practice,"[9] I seek to underscore the connections between the life of charity and the triune God, the church, the theology of the cross, the resurrection of the dead, sacramental mediation, and so on. It is this centrality of charity that allows Paul to say: "If I give away all I have, and if I deliver my body to be burned, but have not love, I gain nothing" (1 Cor 13:3).

The first chapter considers whether the act of charity, as understood by believers in the triune God, is itself an act of exclusion and violence—a critique put forward by an increasing number of scholars, including Regina Schwartz and Laurel Schneider, whose views I examine here. I seek to show that by the act of charity, which points the human person toward loving God and neighbor and away from a self-centered focus on being loved, believers love the goodness of others and love enemies who would otherwise be excluded. Hatred is charity's opposite, but recent popular treatments of Israel's God have portrayed that God as eminently worthy of hatred. My second chapter asks why one would hate God and argues that the answer has to do with a focus on temporal goods. Chapter 3 examines sloth, which as sorrow about spiritual goods negates charity's interior effect of joy. I argue that without faith in the resurrection of the dead, one cannot avoid falling into sloth. Chapter 4 treats envy, which as sorrow over the good of our neighbor also negates joy. I read Aquinas' theology of envy in light of Jewish and Christian exegetical and theological discussions of envy in the book of Genesis, and I suggest that reliance on God as giver of all goodness is the only cure for envy.

Turning to the sins opposed to the interior effect of charity that is peace, chapter 5 examines peace as the solution to discord and contention. I suggest that Aquinas' approach can help us to understand why primarily sociological understandings of the reception of the Second Vatican Council are not sufficient for appreciating the peace that Christ gives to the church despite the presence of discord and contention. Chapter 6 treats schism as opposed to peace, with the goal of understanding why Numbers 16 teaches that liturgical hierarchy enriches rather than diminishes the unity of the people of God. Chapter 7 addresses war. I examine the biblical interpretation that undergirds John Howard Yoder's conclusion that war cannot be other than a sin against charity and Aquinas' conclusion that war, for one side at least, need not be a sin against charity. Chapter 8 takes up scandal, which is opposed to beneficence and fraternal correction. Aquinas understands scandal to be the deliberate effort to cause spiritual downfall, in contrast with René Girard's theory of scandal as mimetic rivalry that leads to the bloody sacrifice of a scapegoat.

The sins against charity oppose dependence on God and thereby undermine human interdependence. Hatred repudiates the infinitely lovable God and prevents us from loving God's goodness in our neighbor; we imagine God to be against us. Sloth sorrows over the healing and deifying gifts of God, and envy supposes that God's gifting operates within a framework of scarcity and stinginess. Hatred, discord, contention, schism, war, strife, and sedition undermine communion. Scandal opposes the providential pattern of beneficence (and fraternal correction) by actively seeking to harm others spiritually. In the sins against charity, we ourselves become the oppressive "god" who does violence to others, the god feared by anti-monotheists such as Schwartz and Schneider. Fortunately, however, "God is love" (1 John 4:16).

Aquinas on Charity: An Overview

A brief summary of Aquinas' theology of charity, including its relation to faith and hope, will prepare for our study.[10] Charity is a supernatural virtue, infused by God in order not only to heal the fallen human will, but also to elevate the human will to a sharing in the love of the Trinity. As a deeper participation in divine love, charity relates the human person in particular to the person of the Holy Spirit, even though as a created effect in the soul, charity is not the same as the Holy Spirit.[11]

Aquinas recognizes that charity is not the sole foundation of love in the human person. Plato, in the voice of Diotima, describes human beings as "lovers of the good" who desire to possess the good forever; love desires the "everlasting loveliness which neither comes nor goes."[12] As Plato summarizes the ascent of *eros*: "Starting from individual beauties, the quest for the universal beauty must find him ever mounting the heavenly ladder, stepping from rung to rung—that is, from one to two, and from two to *every* lovely body, from bodily beauty to the beauty of institutions, from institutions to learning," and from learning to the heavenly form or idea of beauty.[13] Without directly taking up Plato's discussion of the erotic ascent, Aristotle adds to it a rich discussion of friendship in books 8 and 9 of his *Nicomachean Ethics*.

Among the most enduring debates about charity are those about the relationship of Greek philosophical *eros* and *philia* to Christian *agape* (as used in the New Testament to describe self-giving love).[14] In the *Summa Theologiae*, Aquinas discusses *amor* in his treatment of the sense passions that arise in response to a good.[15] He distinguishes *amor* from *dilectio* and *caritas*. *Dilectio* includes the element of free choice, intellectual consent to the good, while *caritas* adds to *dilectio* supernatural elevation of the will to the Trinitarian good, so as to love God and all others in God.[16] For Aquinas every love, not only charity, involves the real union and mutual indwelling of the lover and beloved.[17] Every love involves an "extasis," or going out of oneself toward the beloved.[18] Furthermore, Aquinas appreciates the complex interplay between our sense powers and intellectual powers. The sense passion *amor* is integrated into rational love; charity contains the movement of *eros*.[19]

As Michael Sherwin has eloquently shown, Aquinas holds that to understand charity one must understand faith, since the intellect and the will operate together.[20] Faith unites the intellect to God as "First Truth." Interpreting Hebrews 11:1, Aquinas defines faith as "a habit of the mind, whereby eternal life is begun in us, making the intellect assent to what is non-apparent."[21] First Truth, as the object of faith revealed by God in history, contains the realities of salvation, above all the mysteries of Christ Jesus and the kingdom of God.[22] Aquinas teaches that these mysteries can be known implicitly or explicitly, thereby ensuring that not only those who come after the time of Christ can be saved.[23] The most profound mystery that we know when our minds are raised by the grace of the Holy Spirit to First Truth is the mystery of the divine Trinity. As Aquinas notes, "God's sovereign goodness as we understand it now through its effects, can be understood without the Trinity of Persons: but as understood in itself, and as seen by the Blessed, it cannot be understood without the Trinity of Persons."[24] We do not merely apprehend the Trinity conceptually, but rather the historical missions of the Son and Holy Spirit draw us into the very life of the Trinity.

If faith is the first step in this union with the Trinity, charity is the "form" of faith because our knowing God is ordered to bearing fruit in love of the Father, Son, and Holy Spirit. The end or goal of our faith in the Trinity is that we share in the divine goodness by loving God the Trinity.[25] This goal fuels our hope. Faith teaches us to hope that by his salvific power, God will give us eternal communion with himself, infinite triune goodness.[26] Following Jesus' words to his disciples (John 15:15), and indebted also to Aristotle's *Nicomachean Ethics*, Aquinas identifies this communion with the Trinity as a "friendship": God enables us to love him as his friends by establishing a communication (*communicatio*) and likeness (*similitudo*) between us and God.[27] For Aquinas, as Guy Mansini points out, "*communicatio* means having goods in common" so as to provide the basis for "friendly concourse."[28] By communicating to us his blessedness (that is, himself), God causes in us a likeness in love, "a participation of divine charity."[29]

This communication comes about in Christ and his sacramental body, the church.[30] In Christ and through the grace of his Holy Spirit, believers are configured to God's charitable likeness by means of the sacraments, benevolence, the works of mercy, and so forth. Thus, although charity is beyond our natural powers, and although it orders us to eternal communion with the Trinity, charity is no otherworldly virtue. Rather, charity transforms and elevates our natural love so as to build up communities ordered to the common good, the Trinitarian communion of love.[31] Although in our earthly lives the "communication or fellowship [*conversatio*]" and "likeness" are imperfect—even those who have advanced from the beginning and proficient stages to "perfect" charity still lack the full perfection of charity—the glory of our heavenly sharing in God the Trinity will perfect our charity.[32]

Aquinas denies that the grace of the Holy Spirit gives us charity in proportion to our natural virtue. The gift of charity, while certainly building upon natural virtue, is entirely gratuitous; the fact that we are naturally disposed to friendship does not mean that we have an advantage over others in regards to attaining supernatural charity. As a participation in the divine love, charity enlarges our hearts and enables us always to increase in charity during this life, but charity also can be lost. Certain actions are incompatible with charity. As the Letter of James teaches, we cannot lay claim to charity while neglecting God or our neighbor; we must "be doers of the word, and not hearers only" (Jas 1:22). If we freely act against God's law of love, we thereby lose charity by preferring "sin to God's friendship, which requires that we should obey his will."[33] Given our weakness, the life of charity depends upon the grace of the Holy Spirit, which frees a person to "deny himself and take up his cross and follow me [Jesus]" (Mark 8:34). Servais Pinckaers observes in this regard that "radical self-renunciation is a necessary condition for love of Christ. There is no real charity without detachment and self-renunciation. As love deepens through trial, so its capacity for sacrifice grows stronger."[34]

In charity, we love God and neighbor (as well as ourselves) in the *same* act. Our love for God must always include our love of self and neighbor, and our love for self and neighbor must always be ordered to our love for God. At first glance this might appear to be a strange teaching. When we are loving the infinitely lovable God, must we have in view our far less lovable neighbor, let alone ourselves? Aquinas sees this from an eschatological perspective: "The aspect under which our neighbor is to be loved, is God, since what we ought to love in our neighbor is that he may be in God. Hence it is clear that it is specifically the same act whereby we love God, and whereby we love our neighbor."[35] The same holds with our love of self.[36] Aquinas' perspective is also rooted in the theology of creation. We love our neighbors, including our enemies, because insofar as they exist, they participate in God the Trinity. We love them as creatures called to attain to the fullness of beatific participation in God the Trinity. Thus we can love them without loving their sins.

We do not love irrational animals or demons in this act of charity, because neither irrational animals nor demons can share in the Trinitarian communion; in another sense, however, we do love them in charity by wishing them to endure (and glorify God) as regards their natural being, which is good. Charity has a particular order defined by relation to the good and by obligations that we have with regard to others' welfare.

Aquinas concludes his discussion of charity in the *Summa Theologiae* by exploring the gift of the Holy Spirit that specially enhances our ability to live the charitable life: the gift of wisdom.[37] Following the patristic and medieval exegetical tradition, his understanding of the gift of wisdom relies upon Isaiah and Paul. According to Isaiah, the Davidic Messiah will possess the spirit of the Lord, "the spirit of wisdom and understanding, the spirit of counsel and might, the spirit of knowledge and the fear of the Lord" (Isa 11:2).[38] In Christ, believers share in these gifts. Aquinas cites 1 Corinthians 2, where Paul seeks to show that "we have the mind of Christ" (1 Cor 2:16) because we "receive the gifts of the Spirit of God" (1 Cor 2:14) who "searches everything, even the depths of God" (1 Cor 2:10). In the person who has faith and charity, the gift of wisdom makes it possible to judge the truth of divine realities "on account of connaturality with them," and not merely by study.[39] The gift of wisdom assists in guiding our actions so that they accord with God's law of love. With Augustine, Aquinas associates this gift with the beatitude, "Blessed are the peacemakers, for they shall be called sons of God" (Matt 5:9). Charity and wisdom unite in the effect of peace and configure us to the image of Wisdom incarnate, Jesus Christ.[40]

Sins against Charity

In a general sense, as will be clear, all sins oppose charity. How then does Aquinas identify particular sins against charity? He begins with charity's direct opposite, hatred. He then considers charity's interior and exterior effects. Interiorly, charity causes joy, peace, and mercy. The charitable person takes joy in God's presence, a joy negated by sloth and envy. In a union of wills with God and neighbor, the charitable person experiences peace to the degree that it can be experienced in this life. Love of neighbor leads to mercy, because we take pity on the neighbor's suffering as if it were our own. Peace and mercy are negated by discord, contention, war, and strife. Exteriorly, charity causes three kinds of actions in particular: beneficence, works of mercy or almsdeeds (*eleemosyna*), and fraternal correction. To be beneficent is to do good to someone. The goodwill that the charitable person has for his or her friend leads to beneficence. Almsdeeds consist in helping the needy by bestowing either bodily or spiritual goods. Aquinas lists seven bodily almsdeeds, beginning with feeding the hungry, and seven spiritual almsdeeds, beginning with teaching. The mercy of the charitable person leads to the practice of almsdeeds. Lastly, fraternal correction "is a spiritual almsdeed."[41] Beneficence, almsdeeds, and fraternal correction are negated by scandal, schism, and sedition.

Flowing from the grace of the Holy Spirit, these interior and exterior effects constitute the unity of the people of God in charity.[42] The sins against charity, for their part, directly undo what the unity of charity establishes.

Recent studies of charity have generally neglected the sins against charity, largely because charity in itself provides sufficient material for study. Michael Sherwin focuses on the will's relationship to practical reasoning, the relationship of intellect and will in the act of faith, and charity's relationship to knowledge. Timothy Jackson aims to develop a theology of "strong *agape*" in dialogue with a wide array of literary, biblical, theological, and philosophical voices as well as moral problems. Stephen Pope argues that scientific theories of the evolution of altruism can fit with Aquinas' theology of the order of charity. Paul Wadell employs friendship as the lens for interpreting charity. Eric Silverman shows how love benefits the lover. Benedict XVI's *Deus Caritas Est* focuses on the Christian appropriation of *eros* within *agape* and reflects upon the church's practice of charitable activity in relation to the state's enterprises.[43]

By concentrating on charity rather than on the sins that destroy it, these studies have obviously "chosen the good portion" (Luke 10:42). Even so, is there an advantage to contemplating charity in light of its opposites? Rabbi Joseph Telushkin takes something like this approach in his popular two-volume *A Code of Jewish Ethics* (I discuss a portion of this work in chapter 4). The format of Telushkin's work imitates that of the Mishnah and Maimonides' *Mishneh Torah*, and he also employs the Talmud's practice of including stories and anecdotes illustrating his teaching.[44] He places both volumes under the rubric of "love your neighbor as yourself" (Lev 19:18), whose centrality is signaled by Rabbi Akiva and Rabbi Hillel in the Talmud. In the first volume, titled *You Shall Be Holy*, he has sections on "Basic Virtues and Vices" that include envy, hatred, and humiliation (which he presents as close to scandal). The second volume, titled *Love Your Neighbor as Yourself*, includes the acts of charity that Aquinas specifies under almsdeeds, and also takes up war, strife, and sedition. Both volumes ground the discussion of love upon God the Creator and lawgiver: "Take away the divine foundations for teachings such as 'Love your neighbor as yourself' (the basis for the Golden Rule), and they make no sense."[45]

Consider also part 3 of the *Catechism of the Catholic Church* on "Life in Christ." Like Aquinas, the catechism describes charity as "friendship and communion" (§1829) and identifies the interior and exterior effects of charity as joy, peace, mercy, beneficence, and fraternal correction. The catechism comments that hatred of God views God merely "as the one who forbids sins and inflicts punishments" (§2094); sloth "goes so far as to refuse the joy that comes from God and to be repelled by divine goodness" (§2094); scandal tempts the neighbor into sin (§2284); war is an "ancient bondage" to be avoided if at all possible (§2307); envy consists in "sadness at the sight of another's goods" (§2539). Although the catechism first treats the virtues, including charity, and then treats these sins under the rubric of the Ten Commandments, the catechism's illumination of the charitable life by means of description of sins reflects the value of Aquinas' practice. As Pope Benedict XVI remarks in his encyclical *Caritas in Veritate*, charity is always in danger of being reduced in practice to "sentimentality," to "an empty shell, to be filled in an arbitrary way" (§3).[46] Theological exploration of the sins against charity serves to avert this danger.

In an influential article, Leonard Boyle proposes that Aquinas wrote the *Summa Theologiae* for the purpose of renewing the Dominican order's pastoral explication of moral theology.[47] If so, then the similarities between the approaches of Telushkin, the catechism, and Aquinas may have to do with their shared concern for a pastoral exposition. To exposit love in a pastorally compelling manner requires concrete examples of love's opposites. It is no surprise that in her book on spiritual formation in the context of the seven deadly sins (two of which, envy and sloth, directly oppose charity), Rebecca DeYoung observes, "Reading Aquinas, I found the vices to have revealing and illuminating power."[48]

Reflection upon the sins against charity also enhances dialogue with non-Christians. This is certainly the case in dialogue between Jews and Christians. Even though Jews and Christians disagree about the person of Jesus, it remains the case that, as Markus

Bockmuehl says, "the main features of Jesus' ethics are deeply conversant with Jewish moral presuppositions. . . . Ethics is therefore inalienably theonomous rather than autonomous: both the substance and authority of right behaviour have their source in the God of Israel."[49] For Christians too, charity is inseparable from a theonomous understanding of the moral life. Dialogue with secular theorists likewise benefits from reflecting on sins against charity. For example, inquiring into what "gifts and social solidarity have in common," the Dutch social scientist Aafke Komter argues that "personal and concrete" gifting deepens solidarity.[50] The sins against charity accept an impersonal and abstract understanding of God and other humans, a denial of real gifting (and thus of real solidarity).

The Spiritual Soul and the Sins against Charity

Can remorseless criminality, if caused by neurological damage, be a sin against charity? The answer is no, because severe neurological damage makes impossible the exercise of free will (including charity). Aquinas recognizes that those with healthy brain function will be able to understand better and to will with greater freedom.[51] But does this mean that humans who are burdened with a malformed brain are not persons and are excluded from communion with God in charity?

This is the concern of Hans Reinders in his *Receiving the Gift of Friendship: Profound Disability, Theological Anthropology, and Ethics*.[52] Reinders rightly argues that we need a concept of the "image of God" (Gen 1:27) that includes severely disabled persons who lack any capacity for rationality. He finds that Aquinas' (and the wider Christian tradition's) theology of the *imago Dei* as located in human rationality excludes the severely disabled. At the same time, theologians and biblical scholars such as Nancey Murphy and Joel Green have proposed that the levels of neurological complexity revealed by contemporary study of the brain leave the notion of the spiritual soul without a role to play.[53] Green focuses on how the brain is "sculpted" through our interactions with others, as neural connections are shaped and reshaped (although Green does not address the situation of those whose brains are irreparably damaged).[54] Like

Reinders, Green argues that a relational/covenantal understanding of the "image of God" can do without the spiritual soul.[55]

By contrast, for Aquinas the presence of the spiritual soul is what enables the severely brain-damaged person, as well as children who have not yet reached the age of reason, to be interiorly transformed by God's grace and to share in the communion of charity. Thus, inquiring whether mentally deranged and mentally handicapped persons (*furiosi et amentes*) should be baptized, Aquinas notes an objection: such persons lack the use of reason and therefore should no more be baptized than should irrational animals. In reply, Aquinas points out that such persons "lack the use of reason accidentally, i.e. through some impediment in a bodily organ; but not like irrational animals through want of a rational soul."[56] Whereas empirically a human with severe limbic brain damage is merely "a functionally reptilian organism armed with the cunning of the neocortical brain,"[57] Aquinas allows that even humans with severe brain damage (whether through lack of love as an infant, or in various other ways) are fully human and can be members of the body of Christ in charity due to sacramental grace transforming their spiritual souls. Baptized mentally handicapped persons, "like little children, have the habit of wisdom, which is a gift of the Holy Spirit, but they have not the act, on account of the bodily impediment which hinders the use of reason in them."[58] Aquinas does not dehumanize such persons, nor does he need to follow Reinders' solution and ground their humanity or personhood extrinsically in God's covenantal decree.

Green is certainly correct to highlight the neural activities involved in "memory, consciousness, spiritual experience, the capacity to make decisions on the basis of self-deliberation, planning and action on the basis of that decision, and taking responsibility for these decisions and actions."[59] As regards charity, however, the difficulty with Green's position appears in his repeated insistence that "our identity is formed and found in self-conscious *relationality* with its neural correlates and embodied *narrativity* or formative histories."[60] In comparison with Aquinas' view, this position leaves insufficient room for the human identity—and the Trinitarian participation[61]—of severely mentally handicapped persons.

* * *

Romanus Cessario comments regarding virtue and vice, "The practice of virtue develops a sound and integrated human character, whereas the steady pursuit of vices reduces the self to a disorganized state of potential."[62] In opposition to charity and to its interior and exterior effects, which unite humans to God and each other, the sins against charity result in disorganization and disintegration. "Our soul is bowed down to the dust; our body cleaves to the ground. Rise up, come to our help! Deliver us for the sake of your steadfast love!" (Ps 44:25-26).

CHAPTER 1

Is Charity Violent?

For a growing number of contemporary scholars, charity itself—at least as it has been understood by most Christians over the centuries—is a sin against love. This chapter sets forth these concerns as found in the works of Regina Schwartz and Laurel Schneider, who argue that Trinitarian monotheism imbeds a violent principle of exclusion within human communities. Schwartz and Schneider seek to develop an alternative understanding of charity based on conceptualizing "God" in terms of nonexclusive multiplicity.[1] In light of these concerns, I examine Thomas Aquinas' theology of the act of charity. Does Aquinas' portrait of charity as unitive require the exclusion of those who do not possess charity? Or does charity enable us to love persons who would otherwise be excluded? I conclude by reflecting briefly on the church as the communion of charity.

Trinitarian Monotheism and Empire: Contrasting Views

According to Rémi Brague, it was significant that Constantine was baptized on his deathbed by the leading disciple of Arius, Bishop Eusebius of Nicomedia. Brague argues that Arius' "nontrinitarian monotheism was well suited to the empire."[2] Yet Bishop Eusebius of Nicomedia and his followers failed in their effort to adopt a theology that would have been especially conducive to empire. Agreeing with Brague about the church in the fourth century,[3] Robert Louis Wilken sketches the implications of Trinitarian monotheism for the theology of divine and human love. Wilken points out that both Augustine and Basil the Great emphasize that the Holy Spirit is "love" in the Trinity. He cites especially Basil's exegesis of 1 Corinthians 2:10: "But the greatest proof that the Spirit is one with the Father and the Son is that He is said to have the same relationship to God as the spirit within us has to us."[4] The key for Wilken is that despite the efforts of some, "after the coming of Christ it was not possible to think of God as a solitary monad."[5] God is Trinitarian love who creates and redeems us out of love. As Wilken concludes, "If God is not solitary and exists always in relation, there can be no talk of God that does not involve love. Love unites Father, Son, and Holy Spirit, love brings God into relation with the world, and by love human beings cleave to God."[6]

From the perspective of comparative religion, Guy Stroumsa notes that early Christians denied that the person is "an independent monad, alone responsible—and responsible only—for care of itself."[7] But early Christians enlarged rather than limited the status of the individual self, because the imitation of Christ calls for a renewal that "is no longer reserved for intellectual elites, but is open to every man and every woman, and open to love of the other, by which the love of God now passes."[8] Stroumsa observes that even after Constantine, Christians retained a "deep ambivalence vis-à-vis the political sphere," and he adds that "the opposition between a tolerant paganism and an intolerant Christianity is now recognized for what it is: an idealized and stereotyped image."[9]

By contrast, Regina Schwartz influentially identifies monotheism as a primary cause of violence.[10] Schwartz argues that God's election of one person or one people over others makes the Bible, and cultures influenced by the Bible, deeply violent. She remarks that "over and over the Bible tells the story of a people who inherit at someone else's expense."[11] She begins with the story of Cain and Abel, who compete not for the love of their parents, Adam and Eve, but for God's love. The pattern repeats itself in Jacob and Esau, who are "the eponymous ancestors of peoples" that compete for scarce blessings.[12] The identity of these peoples is formed in violent opposition to the "Other." Schwartz finds that throughout the biblical narrative, cultural identity is formed in this way, thus making the Bible a conduit of personal and communal violence.[13] While she grants that the Bible construes cultural identity in more positive ways as well—and indeed she ultimately blames not the Bible itself but later interpreters who "violated the editors' preference for multiplicity"[14]—she nonetheless decries the "myth of monotheism" for fueling intolerance toward those outside the circle of "*the* Truth."[15]

Echoing this viewpoint, Laurel Schneider argues that "Christian monotheism is empire theology": after Constantine, rulers have employed Trinitarian monotheism in their search for "a divine mirror for their totalitarian dreams of state or of church power."[16] Trinitarianism failed in part, she argues, because despite the efforts of the African theologian Tertullian, "the underlying monotheism was never actually challenged."[17] Instead, Constantine made Christianity into an "empire theology" by insisting upon a single set of orthodox doctrines. The resulting "full-blown warfare" produced a confused and stunted doctrine of the Trinity that was unable to develop further in the direction of multiplicity.[18] Despite the potential of Trinitarianism for further unfolding, it was inevitably placed in the service of divine monarchy (monotheism) so as to justify imperial "monarchical authority."[19] The worst example of this servitude, in Schneider's view, is found in Eusebius of Caesarea, but Augustine too "ends up collapsing the three into the one, and so serves the One in theological imagining, rather than clarifying the multiplicity at work in divinity."[20]

The solution requires deconstructing all efforts to number divinity. For this project Schneider focuses on incarnation, not of course in the Nicene sense but insofar as it names "a divine reality not only implicated in but explicated out of the very fabric of the worlds we inherit and incorporate."[21] She envisions "empire" and "the One" as standing over against the multiplicity of the "gospel" understood as "a mobile and always contextualized message of good news to the poor and disenfranchised."[22] She accepts the need for "functional unities," which are nominal, partial, event-based, temporary groupings that "generate meaning and orientation" and that are good for humans so long as they are not taken up within an absolutized monotheist structure.[23] According to Schneider, when humans attempt to turn a nominal unity into an absolute unity, we end up oppressing others by turning from "the cacophony of embodied existence toward the serenity of unifying concepts in the hope of bringing closure to the world's actual unruly shiftiness."[24]

Schwartz favors the strands of the biblical narrative that she thinks "offer glimpses of another kind of deity, a God of plenitude, of generosity, who need not protect his turf because it is infinite."[25] This God would not be the one God of "exclusive monotheism," because that one God, according to Schwartz, is construed over against others in terms of a "metaphysical scarcity."[26] For Schwartz the answer is to rewrite the biblical canon in a way that "subverts the dominant vision of violence and scarcity with an ideal of plenitude and its corollary ethical imperative of generosity. It would be a Bible embracing multiplicity instead of monotheism."[27] Whereas monotheism serves jealousy and violence in a world of scarcity, multiplicity allows for "God's promiscuous pursuit of lovers—of the world itself."[28] On this view monotheism seeks idolatrously to control and reify God, whereas multiplicity embodies a truly kenotic understanding of love.

As Schneider notes, Judaism, Christianity, and Islam have long been seeking such self-giving love. Indeed, their "instructions of openness to others create a tension with the logic of One and suggest openings to the multiplicity that such a generosity porously creates."[29] With these "openings" in view, Schneider's book concludes with a definition of love based upon her effort to identify multiplicity as "the conceptual shape of divinity."[30] Rather than positing a set of rules for love, she seeks to explore its dimensions of "being-present": "It is grown-up regard; it is deep, physically present recognition of actual others in the world; it is a refusal to be dismissed or erased by others; it is courage to see suffering and a courage to sin in witnessing to it; it is a filling out of space and a making of time; it is relinquishment of stasis and openness to strangers, even the dangerous kind."[31] In other words, love is built upon tolerance and is not defined by moral rules. Love is physically being present to help others in their times of need. Love is unencumbered generosity.[32]

Thomas Aquinas on the Act of Charity

Are Schwartz and Schneider right about the need to move beyond the Christian understanding of charity? In order to explore the relationship of charity and the theology of God, I turn to *Summa Theologiae* 2-2, question 27, where Thomas Aquinas discusses the act of charity. Although my survey is necessarily brief, I propose that Aquinas' valuation of loving over being loved, his recognition of God's supreme lovability, and his connection of loving God with loving one's neighbor result in the repudiation of the self-seeking violence promoted by "empire-theology." Despite their commendable goal of promoting generosity toward others, Schwartz and Schneider are mistaken about Christian theology of love.

"For Me It Is Good to Be Near God"

Inquiring into the "principal act of charity," Thomas Aquinas asks whether this principal act is to love or to be loved. Empire-building rests upon the ambition to be loved (or to be treated as such). Aquinas quotes book 8 of Aristotle's *Nicomachean Ethics*, "Most men however, because they love honour, seem to be more desirous of receiving than of bestowing affection."[33] In book 8, Aristotle goes on to observe that "most men like flattery, for a flatterer is a friend who is your inferior, or pretends to be so, and to love you more than you love him."[34] Yet Aristotle also insists that "in its essence friendship seems to consist more in giving than in receiving affection: witness the pleasure that mothers take in loving their children."[35]

Aquinas goes further than Aristotle by noting that "there is a communication between man and God, inasmuch as He communicates His happiness to us."[36] As sharers in the Trinitarian life, we become God's friends. Aquinas cites John 15:15, where Jesus tells his disciples, "No longer do I call you servants, for the servant does not know what his master is doing; but I have called you friends, for all that I have heard from my Father I have made known to you."[37] Friendship with the omnipotent God occurs through sharing, through God's own gifting, in the self-giving love that characterizes the communion of the Trinity. The unity toward which the act of charitable love tends is a unity of gifting. It is a communion in eternal goodness, infinitely shareable.

Beginning with the Trinitarian friendship that Jesus reveals in John 15:15, Aquinas does not reject the desire to be honored and loved. Rather, he identifies the proper reason for such desire, namely, to have one's goodness (ontological and/or moral) recognized: "By being loved a man is shown to have some good, since good alone is lovable."[38] The charitable person, however, does not focus on being loved. The better the charitable person, the more perfect his or her charity is and so the more strongly he or she loves. This love does not seek one's own, but rather, as Aquinas says, seeks "to love for the sake of loving."[39] In other words, being more lovable means simply loving more; perfection in Trinitarian friendship is not a matter of the will to power, but rather the very opposite.

Exploring the requirements of loving others, Aquinas speaks of benevolence (or goodwill). He notes that "goodwill sometimes arises suddenly, as happens to us if we look on at a boxing match, and we wish one of the boxers to win."[40] Through this example, Aquinas emphasizes that benevolence is a wishing of good to another person that does not presuppose a "union of the affections."[41] The love that binds together friends in Christ includes benevolence, by which (as Aristotle puts it) one "wishes, and promotes by action, the real or apparent good of another for that other's sake" and "wishes the existence and preservation of his friend for the friend's sake."[42] Following Aristotle, however, Aquinas also insists that love, in friendship, requires a unity of affections.[43] Benevolence belongs to friendship, but friendship is more than benevolence. To love means to attain a real union with the beloved.

When love is understood as unitive, however, does it mask dominance on the part of one person? Aquinas is aware that "it would seem that God is loved out of charity, not for himself but for the sake of something else."[44] Most importantly, we hope to receive particular temporal and spiritual goods from God, and we fear that we might not receive these goods. Could it be, then, that we love God simply because we want to be loved by him? Aquinas answers no. Infinitely surpassing any created good, God is "the last end of all things," rather than being ordered to a further and better goal.[45] Similarly, it is not the "form" of goodness that makes God lovable, as though our love of God might arise from attraction to what makes him good. God simply is his goodness. Again, God is the cause of all goodness, and so our love for God cannot be reducible to love for a goodness causally prior to God. In short, we desire union with God for himself (*propter seipsum*).

To love the infinite God we must know him, but we only know God in this life through finite creatures.[46] Can we actually love God for himself, then, rather than loving him for his created effects? Since our knowledge of God is mediated by created things, Aquinas grants the force of 1 Corinthians 13:12, "For now we see in a mirror dimly."[47] If by faith our knowledge of God is only "in part" (1 Cor 13:12), can charity in this life truly unite us in mutual love with the living God? The answer is that love works differently from knowledge.[48] The will tends directly to the thing in itself, whereas the intellect apprehends the thing in the knower. In this life, our intellect can know God only through knowledge gained from the senses; we cannot know God in himself prior to the state of glory. By contrast, we can love God in himself now. Indeed, the union with God in love is such that the will "tends to God first, and flows on from Him to other things."[49] Since God is infinite goodness, we love finite goods in God who is the source and goal of everything. Aquinas observes that "in this sense charity loves God immediately, and other things through God."[50] As support for this position, Aquinas quotes Paul's statement that "Love never ends" whereas knowledge, in its present state, "will pass away" (1 Cor 13:8).[51]

What about the disorder caused by sin, which weakens the will's ability to cleave to its true good? Since God is self-giving love, we must be self-giving lovers if we are to share in his Trinitarian life. But does not our experience suggest that, on the contrary, we are quite weak in willing the good?[52] In discussing our union in love with God, Aquinas observes that charity both removes "aversion from God, which is brought about by sin" and "unites the soul immediately to Him with a chain of spiritual union" (*spiritualis vinculo unionis*).[53] The incarnation of the Son of God inspires our charity and enables Christ to bind up from within, through his sufferings, the wound of injustice that separated humans from

God. Christ solves the problem so powerfully identified in Isaiah's prophecy: "Your iniquities have made a separation between you and your God" (Isa 59:2).[54]

If God's love is supremely expressed by Christ's cross, is love thereby linked too closely with violence?[55] Exploring whether God can be loved wholly (*totaliter*) by us, Aquinas twice quotes Deuteronomy 6:5, "You shall love the Lord your God with all your heart, and with all your soul, and with all your might."[56] When Jesus fulfills this precept of the Torah, why does he do so through suffering? Jesus' love enters into the wound of sin (i.e., human injustice, experienced as punishment in human suffering and death) and heals the wound from within. He transforms the path of suffering and death into the path of life and love.[57]

Inspired by Jesus, Aquinas argues that no creature can love God as much as God is lovable. We cannot exhaust all the ways in which God is lovable; he is always infinitely more lovable than we can grasp. "God is infinitely lovable, since his goodness is infinite."[58] Thus we must "love all that pertains to God" and seek to conform ourselves and our lives entirely to the love of God.[59] In light of Deuteronomy 6:4, "Hear, O Israel: The Lord our God is one Lord," Aquinas observes that oneness for God means "undivided being," in the sense of a negation of division rather than in the sense of numerical quantity. God is the infinite plenitude of being, a plenitude that is not divisible but rather is perfectly simple.[60] God does not stand over against us (as would be the case only if God were a divisible quantity or a multitude of parts), but instead we participate in his supremely simple yet inexhaustible plenitude.

Because of God's infinite plenitude, we should hold nothing back in our love of God. In his teaching on virtuous action, Aristotle observes that "emotions and actions . . . can have excess or deficiency or a due mean."[61] Aquinas notes, however, that love of God, as an internal action, cannot be placed within this portrait of virtuous action. Although external acts of charity (for example, almsgiving) must be measured by charity and by the other virtues, there can be no excess in loving God.[62] Union with God in love can never be too much. This is so because God's infinite lovability makes it impossible for an excess of love to undermine the character of the action. Just as a medical doctor moderates medicine but does not seek to moderate health, so also in loving God "the more the rule is attained the better it is, so that the more we love God the better our love is."[63] It follows that while charity is the measure of other virtues, charity does not itself have a measure. This is how Aquinas understands Paul's teaching that charity is the pinnacle of the life of virtue: "And above all these put on love, which binds everything together in perfect harmony" (Col 3:14).[64] Just like health, charity gives life, as Aquinas emphasizes by quoting Psalm 73:28, "For me it is good to be near God."[65]

Love of Neighbor

In this one interior action of loving God, the love of neighbor is included.[66] Aquinas gives an eschatological reason for the internal unity of love of God and love of neighbor: "Now the aspect under which our neighbor is to be loved, is God, since what we ought to love in our neighbor is that he may be in God. Hence it is clear that it is specifically the same act whereby we love God, and whereby we love our neighbor."[67] On this view, one cannot truly love one's neighbor without referring this love to the neighbor's union with God. Love of the triune God includes love of all rational creatures who enjoy, or who potentially will come to enjoy, a personal communion in the Trinitarian life. Love of God, in other words, is an expansive friendship, including those who are now enemies but who have the potential to be our friends in heaven. Discussing whether it is more meritorious to love an enemy than to love a friend, Aquinas recalls Jesus' teaching on love of enemies, "For if you love those who love you, what reward have you?" (Matt 5:46).[68] As Jesus points out in this passage, those who love God will emulate God's love of sinners: "Love your enemies and pray for those who persecute you, so that you may be sons of your Father who is in heaven; for he makes his sun rise on the evil and on the good, and sends rain on the just and on the unjust" (Matt 5:44-45).

Since love of God is rooted in knowledge of God, however, can the one who loves God avoid dividing the world into people who share one's faith and people who do not? As regards loving both friends and enemies, Aquinas takes an eschatological perspective, calling to mind Paul's statement about the apostolic ministry that "each shall receive his wages according to his labor."[69] Only God, who calls each person to an ultimate destiny of eternal communion in Trinitarian life, can give these eternal "wages." Thus one cannot divide one's neighbors into sheep and goats because one cannot know how God is acting or will act in people's lives. Instead one simply recognizes that each person, called to eternal communion in love, is precious.

What does it mean to love an enemy? One's enemies, Aquinas suggests, can be known by their hatred for one's person.[70] Enemies pose a real threat to one's well-being and happiness, both now and eternally. Aquinas grants that in a certain sense it cannot be helped that we love our friends more, simply because we judge our friends to be more lovable because they are more good. If we have judged correctly that our friends have more goodness, then they are in fact more lovable than our enemies. In this sense, Aquinas' position warrants loving our friends more than our enemies, as indeed would hardly be possible to avoid in practice. He adds that special love of close friends is also unavoidable: "Charity loves with greater fervor those who are united to us than those who are far removed; and in this respect the love of friends, considered in itself, is more ardent and better than the love of one's enemy."[71] Indeed, God is our "chief friend" (*Deus maxime est amicus*) because, as the First Letter of John says, "In this is love, not that we loved God but that he loved us and sent his Son to be the expiation for our sins" (1 John 4:10).[72]

With regard to human friends, however, Aquinas argues that the love of enemy is more meritorious in two senses. First, we have reasons other than love of God for loving our friends.[73] Love of enemy, by contrast, is rooted solely in love of God, because we cannot expect any good from our enemy in return for our love. Second, Aquinas reasons that if both friend and enemy are loved for God, then it is more meritorious—that is, manifests a richer love—when our love extends even to those who are furthest from us.[74] The difficulty of loving enemies makes it the great test of true charity. In these ways, Aquinas repudiates the tendency to love only those who share our perspective and who value us personally. Without denying the existence of enemies, he eschatologically relativizes the friend/enemy distinction, even as he recognizes that in fact some persons have more goodness and therefore are more lovable.

These considerations about love of neighbor lead Aquinas to the question of whether the priority he gives to loving God is misplaced. Does Aquinas' account of charity undo itself by proving instead that it is better to love what is more difficult to love, namely, one's neighbor? If God is infinite goodness, while one's neighbor is flawed like oneself, should not one focus on the more difficult task of trying to love one's neighbor? Why worry so much about loving a transcendent, invisible God who can take care of himself?

In reply, Aquinas notes that the goal of our lives is to share in the eternal Trinitarian communion of love. In this sense, loving one's neighbor does not compare with loving God. No matter how wonderful and/or how needy one's neighbor is, loving him or her cannot suffice as an ultimate end for our lives. When we place all our love in finite creatures without allowing them to point us to the transcendent Creator, we lose our way. Aquinas extends this argument to show that while cleaving to earthly things rather than to God is mistaken, so also is imagining that we can love God without loving our neighbor. Indeed, only love of God that includes love of neighbor is "perfect love of God."[75] Were we to exclude the neighbor, we could only have a profoundly "inadequate and imperfect love of God," not worth calling love of God at all.[76] The point is that the two loves are united and cannot be separated: "If any one says, 'I love God,' and hates his brother, he is a liar; for he who does not love his brother whom he has seen, cannot love God whom he has not seen. And this commandment we have from him, that he who loves God should love his brother also" (1 John 4:20-21).[77] Focus on loving God actually fuels and nourishes love of neighbor, including love of enemy.

Conclusion: Charity and Solidarity

After briefly surveying arguments in favor of Trinitarian monotheism, I set forth Regina Schwartz' and Laurel Schneider's critiques of monotheism as inherently violent due to a "metaphysics of scarcity" that posits "*the* Truth" over against the errors of outsiders. Schwartz and Schneider seek to account for love in terms of a theology of divine multiplicity. Certainly if being loved were the principal act of charity, then Trinitarian monotheism would end in self-centered empire-building. Aquinas shows, however, that to love is the principal act of charity. He explores how charity includes but goes beyond benevolence so as to require a real union of wills. In charity we attain to a personal union with God the Trinity. Loving this God is inseparable from loving our neighbors, including our enemies. Trinitarian monotheism overcomes the violence of disordered empire-building in multiple ways: by the primacy of the act of love for the other, by the focus on mutuality, by the power of God's love in Christ overcoming the world's violence from the inside, by awakening us to the infinitely lovable Trinitarian communion, and by revealing that all human beings are called to share in eternal love.

Even so, if all humans are called to manifest their love within one visible communion, does not this view lead inevitably to the persecution of outsiders?[78] Kelly Johnson observes that the visible life of communion does not validate the persecution of those who are not members, but rather underscores the solidarity of all human beings as (in Johnson's term) "beggars" in need of mercy.[79] Because the gospel proclaims mercy for all, the church offers an order of mercy that contradicts the proud self-sufficiency of "empire-building" and instead demands repentance and self-giving love.

Put another way, God loves us as his friends and communicates his happiness to us by calling us to share in his life of cruciform love. As Aquinas points out, this is what Paul means by saying that "God is faithful, by whom you were called into the fellowship of his Son, Jesus Christ our Lord" (1 Cor 1:9).[80] This eucharistic fellowship comes about because "God's love has been poured into our hearts through the Holy Spirit who has been given to us" (Rom 5:5).[81] This love is sheer mercy, as Paul goes on to say: "While we were yet helpless, at the right time Christ died for the ungodly" (Rom 5:6). Humility involves first and foremost our "subjection to God," but this does not mean abasement.[82] Rather it means learning how to receive God's gifts rather than seeking to grasp them by our own power. When we perceive with the eyes of faith the humility of Jesus (Phil 2:5-11), we discover the Trinitarian pattern of love that liberates us from enslavement to empire-building.[83]

CHAPTER 2

Hatred and the God of Israel

The first sin against charity treated by Thomas Aquinas is hatred. Hatred of God would not be possible if we knew God in himself, because he is infinite goodness. We can hate God because in this life we know God only through his effects. Our experience of these effects can be unpleasant, and this experience can lead us to hatred. After examining Aquinas' theology of hatred, I explore the eminent literary critic Harold Bloom's avowed hatred for "Yahweh." Bloom blames the literary Yahweh for the Jewish people's long history of suffering, for the violent fanaticism of believers, and for ruining human lives rather than creating and enhancing them. Without suggesting that Bloom hates God—since he thinks of "Yahweh" solely as a literary character—Bloom's concerns raise the question of whether human history validates hatred of God. Does Aquinas' theology of hatred help with such matters?

Hatred and Rebellion against God

Since charity is about love of God (and love of neighbor in God), Aquinas' discussion of hatred begins by asking whether it is possible for anyone to hate God. The answer is clearly no as regards God in himself: God is infinite goodness, and no rational creature

who sees God directly could be repulsed, given our natural inclination toward goodness. Aquinas quotes Romans 1, however, where
Paul describes hatred of God in light of the human capacity to
know God's attributes "in the things that have been made" (Rom
1:20). Differentiating among God's created effects, Aquinas comments that we do not hate God for being, life, and understanding;
these are "desirable and lovable to all."[1] Rather, we hate him for
things that we experience as unpleasant, for example "the infliction
of punishment, and the prohibition of sin by the divine law."[2] God's
law prohibits and punishes sinful actions, and therefore sinners hate
God as the author of this prohibition and punishment. As Aquinas
comments, "Such like effects are repugnant to a will debased by sin,
and as regards the consideration of them, God may be an object of
hatred to some, in so far as they look upon Him as forbidding sin,
and inflicting punishment."[3]

Aquinas further explains hatred by means of Psalm 74:23, which
has to do with the seeming flourishing of those who hate God.[4] The
psalmist wonders whether hatred of God will ever be punished.
Speaking on behalf of the Israel of God, the psalmist bewails the
destruction of the temple by Babylonian idolaters: "They set thy
sanctuary on fire; to the ground they desecrated the dwelling place
of thy name" (Ps 74:7). He begs God to act powerfully, as God did
in creating the world. By acting on behalf of his covenantal people,
the psalmist says, God will rid the land of "the habitations of violence" and lift up the downtrodden and the needy. Throughout the
psalm—including verse 23, which Aquinas quotes—the key question is why God is permitting so much hatred. The psalmist urges,
"Arise, O God, plead thy cause; remember how the impious scoff
at thee all the day! Do not forget the clamor of thy foes, the uproar
of thy adversaries which goes up continually!" (Ps 74:22-23). The
enemies of Israel hate God, it seems, with impunity; hatred thrives
in this world.

In the same *sed contra*, Aquinas also quotes John 15:24, "If I
had not done among them the works which no one else did, they
would not have sin; but now they have seen and hated both me and
my Father." Psalm 74 is about Israel's Babylonian enemies, whereas
John 15:24 has to do with the worldly (cf. John 15:18). Those who

are in rebellion against God find in God primarily a punisher and a prohibiter. They fail to recognize the divine goodness, which God's law aims to share with humans.

Aquinas goes on to explain that hating punishment need not mean that we hate God. Hatred of God requires turning away deliberately and directly from "the giver of all good things."[5] Insofar as every human experience of suffering is in some sense a punishment (either of original or actual sin), we do not need to like the suffering so long as we endure it patiently. If we lose patience and curse God for the suffering we endure, however, we fall into hatred of God.

Aquinas' quotations from Psalm 74 and John 15 present a stark contrast between those who love God and those who hate God, between Zion and Babylon, between Jesus' disciples and "the world." Should those who love God hate those who hate God? In an objection in the third article of his question on hatred, Aquinas quotes Luke 14:26, where Jesus states, "If any one comes to me and does not hate his own father and mother and wife and children and brothers and sisters, yes, and even his own life, he cannot be my disciple." Does this mean that hatred of other people can be consistent with love of God? Quoting 1 John 2:9, "He who says he is in the light and hates his brother is in the darkness still," Aquinas answers that no hatred of other people is consistent with charity.[6] He also quotes 1 John 3:15, which makes clear that hatred cuts off a person from eternal life: "Any one who hates his brother is a murderer, and you know that no murderer has eternal life abiding in him."[7]

But why could we not hate a neighbor without hating God's law, especially when the neighbor is a notorious breaker of God's law? Love of God, Aquinas replies, requires loving all that shares in God's goodness by existing. We love our neighbors by loving their goodness and by willing that they might come to be perfected in goodness. We therefore cannot hate a neighbor without hating God, both as the giver of created being and as the lawgiver.

Despite his awareness of the extent of hatred among humans, Aquinas holds that love of the good is by far the deeper inclination. We love good things. Rationally speaking, it is natural for us to love God, who is infinite goodness, above all things. Even sinful actions seek to obtain some good. Hatred of God is not therefore a vice from which other sins originate. Rather, it is a vice which is the culmination of other sins: "Hatred of one's connatural good cannot be first, but is something last, because such like hatred is a proof of an already corrupted nature."[8] In this regard Aquinas distinguishes hatred of evil, which is natural, from the corruption that is hatred of good, described in Romans 7:5's reference to "our sinful passions . . . at work in our members to bear fruit for death."[9] When our neighbor possesses much goodness, this should arouse love, since we naturally love what is good. But when our nature has been corrupted, our neighbor's goodness instead displeases us. God's providential ordering, his sharing of his goodness, becomes hateful to us. We hate God as an opponent of our own good because God has blessed our neighbor. Aquinas explains that "since envy of our neighbor is the mother of hatred of our neighbor, it becomes, in consequence, the cause of hatred towards God."[10]

Harold Bloom and Hatred for Israel's God

Although he does not believe in God, Harold Bloom sets forth in his *Jesus and Yahweh* a case for hating the biblical God. He argues that both Judaism and Christianity are intelligible in terms of a sadistic god who nonetheless is a powerful literary character. On a literary level, Bloom commends what he terms the "Book of J" for presenting Yahweh as a "flamboyant personality."[11] He criticizes Philo of Alexandria and later theologians for distorting and taming the literary character Yahweh. According to Bloom, Philo "invented" theology "in order to explain away Yahweh's human personality"[12]—or personalities, since Bloom later specifies that Yahweh has not one personality but at least seven.[13] As a literary character, Yahweh is too important to the Western aesthetic tradition to be tamed theologically. Bloom gives the highest praise he possesses to Yahweh as a literary character: "If Yahweh is a fiction, he is much the most disturbing fiction the West ever has encountered. Yahweh is, at the least, the supreme fiction, the literary character (to call him that) more endless to meditation than even Jesus Christ, or the most capacious Shakespearean characterizations."[14] Here "disturbing" functions as a compliment: the character of Yahweh commands attention and stimulates creative reflection.

What Bloom most appreciates is the fallen humanity of Yahweh; as he puts it, "J's Yahweh is wonderfully anthropomorphic."[15] This humanity of Yahweh expresses itself most forcefully in Yahweh's "uncanniness," which allows him always to surprise. Yahweh is eminently this-worldly: "Heaven on earth is his promise; *his* Kingdom decidedly is of this world."[16] He has no theological attributes such as omniscience or omnipotence. Rather, he is "an ambivalent creator and destroyer," "a swordsman," marked by complexities that "are infinite, labyrinthine, and permanently inexplicable."[17] Yahweh is unintelligible but endlessly interesting as a tricky "creator and destroyer."

Yet Bloom is not content to leave Yahweh entirely at the literary level, because even though Yahweh does not exist, he "exists" in the minds of believers and in what he has wrought through the force of his (literary) character. In this respect Bloom repudiates both Yahweh and Judaism. Writing from the perspective of "a literary critic divided between Judaic heritage and a Gnostic discomfort with God,"[18] Bloom observes with regard to Moses' fate, "Yahweh, who generally is bad news, is the worst possible news when he ends Moses. But then, he has been a personal disaster for Moses from the start. I regret suggesting that he has been a disaster for his champions more often than not, but that is the long story of the Tanakh, and of most Jewish experience since."[19] Yahweh the literary character, when treated by believers as more than a literary character, becomes worthy of real hatred.

On a personal level, Bloom has some scores to settle with the character Yahweh. As he remarks, "My own mother *trusted in* the covenant, despite Yahweh's blatant violation of its terms."[20] For centuries, he thinks, Jews have trusted in vain. As he comments regarding centuries of unimpeded and often horrific violence against Jews,

> The Tanakh's question always is "Will Yahweh act?" The ultimate answer implied is that he will not, and has deserted us, perhaps because he is caught up in the contradictions of his own character and personality. The Sages of the Talmud would not agree with such an interpretation, and yet post-Holocaust Jewry

is confronted by this enigma. The Roman Holocaust of the Jews, with its first climax at the fall of Jerusalem and destruction of Yahweh's Temple, and a second one after the even larger-scale devastation of the Bar-Kochba rebellion, resulted in the rise and persistence of Rabbinical Judaism. A remnant of that faith still struggles on, yet many of its adherents avert themselves from asking, Is it possible still to trust in a Covenant that Yahweh pragmatically has forsaken? If you have lost your grandparents in the German death camps, are you to trust a Yahweh who must be either powerless or uncaring?[21]

The literary Yahweh, Bloom finds, does not love anyone and never has, with the possible exceptions of Joseph and David. In the sense that Yahweh "exists" in his believers, Yahweh consistently causes harm to them. He never shows his love for his covenantal people, and those who depend upon him find themselves stranded. Bloom remarks, "I am compelled to conclude that Yahweh has exiled himself from the Original Covenant, and is off in the outer spaces, nursing his lovelessness."[22] Yahweh's ferocity and unpredictability mean that believers should hate him, for he is not lovable or good. For Jewish believers, "Yahweh is bad news incarnate. . . . It is an awful thing to fall into the hands of the living Yahweh."[23]

Even so, Bloom cannot rid himself or the world of Yahweh. He remarks, "I very much want to dismiss Yahweh as the ancient Gnostics did, finding in him a mere demiurge who had botched the Creation so that it was simultaneously a Fall."[24] Yahweh continues to haunt Bloom in nightmares, however. Most crucially, Bloom fears that Yahweh is on the side of death and of all that constrains human beings, not only as a literary character sanctifying "the tyranny of nature over women and men," but also in his offspring Allah: "If Yahweh is a man of war, Allah is a suicide bomber."[25] For Bloom, therefore, it is imperative not to confuse the literary Yahweh with a truly living God. No such God exists. As he emphasizes, "The Tanakh has *no* theology, and Yahweh, to keep repeating the obvious, is not at all a theological God."[26] The danger is that Jews, even today, continue to be misled by their trust in the covenant. Those who trust have not understood that Yahweh is simply a literary character, and an ambivalent and untrustworthy one at that.

Is Bloom therefore advising Jews to cease being Jews? No. In addition to taking pride in Yahweh as a literary character, he fears that Jews would simply be assimilated into the religions of one or the other of Yahweh's lesser literary offspring, Jesus or Allah, neither of whom holds out hope for future humanity.[27] For Bloom, Jesus (and the polytheistic God of Christianity, a radical distortion of Judaism[28]) is as unintelligible as Yahweh, but less interesting as a literary character. Bloom can praise Jesus for his "enigmatic wit,"[29] but he observes that in contrast to the gentle sage Hillel, Jesus divided "the populace into sheep and goats."[30] A proto-theologian, Jesus was fiercely disappointed that Yahweh was not the perfect God he desired and that Israel was not a perfect people. Such fierce perfectionism is destructive of human beings.

To those who think that Jesus images God's love, Bloom insists on the contrary, that Jesus images God's hatred. Asking whether the Trinity is a mythical "dream of love," Bloom answers his own question: "God the Father, a mere shade of Yahweh, has the primary function of loving his Son, Jesus Christ," but instead God the Father (Yahweh's "shade") kills his son.[31] As Bloom says, "Yahweh intervened to save Isaac from the over-literalist Abraham, most obedient of Covenanters, but was not available to save Jesus from God the Father."[32] For Bloom, the narratives of the cross are only intelligible as a continuation of the story of Yahweh, who now assumes the murderous role of God the Father who "himself tortures and executes Jesus."[33] Christianity is the religion par excellence of child sacrifice.[34]

On Bloom's reading, then, the God of Judaism is, when the biblical texts are read carefully, a crazed, untrustworthy, and loveless failure, although worth keeping as a literary masterpiece, and the God of Christianity is a polytheistic myth whose identity is formed in child sacrifice. No wonder, then, that Bloom concludes by associating Jewish-Christian dialogue with the Holocaust: "There are doubtless political and social benefits, ongoing and crucial, that stem from the myth of 'the Judeo-Christian tradition,' but delusions finally prove pernicious, as they did for German-speaking Jewry. 'Christian-Jewish dialogue' isn't even a myth, but invariably farce."[35] It is farce not only because Judaism and Christianity share almost nothing, but also, and more importantly, because they both worship imaginary gods who—whatever their literary value—sanctify murderous tyranny and the slaughter of the innocent.[36]

Aquinas and Bloom

Without suggesting that Bloom hates the living God, since he knows only the literary character Yahweh (distorted further, in his view, by followers of Jesus and Muhammad), one can ask why Bloom thinks Jewish and Christian believers should hate the God in whom they believe. First, he observes that the Jewish people suffered in history because of their belief in this fictional God. Without denying that human suffering is endemic, he appeals to the historical record to suggest that Jews have suffered far more than most—even though he grants that the state of Israel may now inflict harm on others as one more noxious effect of belief in the covenant. Jews underwent much horrific suffering because they would not renounce their adherence to this God, and this suffering was entirely pointless because their God did not exist (except in their minds) and could not help them.

Second, in Bloom's view Israel's God is hardly the "giver of all good things." Rather, Bloom's Yahweh is generally on the side of the forces that constrict the human person. As a literary character, Yahweh does not love his people, but instead grows more and more isolated and wrathful. The literary character Yahweh is prone to violence against his people, and whenever he appears on the scene, those who trust in him suffer needlessly and fail to find fulfillment. Far from being the fount of all good things, this literary character is "bad news" both in Scripture and for those who believe in him as a living God.

Third, for Bloom, not only is the literary character Yahweh malevolent, but also the people who believe in him become distorted. They become like what they worship. Thus Yahweh's support for war and for rigid gender codes, along with Yahweh's irrationality, are reflected in the fanaticism of Yahweh's adherents. This goes not only for Jews, but also far more for Christians and Muslims, since Christians extend Yahweh's literary and historical life in the direction of polytheism and child-killing, while Muslims magnify the violent streak of Yahweh's personality in the character of Allah. The result is that Christians and Muslims become sanctimonious in their rampant violence against each other and against outsiders (even if strands of both religions attempt to claim the mantle of peace). Much better than all these fanaticisms that plague the human race would be an end to this violent God, despite the permanently impressive literary qualities of Yahweh as a fictional character.

On this basis, we can compare Bloom's hatred for the literary character Yahweh, as Bloom understands him, with Aquinas' theology of hatred—*mutatis mutandis*. Bloom sees the literary character Yahweh in his effects, and finds that those effects have been largely negative. Had Yahweh been a real God, he would not have permitted inexplicable sufferings such as the Holocaust to ravage his covenantal people. Nor would he have punished his people so ruthlessly for doing forbidden things, especially since in Bloom's view many of the forbidden things were hardly as wicked as many things (such as war) that the literary character Yahweh does at times encourage. Lastly, Bloom hates the literary character Yahweh in the effects that he has upon sincere believers (not only Jews but also Christians and Muslims), whose lives are distorted in fanatical and violent directions that produce a devastating impact upon the world as a whole.

If we compare these reasons for hating the literary character Yahweh to the reasons that Aquinas gives for why people might hate God, we find affinities. Bloom implicitly suggests that had the literary character Yahweh never been invented, the human race as it currently stands would have been less violent (even if perhaps also less creative). At least as regards violence, he begins by assuming that his non-Yahwist neighbor's cultural endowments are greater than his own. To the degree that Yahwist cultures are plagued by fanatical violence, he hates what the fictional character Yahweh has given to these cultures, and he hates the fictional character Yahweh (while as a literary critic admiring the character for its complexity). One could say that envy of his less-violent hypothetical neighbor leads him to hatred of the fictional character Yahweh.

Bloom also holds the fictional character Yahweh largely responsible for the particular sufferings of the Jews over the course of history. Just as Bloom is able to imagine better humans than the violent ones he sees around him, so also he is able to imagine a better god. Such a better god would have acted, out of sheer love, on behalf of his people. A better god would have had a broader understanding of human morality, would have punished less, and would not have permitted such an outrageous amount of suffering, especially on the part of his chosen people. A better god would not have, in the Christian version, killed his own son as part of a perfectionist crusade. Able to imagine better historical effects, Bloom is able to imagine a better divine author of these effects. He therefore hates the fictional character Yahweh in relation to his effects, which seem profoundly out of joint with what one might expect from a loving and trustworthy god.

By contrast, Aquinas holds that far from having a greater propensity to unjust violence, biblical cultures encourage us to bear witness to God by standing against unjust violence. The charge that the Gospels depict the killing of Jesus by "Yahweh" in the guise of God the Father misses the central point of these narratives. Neither God the Father nor Yahweh kills Jesus. Rather, God nonactively permits the unjust violence of humans (Gentiles and Jews) against Jesus, and Jesus with perfect freedom and charity endures this unjust violence in order to accomplish the forgiveness of sins.[37] God thereby enters into our broken condition from within and turns it inside out: the path of death becomes in Jesus the path of life (resurrection), and the injustice of humans becomes in Jesus the glorious justice of new creation. God's permission of suffering has to do with the preparation of this new creation through the charity of the saints.

Since Bloom does not believe in a living God, these answers may not console him. But once rid of the myth of less-violent non-Yahwist cultures, envy for the non-Yahwist neighbor might subside. Given the scope of human injustice, it is no wonder that a people bearing witness to God's holiness would suffer. Such suffering can be seen as a path of life, however, only if God's effects in this world appear in light of the new creation that his love is bringing about. The fictional God must inevitably be hated. The living God, by contrast, merits a closer look.

CHAPTER 3

Sloth and the Joy of the Resurrection

Rebecca DeYoung identifies biblical examples of the vice of sloth "in the Israelites' resistance to embracing their new home in the promised land, and in Lot's wife turning back to the familiarity of Sodom while angels attempted to rescue her."[1] In both cases, she connects sloth with a failure to trust in God's redemption. This chapter extends DeYoung's insight by connecting sloth with agnosticism about the resurrection of the dead. I argue that without faith in resurrection, we cannot sustain the joy that flows from charity, but instead fall into the sin of sloth regarding what God is doing for us.[2]

It would seem, however, that loving God for his own sake requires that our joy in God be unrelated to whether God has conquered death for us. Immanuel Kant describes the nature of *"pure morality"* by telling a story whose moral, he thinks, will be evident to a child.[3] The story is about an effort to corrupt an honest man into doing something wrong. First the honest man is offered enticing rewards; then he is threatened with dire punishments, and even his family implores him to yield. Despite his agony, he persists steadfastly in the path of honesty. Kant imagines that "my young listener will be raised step by step from mere approval to admiration, from that to amazement, and finally to the greatest veneration and a lively wish that he himself could be such a man."[4] In this costly action, Kant suggests, the boy will be able to identify pure morality, lacking any tinge of incentive or self-interest. Kant adds that the immortality of the soul is a postulate of practical reason, a postulate without which we would despair.[5] But Ludwig Feuerbach deconstructs this practical postulate as simply another instance of the human pursuit of self-interest. As Feuerbach depicts the believer's worldview: "God is the certainty of my future felicity. The interest I have in knowing that *God is*, is one with the interest I have in knowing that *I am*, that I am immortal. God is my hidden, my assured existence."[6]

Accepting Kant's critique of self-interest, Timothy Jackson argues that charity requires agnosticism about resurrection and life after death. In what follows, I consider Jackson's argument in light of Aquinas' theology of joy, the interior effect of charity that is opposed by sloth. Aquinas' presentation of joy and sloth helps to reveal the intrinsic relation of charity to faith that God will resurrect us from the dead. Without faith in the resurrection, we almost inevitably sin against charity by falling into sloth. The vice of sloth requires the strong spiritual medicine brought by Jesus Christ.

Timothy Jackson on Charity and Eternal Life

Charity Is Its Own Reward

In two recent books, *Love Disconsoled* and *The Priority of Love*, Timothy Jackson suggests that Christian charity should be dissociated from faith in life after death. His aim is to show that the reason we practice self-giving love is not because we hope for an eternal reward; rather, self-giving love is simply worth practicing for its own sake.

In *Love Disconsoled*, Jackson notes Boethius' view that if humans do not live forever, we cannot hope to experience real happiness. For Boethius, the happiness we experience in this short life is too fleeting to merit the name "happiness." In response, Jackson insists that even without "certainty about one's endless longevity," we can still live a life of grateful charity.[7] God does not owe us eternal life, since our life is his gift. In gratitude for this gift we owe God (and our neighbor in God) self-giving love or charity.

As Jackson observes, Feuerbach's early work *Thoughts on Death and Immortality* suggests that the desire for immortality, as found in Christian faith, is self-centered and prevents Christians from freely surrendering themselves to the whole. Feuerbach considers death to be the physical analogue of the spiritual self-giving that is love. Against this view, Jackson warns against the danger of valorizing death. Charity should not be equated, as in Feuerbach, with "the absorption of the personal into something infinite, universal, and impersonal."[8] In other words, even if self-giving love makes life meaningful in the face of eternal death (pace Boethius), death is not a personal good. In itself, death is far from being the mirror of charity.

Jackson's solution is to argue that charity fulfills human beings by turning our lives into expressions of care for others, whether or not we are going to be everlastingly dead or alive forever in God. Humans should act charitably without needing the extra stimulus of an eternal reward. We love God (and our neighbor in God) not because we want a reward or fear a punishment, but because God has created us. As Jackson says, "To be charitable is already to know God . . . regardless of what (if anything) follows this life."[9] If we already enjoy God in and through the life of charity, we need not suppose that charity makes sense only if God enables us to continue to enjoy him after our earthly life is over. Rather, enjoying God in the present moment should suffice. Everlasting death would not make meaningless what God graciously gives us now in and through the life of charity. The meaningful life made possible by self-giving love does not require, although it does allow for, eternal life as a hope. By practicing self-giving love—itself God's gift—humans can have a fulfilling life here and now without the need of appealing to an eternal life with God.

Jackson is aware that in taking this position, he differs from St. Paul, the Fathers, and almost all Christian thinkers across the centuries. But his point is that charity already, here and now, possesses sufficient meaning: the practice of charity, as a communion with God, is its own reward. As he puts it, "To think that the future finality of death would evacuate present love of all meaning is to deny that *agape* is motivated by the well-being of finite others here and now."[10] Charity does not require any further reward or any further motivation. If it comes about, eternal life with God will be a pure gift, just as the present life is. Jackson has an optimistic view of the quality of a life marked by self-giving love for God and neighbor: it is "anything but wretchedness" and it brings about "the present plenitude of the self."[11] On the other hand, against Feuerbach's glorification of death as intrinsic to love, Jackson grants that "all things being equal, we would prefer a lasting communion with those we care for."[12]

Jackson critically surveys two other views regarding love, death, and eternal life. On the one hand, Walter Kaufmann proposes that a life well lived, an intense life filled with love, creativity, and suffering, wears us out and enables us to welcome death as the proper end of such a life. In reply, Jackson argues that eternal life might be something "qualitatively better" and therefore might not simply be an exhausting continuation of earthly striving.[13] On the other hand, C. S. Lewis suggests that the desire for heavenly reward grows with the life of charity, so that this desire is intrinsic to charity. Jackson finds that Lewis' view denigrates life on earth and weakens our desire for earthly justice. Jackson also argues that desire for eternal life is not an intrinsic component of charity: "It is unclear that endless life is such an inherent 'consummation' of Christian discipleship—what I have called 'putting charity first'—that its absence would undermine the meaning of that discipleship."[14]

In a brief overview of the biblical testimony, Jackson emphasizes that the notion of life after death is absent from much of the Old Testament and appears only around the sixth century B.C. Suggesting that the notion of personal immortality arose from an emphasis on each person's accountability to divine justice, Jackson thinks that God's presence here and now suffices for such accountability. Jackson contrasts Jesus' view of the relationship of charity to eternal life with Paul's (especially 1 Cor 15:12-19), and finds that Jesus values more the present participation in God's life made possible by the Holy Spirit: "Individuals may have 'eternal life' here and now, in love."[15] Without positing a fully realized eschaton in this life, God's presence here and now, in charitable believers, can be termed "eternal life" in the sense that God is with us now and so our lives are meaningful insofar as we are engaged in self-giving love.

Even if one takes literally the resurrection accounts, Jackson argues, it does not follow that Christians need have (or can have) certainty about their own "endlessness."[16] It suffices that the kingdom of God is experienced as a present reality. This experience provides ample motivation for the life of charity. Against Plato's arguments for the soul's immortality, and Paul's arguments for eternal life as an intrinsic motivation to charity, Jackson prefers to leave eternal life as a hope or intuition, separate from the rationale for living charitably in the here and now.

Jackson similarly considers that sin, not death, is the primary enemy overcome by the good news of Christ Jesus. During our earthly lives, self-giving love provides a meaningful "inkling of divine fullness and a partial remedy for human neediness."[17] Even if death annihilates individual humans, love remains meaningful in the here and now. Indeed, appeal to eternal life may weaken self-giving love in the here and now by supposing that justice will be done in the afterlife. Love fulfills the human person to such a degree that "we need not fear dying (however permanently)."[18]

Yet, why would not a loving Creator bestow eternal life upon us? Would it not be more loving for him to do so? Are not humans made to share in the life of God, and if so wouldn't a loving God bring this about? Jackson answers that charity, not immortality, is God's greatest gift. Therefore, a loving God gives what is necessary for and intrinsic to the possession of charity during one's life. Since eternal life is not necessary for or intrinsic to such charity, however, God does not need to bestow eternal life upon us. We can have charity without having it after our earthly existence. As Jackson says, "Even if friendship with God is seen as the key virtue, it need not be permanent to be real."[19] God's goodness in granting us friendship with him here and now, in charity, shows God's love for us; he does not owe us further communion with him after death. Arguing against John Hick's argument that life after death is required for God to be just, Jackson notes that the incarnation demonstrates that "God loves creation and has extended to creatures the wherewithal to love God in return (even in and through their affliction)," and this ability to love God is gift enough, although in freedom we may reject it.[20] Having given us the ability to have charity in this life, God does not need to bestow the further gift of eternal life.

What about those who, due to no fault of their own, seemingly have no opportunity to exercise charity—those killed as infants, for example? Jackson proposes that "even the radically harmed and harmful, however, may be loved by God in ways that do not entail an afterlife. (God may simply grant them release, for example.)"[21] God is not responsible for the damage that the misuse of human freedom has inflicted upon the human race. Having acted for our good, God does not constrict our freedom.

Jackson sums up his position by observing that "in the absence of an internal connection between endless duration and our own ability to love," eternal life "is not required by God's charity."[22] God might give us eternal life, but if so this would be pure gift rather than anything required for the fulfillment of charity. Charity fulfills us here and now. Here and now, God has given us the greatest good—namely, the ability to love God and neighbor in the present moment: "We are able to love love, so to speak, because God loves us first."[23] There is no need to add everlasting duration to this greatest good, even though it is possible that God might do so. Jackson expresses his hope for love's sufficiency here and now: "We may yet, with Love's help, take joy in our imperfect lives without lapsing into Boethian false consolation."[24]

In a more recent book, *The Priority of Love*, Jackson takes up this issue again, in the context of a chapter on whether God is just. Having freely created, God freely binds himself (in love for us) to obligations of justice vis-à-vis humans. Is eternal life one such obligation of justice?

Jackson begins by arguing that Paul, in 1 Corinthians 15:12-34, tends to instrumentalize charity and devalue the present life. He comments, "As communion with God and service of neighbor, agapic love is more intrinsically good, more self-justifying" than Paul recognizes, and he goes on to say that charity is "its own reward."[25] As its own reward, charity should be practiced for its own sake.

He then raises an objection, drawn from Henry Emerson Fosdick and indebted to Kant. If God creates us with intellectual and moral potentialities that at best are only beginning to flourish during this brief life, does not God owe it to us, in love for us, to preserve us in existence after death? Jackson replies that this would only be the case had God promised immortality to us. As Jackson interprets the gospel of John, however, Jesus may promise a qualitative rather than quantitative "eternal life." Qualitatively, Jackson says, " 'eternal life' can be taken as readily to mean an existence permeated by, and imitative of, the loving presence of God here and now as to mean a remote and endless afterlife."[26] Eternal life is present here and now in the life of charity, and our present enjoyment of this life should fulfill us. As in his earlier book, Jackson sees a significant opposition between Jesus and Paul, and he emphasizes that belief in an after-life tends to undermine concern for justice in this life.

As before, too, Jackson refuses to glorify death. He notes that although we should find meaning in our relationship with God and neighbor here and now, nonetheless death "threatens the oblivion of all our life's projects and thus is inherently dreadful."[27] Yet death's threat of annihilation inspires a Christ-like love because it requires us to love others without counting on a personal benefit other than that to be found in love itself. In Jackson's view, Jesus' words in the garden of Gethsemane and on the cross indicate profound fear of death rather than serene confidence in resurrection.

What about the problem of suffering? Does the suffering that we experience here through no particular fault of our own require God, in justice, to reward us (or at least to reward the righteous) with an eternal life free from suffering? Jackson answers no, on the grounds that this position supposes that God is to blame for our suffering. Charity should love God without expecting anything more than we already have from him, namely, the extraordinary gift of his love and presence here and now (a presence that in Christ Jesus enters into the heart of our suffering). In this book as in his earlier one, therefore, Jackson holds that we can hope for eternal life, but not in a way that makes our charity dependent in any way upon this hope.

Evaluation

When Jackson observes that self-giving love brings its own rewards, that charitable persons are not focused on their own gain, and that supposing that God will make things right in the life to come should not dull the quest for justice here and now, his position is unobjectionable. Yet Jackson overstates his case. For example, consider his statement "Putting charity first means that love's willing the good for others insures only the present plenitude of the self."[28] In speaking of the charitable person's "present plenitude," Jackson does not sufficiently account for our lack of wholeness, our longing for a deeper and permanent communion with God and others in God. Furthermore, how could we have a "present plenitude" if we suspect that our divine friend, to whom we are allegedly beloved, intends to annihilate us? How could we not feel profound sadness at the thought of this emerging relationship being suddenly cut off forever?

Although Jackson elsewhere interprets the book of Job as a rejection of the thirst for eternal communion with God,[29] I am struck by Job's plea, in the midst of his sufferings, for an ongoing relationship with God: "Oh that thou wouldest hide me in Sheol, that thou wouldest conceal me until thy wrath be past, that thou wouldest appoint me a set time, and remember me! If a man die, shall he live again? All the days of my service I would wait, till my release should come. Thou wouldest call, and I would answer thee; thou wouldest long for the work of thy hands" (Job 14:13-15). Will God long for us, as one longs for a beloved after his or her death? Or will God cast off the personal communion that he once shared with us? Will God, in Job's extraordinary words, remember me and call for me so that I can answer? Or does God simply send us away so that we perceive nothing more forever (cf. Job 14:20-21)?

Jackson's admission that "all things being equal, we would prefer a lasting communion with those we care for" is a massive understatement, especially as regards our communion with God.[30] Job at least recognizes our powerful longing to be remembered by God, so that God calls us again and we can respond, rather than being eternally annihilated. One recalls Jesus' affirmation of the resurrection of the dead: "Have you not read what was said to you by God, 'I am the God of Abraham, and the God of Isaac, and the God of Jacob'? He is not the God of the dead, but of the living" (Matt 22:31-32). Abraham, Isaac, and Jacob live in the presence of God. God does not renounce his communion with them after their deaths.

Similarly, I wonder about Jackson's conclusion that "we may yet, with Love's help, take joy in our imperfect lives without lapsing into Boethian false consolation."[31] Is it really possible to experience "joy" while at the same time finding it likely that God will annul our relationship with him when we die? If God will toss us aside in this fashion, can we really be joyful other than in the weaker sense of enjoying the good things of this world, including our good ability to help others? Although Jackson often finds himself in strong disagreement with Paul, like Jesus Paul believed in the resurrection of the dead. Only in light of the resurrection does Paul urge the Philippians to be joyful: "Rejoice in the Lord always; again I will say, Rejoice" (Phil 4:4). Without the resurrection, such joy would not be possible for Paul, because Paul eagerly anticipates—without thereby undermining his commitment to this-worldly justice and holiness of life—the eternal fulfillment of his present communion with the Father, Son, and Holy Spirit.[32]

The biblical scholar Dale Allison, who is at best uncertain about Jesus' bodily resurrection from the dead (or our own), nonetheless observes that "hope for something more than death's wanton and cruel negation of life seems necessary if Jesus' belief in God's loving-kindness is to ring true."[33] He goes on to explain that this intuition is rooted in more than mere dismay over the harshness of death. Rather, it is rooted in a basic element of interpersonal communion, namely, that true friends wish for an ongoing communion with their friend rather than the utter annihilation of their friend. He explains, "Such hope [for life after death] is also, I have come to believe, a correlate of Jesus' demand that I love my neighbor and live by the golden rule. For to love others and to desire for them what I desire for myself is to wish them well, and if they are well, I can hardly want them to go out of existence."[34] Allison would also disagree with Jackson's juxtaposition of Jesus and Paul. According to Allison, Jesus focuses on the life to come without thereby being unconcerned with this-worldly justice. As Allison comments, "For

Jesus, meaning resides principally in the heavenly Father and in the world to come, and in their light he perceives and understands everything else."[35]

Given these concerns, I find inadequate Jackson's view of the "present plenitude" and "joy" available to charitable persons who do not affirm that their present communion with God the Father in Christ and the Holy Spirit will continue beyond their death. In seeking to understand why Jesus and Paul grant such importance to the world to come, I turn to Aquinas' theology of joy (*gaudium*) and sloth (*acedia*). As noted above, Aquinas understands sloth as directly opposed to the joy that is an effect of charity. When sloth characterizes not only our passions but also our rationality, we consent "in the dislike, horror and detestation of the divine good."[36] Such sloth is a mortal sin because it "destroys the spiritual life which is the effect of charity, whereby God dwells in us."[37]

Thomas Aquinas on Joy and Sloth

Joy: Earthly and Eschatological Dimensions

In the first article of his question on joy, Aquinas observes that one might think that mourning, not joy, would be the appropriate interior effect of charity. He has in view such biblical passages as Matthew 5:4, "Blessed are those who mourn, for they shall be comforted," and 2 Corinthians 5:6, "While we are at home in the body we are away from the Lord."[38] As Paul goes on to say, "We would rather be away from the body and at home with the Lord" (2 Cor 5:8). Paul puts the point even more strongly at the beginning of this discourse on death: "Here indeed we groan, and long to put on our heavenly dwelling, so that by putting it on we may not be found naked. For while we are still in this tent, we sigh with anxiety" (2 Cor 5:2-4). The deeper our love for God, the more we wish for a deeper and lasting communion with him, beyond the relatively weak and fleeting communion that we experience in this life. This sorrow for the incompleteness of our communion with God, a sorrow fueled by charity, is largely absent in Jackson's discussion. While allowing one to hope for this deeper union with God,

Jackson assumes that the communion with God that we experience here and now suffices for joy.

Aquinas holds that life in Christ and the Holy Spirit is not primarily characterized by spiritual sorrow for what we lack. In this regard Aquinas cites Romans 5:5, "Hope does not disappoint us, because God's love has been poured into our hearts through the Holy Spirit who has been given to us," and Romans 14:17, "For the kingdom of God does not mean food and drink but righteousness and peace and joy in the Holy Spirit." In light of Paul's words, Aquinas reasons that the presence of God's love in our hearts produces joy. The "kingdom of God" is already present here and now. Nonetheless, the kingdom of God is not fully present. We hope for the arrival of the fullness of the kingdom of God, and in this sense we "groan" for the joy of our "heavenly dwelling," a joy whose perfection flows from the degree of our charity. In this way Aquinas interprets Romans 12:12, "Rejoice in your hope, be patient in tribulation, be constant in prayer."[39]

How can we "groan" and "mourn" while still experiencing the joy that flows from charity (that is, from the presence of the Holy Spirit dwelling in us)? Consider Julian of Norwich's vision of Jesus' passion:

> I, beholding all this by his grace, saw that the love in him was so strong which he has to our soul that willingly he chose it with great desire and mildly he suffered it with great joy. . . . Suddenly, I beholding in the same cross, he changed in blissful visage [blessydfulle chere]. The changing of his blessed visage changed mine, and I was as glad and merry as it was possible.[40]

In this vision, Jesus' supreme sorrow does not negate his perfect joy, and likewise Julian both mourns and rejoices. Since our joy is not yet perfect, it can coexist with deep sorrow.

Indeed, Aquinas in an objection proposes the view that joy in this life always possesses "an admixture of sorrow" because we are not yet fully with Christ. He cites Philippians 1:23, "My desire is to depart and be with Christ, for that is far better."[41] In the same objection, he quotes Psalm 120:5, which in the Vulgate reads, "Woe is me that my sojourning is prolonged."[42] Does it follow that joy, which flows from charity, is *mixed with* sorrow in this life?

Aquinas answers no. The joy that flows from charity has to do with divine realities. When we love God, we rejoice in what we love; there is no sorrow mixed with this joy. Here Aquinas recalls a passage from Wisdom of Solomon in praise of wisdom: "When I enter my house, I shall find rest with her, for companionship with her has no bitterness, and life with her has no pain, but gladness and joy" (Wis 8:16). Since there is no evil or deficiency in God, our joy in the God we love has no taint of sorrow. For this reason, Aquinas suggests, Paul can command, "Rejoice in the Lord always" (Phil 4:4), even though Paul writes from prison and warns the Philippians to "look out for the evil-workers" (Phil 3:2).

While joy is not mixed with sorrow, however, joy does coexist with sorrow. Our love for God causes nothing but joy, as we rejoice in his goodness. Yet we sorrow when we experience things that hinder us from fully rejoicing in God's goodness. Although God created us to participate in his goodness, our participation in God's goodness is not now full because of the evils that characterize the human condition. Aquinas states that "the joy of charity is compatible with an admixture of sorrow, in so far as a man grieves for that which hinders the participation of the divine good, either in us or in our neighbor, whom we love as ourselves."[43]

In what way do suffering and death hinder our joyful "participation of the divine good"? For Jackson, of course, death may well end our participation entirely, thus bringing our joy completely to an end. As we have seen, Aquinas insists that the joy that we experience here and now in loving God is real joy, because we truly participate in God's goodness through charity. Yet he also recognizes that sin and suffering limit our participation in God's goodness, and thereby limit our joy. As he remarks in view of Paul's longing for eternal life in Philippians 1:23: "The unhappiness of this life is an obstacle to a perfect participation in the divine good: hence this very sorrow, whereby a man grieves for the delay of glory, is connected with the hindrance to a participation of the divine good."[44] For Aquinas, then, our communion in love with God causes joy, but at the same time we also long for a deeper, permanent communion with God. The limitation that we experience with respect to our participation in the goodness of God causes sorrow insofar as we yearn for the fulfillment of our joy in eternal life. In this way, charity is connected both with joy and with sorrow.

It follows that charity is internally connected with eternal life. Here and now, our communion with God suffices for joy but also inspires sorrow over the relative weakness and impermanence of this communion. Our love for God (and for our neighbor in God) is such that far from desiring this communion to end or to become weaker, we yearn for eternal communion, for a more perfect participation in God's goodness through charity. In this regard, Jackson's connection of self-giving love with "the present plenitude of the self" and with a joy that is separable from longing for eternal life seems insufficient, whereas Allison's observation that friendship entails desiring a continuation of the friendship appears closer to the mark.

Jackson seeks to emphasize that charity's joy does not depend upon anything else: the joy that we experience in love is not lessened, in itself, by limitations extrinsic to the joy of self-giving love. But Jackson underestimates the truth that bound up in love is the desire to love more perfectly, to be in a more perfect communion with the divine lover. So long as earthly sufferings and limitations deprive us of eternal communion, joy is joined to sorrow and we lack true "plenitude."

In pressing the point that "charity is its own reward," Jackson grants that "all things being equal, we would prefer a lasting communion with those we care for."[45] Yet for Jackson, disagreeing with Paul, "there is no internal relation between charity and an afterlife; they neither require nor exclude one another."[46] Given our preference for "a lasting communion," however, charity does have an internal relation to eternal life, rooted in the dynamism of love itself, which seeks more and more perfect interpersonal union with the beloved and which sorrows when this love is impeded. Jackson is right to hold that the joy that flows from loving does not depend in itself upon whether our charity continues after death, but Jackson should add that joy is hindered insofar as we grieve "for that which hinders the participation of the divine good, either in us or in our neighbor, whom we love as ourselves."[47] Love desires a greater participation in God both for ourselves and for others. Since this is true, there is indeed an internal relation between love and eternal life, since the greater participation in God that we desire for ourselves and others is hindered in this life, and we long for God to bring it about in eternal life.

Indeed, Aquinas does not envision the joy that flows from charity without at the same time considering its fulfillment in eternal life. The communion of charity in this life aims at what Aquinas calls "full enjoyment of God," which is possible only in the complete and lasting communion of the life to come.[48] In the gospel of John, which Jackson reads as promoting a here-and-now "eternal life" rooted in charity, Jesus tells his disciples that they should abide in his love so "that my joy may be in you, and that your joy may be full" (John 15:11).[49] The promise by which Jesus began this discourse, however, goes beyond the here and now: "In my Father's house are many rooms; if it were not so, would I have told you that I go to prepare a place for you? And when I go and prepare a place for you, I will come again and will take you to myself, that where I am you may be also" (John 14:2-3). In pondering the fulfillment of charity and joy, Aquinas also thinks of Jesus' promise (in a parable) that the Lord will tell his faithful ones, "Well done, good and faithful servant; you have been faithful over a little, I will set you over much; enter into the joy of your master" (Matt 25:21).[50] In this parable, eternal life is sharing fully in God's joy, not merely an "afterlife" unrelated to the present life of charity.

From this perspective, the experience of joy and love in this life makes sense as a foretaste of the divine fullness. This is so not because an a priori necessity compels God to give us a lasting participation in his life, but because the gift of charity is a dynamism that carries within itself a yearning for completion and that expresses the divine Lover's will to make us his friends in Christ and the Holy Spirit. As "friends" of Christ (John 15:14), our lives have a touchstone beyond the grave; God does not abandon his friends to death, because he loves them. In order to highlight the glorious character of "the joy of [our] master," and thus to make clear that eternal life differs from mere endless duration of our present life, Aquinas in the same place quotes Paul (who in turn is quoting Isaiah): "What no eye has seen, nor ear heard, nor the heart of man conceived, what God has prepared for those who love him" (1 Cor 2:9).[51]

Does this mean that our reward for charity, our "joy," is otherworldly? On the contrary, insofar as we participate in God's goodness already through charity, we rejoice. But this joy will be far greater, in eternal life, than what we can imagine. Regarding this overflowing joy arising from self-giving love, Aquinas also cites Jesus' words according to the gospel of Luke, "Give, and it will be given to you; good measure, pressed down, shaken together, running over, will be put into your lap" (Luke 6:38).

Sloth: Sorrow about the Gifting God

Sloth is the opposite of joy in divine realities. As Aquinas defines it, sloth is "sorrow about spiritual good."[52] For the charitable person, life in Christ is delightful and desirable. By contrast, the slothful person has "sorrow about spiritual good inasmuch as it is a divine good."[53] So long as sorrow is only in the passions rather than in the will, it need not destroy charity, but may instead instance solely a certain "opposition of the flesh to the spirit."[54] But when the person, in his or her rational will, consents to this sorrow, then sloth has cast out charity. Sloth in this sense manifests a dislike for what is rationally speaking most desirable—namely, friendship with God—because the slothful person finds the requirements of this spiritual good to be too burdensome.[55]

If we knew that God's friendship with us did not extend to wishing us communion with him beyond the short and difficult span of our earthly life, could we avoid finding the arduous quest for spiritual goods to be repugnant? If God's love for us were conceived as not entailing (on his side) the desire for ongoing communion, could we respond positively to this love without being "sorry to have to do something for God's sake"?[56] Put another way, if death ended all, would the resulting portrait of divine friendship be sufficiently attractive, or would divine friendship understood in this way foster "dislike, horror and detestation of the divine good, on account of the flesh utterly prevailing over the spirit"?[57]

Wisdom of Solomon provides a warning in this regard. For Wisdom of Solomon, those who consider death to be the annihilation of the person end up thinking that life is about maximizing earthly pleasure and power, on the grounds that "what is weak proves itself to be useless" (Wis 2:11). Likewise, this concern seems to be behind Paul's protestation, criticized by Jackson, that "if for this life only we have hoped in Christ, we are of all men most to be pitied. . . . If the dead are not raised, 'Let us eat and drink, for tomorrow we die'" (1 Cor 15:19, 32). If humans have only this life, in which sin and suffering largely rule the day, then why should Paul rejoice in spiritual goods to such an extent that he is willing to fight "with beasts at Ephesus" (1 Cor 15:32) and risk his life in many other situations? If God does not will for our spiritual goods—the goods by which he befriends us—to endure past this short life, why should Paul not instead have sorrow regarding spiritual goods?

In his treatment of sloth, Aquinas focuses on the resources of the patristic tradition: John Cassian and Gregory the Great are cited most frequently, and John of Damascus and Isidore of Seville appear as well. Aquinas also draws upon Aristotle's *Nicomachean Ethics* for the observation that "those who find no joy in spiritual pleasures, have recourse to pleasures of the body."[58] Among the vices arising from sloth, Aquinas (indebted to Gregory) identifies despair, faintheartedness, spite, malice, sluggishness about the precepts, and wandering after unlawful things. As Aquinas states, "sloth seeks undue rest [*quietem indebitam*] in so far as it spurns the divine good."[59] These means of "undue rest" express a heart that cannot find rest in God. But can human beings find rest in God if God wills that this communion be utterly cut off at death? Can love will the annihilation of a friend?

Aquinas' use of Scripture in his question on sloth helps, I think, to answer this question. In an objection in the first article, Aquinas quotes Sirach 21:2, "Flee from sin as from a snake; for if you approach sin, it will bite you";[60] to which he adds (in the response to the objection) 1 Corinthians 6:18, "Shun immorality" (Vulgate: *fugite fornicationem*). Although Aquinas uses both texts to distinguish flight from sin from resistance to sin, the text from 1 Corinthians 6 has strong eschatological overtones: "The body is not meant for immorality, but for the Lord, and the Lord for the body. And God raised the Lord and will also raise us up by his power" (1 Cor 6:13-14). Immorality should be avoided because God will raise us from the dead. This resurrection will not merely reveal the condemnation of immorality; it will also reveal the unity (in charity) of believers in Christ. As Paul says, "He who is united to the Lord becomes one spirit with him" (1 Cor 6:17) because of the indwelling Holy Spirit who unites the body of Christ in love.

The choice of Sirach receives further significance in the *sed contra*. The *sed contra* hinges upon Sirach 6:25's teaching about wisdom: "Put your shoulder under her and carry her, and do not fret under her bonds." Here wisdom appears as a burden, an enslavement. If wisdom must be carried like a burden, whereas sin offers pleasures, why flee from sin rather than from wisdom? Sirach answers that wisdom (God's law) will eventually reward those who subject themselves to it. Sirach promises that "at last you will find the rest she [wisdom] gives, and she will be changed into joy for you. Then her fetters will become for you a strong protection, and her collar a glorious robe. Her yoke is a golden ornament, and her bonds are a cord of blue. You will wear her like a glorious robe, and put her on like a crown of gladness" (Sir 6:28-31).

If everlasting death intervenes before one finds such rest, however, of what use is wisdom? Since many people experience the life of wisdom as mere "fetters," wisdom cannot simply be presented as its own reward. In order to be experienced as a reward, wisdom requires an apprenticeship or formation. As described by Sirach, the reward of wisdom has eschatological overtones: "a golden ornament," "a glorious robe," "a crown of gladness." By contrast, sin receives an eschatological punishment, depicted as "fire and worms" (Sir 7:17).

Thus, rather than depicting joy as arising in an experientially clear manner from the life of charity, Aquinas chooses biblical texts that recognize the temptation of spiritual sloth. We require spiritual apprenticeship in order to appreciate the joy of self-giving love, and so Sirach underscores charity's internal relation to an eschatological reward.

This eschatological dimension receives further emphasis through Aquinas' selection of Psalm 107 to illustrate the "weariness of work" that characterizes spiritual sloth.[61] This psalm has to do with God's "steadfast love" that "endures forever" (Ps 107:1) and brings about the redemption of his people. In depicting sloth, Aquinas quotes Psalm 107:18, "They loathed any kind of food, and they drew near to the gates of death." As Aquinas points out, the medieval gloss on this text applies the loathing of "food" (in the spiritual sense) to the slothful person. Joy, not sloth, should flow from communion with God because God's love is "steadfast." After describing those who loathe "food" and are heading toward "the gates of death," the psalm continues by stating that God "sent forth his word, and healed them, and delivered them from destruction" (Ps 107:20). God's "steadfast love" manifests itself by healing those who are near death, a healing that God accomplishes by sending forth "his word." This psalm measures the steadfastness of God's love by the willingness of God to deliver his people from death. The slothful are on the path of death; their deliverance comes about when God manifests his everlasting love for them through his word. Such love conquers death, thereby producing the rejoicing of God's (previously slothful) people: "Let them offer sacrifices of thanksgiving, and tell of his deeds in songs of joy!" (Ps 107:22).

Aquinas complements his quotation from Psalm 107 with a quotation from 2 Corinthians. In a manner similar to that of Psalm 107, 2 Corinthians describes the power of God's love to redeem his suffering people. Urging the Corinthians to depend upon God's love in Christ, Paul appeals to the example of his own suffering: "We do not want you to be ignorant, brethren, of the affliction we experienced in Asia; for we were so utterly, unbearably crushed that we despaired of life itself. Why, we felt that we had received the sentence of death; but that was to make us rely not on ourselves but on God who raises the dead" (2 Cor 1:8-9). Paul's suffering causes him sorrow without extinguishing his joy, because he relies on "God who raises the dead." By contrast, Paul is aware of a kind of suffering that extinguishes the joy of charity. He explains that a formerly wayward member of the Corinthian church needs comforting from his brethren, lest he "be overwhelmed by excessive sorrow" (2 Cor 2:7) and leave the church. Aquinas cites this text from 2 Corinthians as an example of the sloth that can arise when spiritual goods no longer rejoice our hearts.[62] Against the onset of such sloth stand not only one's fellow believers, but also, and most importantly, the "God who raises the dead."

Before he moves in the fourth and final article to evaluating Gregory the Great's (and Isidore of Seville's) portrait of sloth as a "capital vice," Aquinas cites 2 Corinthians 7:10 in the *sed contra* of article three. In 2 Corinthians 7:10, Paul compares godly and worldly grief: "For godly grief produces a repentance that leads to salvation and brings no regret, but worldly grief produces death." Such "worldly grief," Aquinas comments, is spiritual sloth. Paul goes on to say that worldly grief does not lead to repentance and to spiritual zeal. Instead, worldly grief, or sloth, bogs down the sinner in his or her sins, from which the sinner makes no effort to escape. For his part, Paul refuses to "lose heart" (2 Cor 4:16) because he knows that "this slight momentary affliction is preparing for us an eternal weight of glory beyond all comparison" (2 Cor 4:17). With the resurrection of the dead in view, Paul warns against the sloth (or "worldly grief") that imprisons humans in their sins by causing them to lose heart in the midst of sin and suffering.

Aquinas' biblical quotations in his treatment of sloth undermine Jackson's view that "charity is its own reward" or that "there is no internal relation between charity and an afterlife."[63] If charity were easily experienced as "its own reward," then sloth would not be a real temptation; we would all go joyfully about loving God and each other. Sloth is a real temptation because it may often seem that sin and death, not love, ultimately conquer. To learn the joy of charity in the midst of suffering entails not simply relating to God and neighbor here and now. Rather, experiencing joy and avoiding sloth involves an apprenticeship or formation in God's steadfast love. In Christ and the Holy Spirit, God overcomes sin and death for us. God truly cares for us, rather than leaving us subject to annihilation. Receiving such powerful love, we enter into the communion of the Trinity, a communion in which we find our eternal home.

Sloth supposes that this eternal communion of love is ultimately not for us. Joy knows that God, the infinite Lover, calls us to an eternal communion with him. As Aquinas describes God's communication of his life to us in Christ Jesus: "Some kind of friendship must be based on this same communication, of which it is written (1 Cor. 1:9): 'God is faithful: by Whom you are called unto the fellowship of His Son.' The love which is based on this communication, is charity."[64]

Conclusion

Recall Aquinas' point that "the joy of charity is compatible with an admixture of sorrow, in so far as a man grieves for that which hinders the participation of the divine good, either in us or in our neighbor, whom we love as ourselves."[65] This way of putting it differentiates his position from Jackson's. On the one hand, he can agree with Jackson's insistence upon the sufficiency of charity (and joy) because charity and joy have God for their object. Communion with God in charity is indeed its own reward, and it suffices for real unalloyed joy even in the midst of suffering. On the other hand, his emphasis on our "participation of the divine good" reminds us that charity—and joy—can always increase in this life, because in this life they only inaugurate our relationship with the gifting God. Charity leads us to desire greater charity and greater joy through a more profound and enduring communion with the Trinity. As Aquinas comments, "The capacity of the rational creature is increased by charity, because the heart is enlarged thereby, according to 2 Cor. 6:11: 'Our heart is enlarged.'"[66] Charity desires its own eschatological perfection: "The increase of charity is directed to an end, which is not in this, but in a future life."[67] This is so because charity is personal communion with God the Trinity, and so charity desires to expand this friendship. In short, charity has within itself a relation to eternal life because charity "is a participation of the infinite charity which is the Holy Spirit."[68]

As Jackson might expect, Aquinas draws deeply upon the writings of Paul. His theology of joy as an effect of charity contains ten quotations from Paul, along with four quotations from the Gospels that contextualize Paul's connection of joy and charity with eternal life, above all John 15:11, "These things I have spoken to you, that my joy may be in you, and that your joy may be full," and Matthew 25:21, "Well done, good and faithful servant; you have been faithful over a little, I will set you over much; enter into the joy of your master." As we have seen, Aquinas' theology of joy contains room for earthly suffering while focusing on our participation in God's goodness through friendship with the Trinity. In his discussion of joy's opposite, sloth, he shows how people give up on God's gifting. Both his Old Testament texts and his New Testament texts (the latter drawn entirely from the Corinthian correspondence) highlight Scripture's appeal to us to rely on the power of God's redemptive love rather than sorrowfully turning away from God in the midst of our sins and sufferings. Here a key element is Paul's distinction between godly grief, which produces repentance and zeal, and worldly grief, which produces spiritual death by imagining that we cannot rely "on God who raises the dead" (2 Cor 1:9) to conquer bodily death for us.

Aquinas describes sloth as our rational consent "in the dislike, horror and detestation of the divine good, on account of the flesh utterly prevailing over the spirit."[69] When sensible goods (the pleasures of this world) come to seem better than spiritual goods (friendship with God), the result is that we become "sorry to have to do something for God's sake."[70] Rather than taking joy in the relationship with God that charity enables, we turn away from such a relationship. As Aquinas shows, if our participation in God's goodness is only for this life, then our relationship with God—charity's internal dynamism—would be stunted from the outset. Why would God only love us and care for us for such a short time, and then assent to our utter annihilation? How could a friend or lover do that, and how could our love be nourished within such a context? With Paul, Aquinas answers that it could not: we would succumb to sloth, toward which we often tend anyway. Paul rejoices that "we know that if the earthly tent we live in is destroyed, we have a building from God, a house not made with hands, eternal in the heavens" (2 Cor 5:1). Yet Paul recognizes that were this not the case, the love of God poured out in Christ through the Holy

Spirit would not be the perduring gift that Paul knows it to be; and so Paul rightly observes, "If Christ has not been raised, your faith is futile and you are still in your sins. Then those also who have fallen asleep in Christ have perished. If for this life only we have hoped in Christ, we are of all men most to be pitied" (1 Cor 15:17-19).

CHAPTER 4

Envy and God-Reliance

Introduction

Remarking upon the presence of ambition in each human being, Ralph Waldo Emerson states, "We honor the rich because they have externally the freedom, power, and grace, which we feel to be proper to man, proper to us. So all that is said of the wise man by Stoic or Oriental or modern essayist, describes to each reader his own idea, describes his unattained but attainable self."[1] Throughout his career, Emerson responds to the impulse to honor others by urging us to honor our true selves. We must seek perfection within ourselves: "There is a time in every man's education when he arrives at the conviction that envy is ignorance; that imitation is suicide; that he must take himself for better, for worse, as his portion. . . . Trust thyself: every heart vibrates to that iron string."[2] For Emerson, envy is the sign of cowardly lack of "self-reliance."[3]

I want to contest this portrait of envy as a cowardly underestimation of one's own resources. Indeed, when we rely upon our own resources, we set ourselves up for envy. We soon find that we cannot attain to the status we think we should attain and that we see in others around us. What we require instead is an understanding of the good of others as participating in the goodness of the divine giver, whose love for each of us is superabundant. By learning to rely upon the divine giver who pours forth a diversity of gifts and calls us to eternal communion in him, we can learn to love the good we see in others rather than sorrowing that others possess more good than we do.

In exploring the sin against charity that is envy, I begin with the book of Genesis. Reading the stories of Cain and Abel and Joseph and his brothers (among others), Jewish and Christian scholars have proposed valuable ways of avoiding and overcoming envy. In light of Genesis, I turn to a detailed reading of Thomas Aquinas' theology of envy. Aquinas teaches God-reliance as the solution to envy, a God-reliance rooted in love of God and neighbor as modeled by Christ Jesus, who reverses Cain's murderous envy.

Overcoming Envy: Beginning with Genesis

In a recent popular handbook of Jewish ethics, Rabbi Joseph Telushkin devotes a chapter to envy in which he examines various stories from Genesis.[4] The most well-known is that of Cain and Abel: when the Lord approves Abel's offering but does not approve Cain's, "Cain was very angry, and his countenance fell" (Gen 4:5). Envious of his brother, he murders him. Telushkin also mentions the Philistines' envy of Isaac's great possessions (Gen 26:14), Rachel's envy of Leah due to Leah's having many children while Rachel remains childless (Gen 30:1), Leah's envy of Rachel because of Jacob's greater love for Rachel (Gen 30:15), and the jealousy of Joseph's brothers because of Jacob's greater love for Joseph (Gen 37:11).

According to Telushkin, entirely avoiding envy is not possible. In support of this position he cites two texts from the Talmud, one of which suggests that only God can preserve us from envy (both our own and that of others toward us), while the other states that we will envy everyone except our children and our students, whose success we can bear with equanimity. The biblical example of lack of envy for our children is David's assent to his servants' prayer that Solomon's reign be greater than David's (1 Kgs 1:47); the biblical example of lack of envy for our students/disciples is Elijah's consent to Elisha's prayer to receive a "double share" of Elijah's spirit

(2 Kgs 2:9). But if only our children and our close disciples escape our envy, how can we avoid the corrosive and violent consequences of envy in our lives?

This question is the main burden of Rabbi Telushkin's chapter. Following Daniel Taub, he observes that the reason why we often do not envy the success of our children and close students is that we feel that we have contributed to, and thereby share in, their success. The first way to diminish envy, therefore, is to focus on helping others, so as to be successful oneself through the success of others. Second, Telushkin learns from Rabbi Nachman of Bratslav (1772–1810), who taught that we should focus on the good points of others, thereby enabling us to see why their success was fully deserved. Third, religious persons will desire to observe God's command, "you shall love your neighbor as yourself" (Lev 19:18; cf. Mark 12:31). This desire to obey God's command should lead us to pray for the success of those we envy. Prayer will reduce our envy and enable us to succeed more fully in obeying God's command. Fourth, when we envy someone for their successes, we should ask ourselves whether we would want to have not only their successes but also their sufferings and problems.

As further practical tactics for overcoming envy, we should consider that we possess certain abilities and blessings that the person we envy lacks; we should compare ourselves with those less fortunate than ourselves rather than only with who seem to have been more fortunate; we should seek to improve our lives by emulating the merits of the person we envy (in this sense envy, when reoriented, can be a creative catalyst); and we should meditate on ways that our envy can harm ourselves and others. Perhaps most importantly, we should strive not to incite others' envy. Thus we should downplay our accomplishments, we should show interest in other people's lives, we should show appreciation for the work of others who are less widely appreciated, we should share our wealth with others, and we should treat our children equally. As Telushkin observes with regard to our behavior toward our children, "One suspects that, during Joseph's days as a slave and prisoner in Egypt, he did not remember Jacob's favoritism with gratitude."[5]

Reflecting on the story of Cain and Abel, the Old Testament scholar Walter Moberly concentrates on the inequities that we experience in our lives, inequities that are so often out of our control—for example, differences in health, in bodily appearance, in intelligence, and in the circumstances in which one lives one's life. The "unfavored" person tends enviously to ask the backward-looking question of why he or she is less favored than another person, whereas the biblical story insists upon looking forward. Cain is crestfallen now, but if he does well in the future he will be "accepted" or "lifted up."[6] The key is to learn how to love. Moberly offers a similar reading of Joseph's development. Joseph exacerbates the envy that his brothers feel for him by boastfully describing his dreams in which he receives dominion over his brothers and parents (see Gen 37:5-11). A more mature Joseph, however, learns that the fulfillment of such dreams means not domineering dominion but life-giving service (Gen 45:5).[7] When success is understood as service, envy can be overcome.

The Jewish ethicist Leon Kass treats Cain's envy in the context of Cain's expectations as the firstborn: "The bitterness of not having his own gift respected is nothing compared with seeing the greater success of his (lesser) brother."[8] After murdering his brother, however, Cain begins to understand the real meaning of brotherhood, namely, the sharing of blood. The horror caused by Cain's shedding of his brother's blood makes clear that envy arises from differences that are trivial in comparison to what should bond brothers together. With a focus on the tensions that arise because of Jacob's actions, Kass comments as well upon Rachel's experience of the "ugly green monster" of envy.[9] Rachel's envy, and the rivalry within Jacob's family, is exacerbated by Jacob's consent to have intercourse with Rachel's slave Bilhah in order to obtain surrogate children for Rachel. In Kass' view, Rachel and Leah enact a sisterly rivalry "for love and 'creativity'" comparable to that of the brothers Cain and Abel.[10] Rachel is the beautiful one, Leah is the one blessed with children; at issue is how to negotiate and channel the envy of each for the other. Kass places Joseph's situation likewise within the context of how to form human community. At the outset, Joseph is "deaf to all political tones" and "imprudent in the extreme": Kass finds Joseph's dreams to reveal the ambition of "cosmic mastery," so that "the heavens do not declare the glory of God but instead bow to the superiority of Joseph."[11] Whereas Moberly argues that Joseph's later revelation of his identity to his brothers in Egypt indicates a mature overcoming of the pattern of domineering (on Joseph's side) and envy (on his brothers' side), Kass is not so sure.[12]

The seriousness with which Rabbi Telushkin takes envy, then, is echoed by Moberly and Kass as biblical commentators. Telushkin argues that envy is bad because it distorts our relationship with our neighbor and with God. So as not to have our lives crippled by envy, we need to practice helping others, to realize that others' successes are often deserved, to pray for the success of those we envy, to be aware that their successes come with problems and difficulties, and to be careful not to boast. Moberly finds similar messages in Genesis' presentation of Cain and Abel and of Joseph and his brothers. God calls Cain to overcome his envy by looking forward, by learning how to love. Joseph develops from the immaturity of boasting to the mature realization that power is about life-giving service rather than about domineering. Kass, too, reflects upon the consequences of boasting, although he thinks that Joseph remained subject to this vice. For Kass, envy is conquered by the recognition of the unity of the whole human community as well as by the recognition of the family's unity.

Thomas Aquinas on Envy

Envy and Zeal

When the joy of charity has to do with the divine good, joy's opposite is sloth; and when the joy of charity has to do with the neighbor's good, joy's opposite is envy (*invidia*). Following John Damascene and Aristotle, Aquinas defines envy as sorrow regarding the good of our neighbor, a sorrow that comes about because the good of our neighbor seems to constitute an evil for ourselves. When our neighbor possesses a good, it may seem to lessen our "own good name [*propriae gloriae*] or excellence."[13] On this view the better our neighbor is, the worse we are. Desiring reputation for ourselves, we feel lessened when our neighbor possesses greater reputation. Aquinas explains that a person "is envious of those only whom he wishes to rival or surpass in reputation."[14] For this reason we envy those whose position in life is in some way similar to ours. We do not envy those whose position is significantly different from ours, because their reputation does not compete with ours. Envy is dangerous because it is so concrete: a person envies those "whom he strives to rival or surpass."[15] A professor envies other professors.

Does this portrait of envy overestimate most people's competitiveness? Does envy perhaps only afflict the ambitious? In answer, Aquinas observes that all people have at least some ambition. Because envy has to do with peers, envy threatens everyone. We are all prone to thinking that we can do better than the colleague or the neighbor. Although everyone is susceptible to envy in some degree, however, people who have greater ambition are more susceptible. In addition, cowards (*pusillanimes*) are more susceptible to envy, because they consider all goods to be hard to attain and therefore they more easily consider that others are greater than they are.[16]

What about those who no longer strive after reputation? Following Aristotle, Aquinas replies that envy does indeed remain a threat even after the quest for reputation has become less heated. For example, older people, having lost the good of youthful health, can envy younger people. Aquinas comments, "Recollection of past goods in so far as we have had them, causes pleasure; in so far as we have lost them, causes sorrow; and in so far as others have them, causes envy, because that, above all, seems to belittle our reputation [*quia hoc maxime videtur gloriae propriae derogare*]."[17] When others have more, we appear to have less. We want to be the ones who have more. Similarly, even when we possess the same reputation as another person, we can envy the other person because he or she gained this reputation without incurring the losses that we incurred.

But what is wrong with wanting to have more reputation or glory than another person? How would we improve ourselves in virtue, for example, if we did not measure ourselves against others and try to attain to their level or even to outdo them? If the student does not wish to learn more than the teacher knows, then the student's zeal for knowledge is inadequate. Quoting Psalm 69:9, with its Chris-tological reference (see John 2:17 and Rom 15:3), Aquinas points out that zeal can be good: "Zeal for thy house has consumed me."[18] He goes on carefully to distinguish envy from zeal. Being sorrowful when one sees that another person has a good is not necessarily sin-ful. For example, righteous sorrow over another's good arises when we know that the good will be misused, as when a demagogue gains political power. Similarly, righteous sorrow may be produced by see-ing another's good, not because the other person possesses the good, but because we lack that particular good and wish also to have it. Aquinas cites Paul in support of such zeal: "Make love your aim, and earnestly desire the spiritual gifts" (1 Cor 14:1).[19]

Aquinas also mentions the sorrow for another's good that Aris-totle calls *nemesis*. This kind of sorrow arises when a person sees an unjust person receive a temporal good, such as wealth, that many just persons lack. Aristotle holds that one can justly be sorrowful at such an event, not because the newly wealthy person will neces-sarily use the wealth badly, but because the newly wealthy person is unworthy to receive such wealth while worthier persons remain poor. In Aristotle's view, the uneven distribution of temporal goods is a cause for just sadness on the part of the just person who knows that he or she merits more temporal goods.

Aquinas argues that Aristotle's understanding of *nemesis* fails to appreciate the providential ordering of rational creatures to eter-nal rather than temporal goods. As Aquinas explains, God may in fact be punishing the unjust wealthy person by giving the tempo-ral good. By withholding the temporal good, God may be assisting the worthy poor person toward the attainment of eternal good. It would therefore be the sin of envy rather than a just sadness (*nem-esis*) if one were to be sad about another's good because the other person is unworthy. Aquinas appeals here to psalms which warn that sorrow over the good of an unworthy person undermines one's faith in God's providential care: "Fret not yourself because of the wicked, be not envious of wrongdoers!" (Ps 37:1); "But as for me, my feet had almost stumbled, my steps had well nigh slipped. For I was envious of the arrogant, when I saw the prosperity of the wicked" (Ps 73:2-3).

In short, charity promotes zeal for virtuous goods, and in this regard we should be sorrowful that we do not possess the good that we see in our neighbor: as Paul urges us, "Be imitators of me, as I am of Christ" (1 Cor 11:1). Charity also ensures that we will not be envious of the temporal goods of unworthy persons, because we seek eternal goods and have faith in God's providence. But charity requires that we sorrow when we see an unworthy person receive a temporal good that he or she will use to harm the common good, so long as our sorrow has to do with the harm that we foresee. Envy arises only when we sorrow for our neighbor's good "in so far as his good surpasses ours."[20] Rather than imagining ourselves to be in competition with our neighbor for reputation, we should rejoice in the good that our neighbor possesses. The good that our neighbor possesses, insofar as it is good, is due to God's gifting. Therefore our response in charity must be joy. If our neighbor is greater than we are, our response must be greater joy due to the greater good, which in itself is the effect of God's gifting.

The Gifting God and the Parsimonious "God"

In exploring the harm that envy does to us, Aquinas begins with our experience of charity, as set forth in 1 John 3:14: "We know that we have passed out of death into life, because we love the brethren."[21] Charity gives life in communion with the Trinity and our neighbor; lack of charity means that we remain in our sins, enslaved to patterns of behavior that are spiritually death-dealing. In charity, we love God, and our neighbor in God, for God's goodness. We love God's goodness and all who share in it. Charity provides a new way of seeing reality. David Bentley Hart puts it well: "The Christian should see two realities at once, one world (as it were) within another: one the world as we all know it, in all its beauty and terror, grandeur and dreariness, delight and anguish; and the other the world in its first and ultimate truth, not simply 'nature' but 'creation,' an endless sea of glory, radiant with the beauty of God in every part, innocent of all violence."[22] By contrast, in envy we see our neighbor's good and instead of rejoicing in God's good gifting, we sorrow. As Aquinas says, "charity rejoices in our neighbor's good, while envy grieves over it."[23]

Does every envious feeling destroy charity? Aquinas distinguishes the movement of the passions from the full consent of the will. Some movements of envy, arising in the passions, are sins, but because they do not receive the full consent of the will, they do not destroy charity and so are "venial" rather than "mortal." Aquinas here probes further into envy's relationship to Aristotle's *nemesis*. In his *Rhetoric*, Aristotle grants that "envy is closely akin to indignation [*nemesis*], or even the same thing."[24] But as we have seen, Aristotle distinguishes the two on the grounds that *nemesis* consists in sorrow or pain at seeing the undeserving receive a good, whereas envy consists in seeing the prosperity of those who are like oneself. For Aristotle, we must rejoice only "at the prosperity of the deserving."[25] Aquinas corrects this position to take into account the scope of human sinfulness, as well as the creature-Creator relationship. In a real sense, no one is deserving; all good is God's gift and we must rejoice in it as such. Furthermore, the charitable person need not be indignant at the prosperity of the wicked person; such grieving would only be appropriate were there a fundamental injustice in the ordering of temporal goods. As Aquinas argues, there is no such injustice in God's providential gifting, although the temporal ordering often appears unjust. The justice of God's gifts of temporal goods can only be measured in light of the final end toward which all God's gifting aims.

God's gifting here and now aims at leading humans to the eternal communion of charity. To sorrow enviously about others' goods is to turn away from the gifting God and to worship instead a parsimonious god whose gifts are scarce and zero-sum, whose gifts need to be jealously hoarded. We could not approach such a god as a friend, nor could such a god truly befriend us in love. William Cavanaugh explains this in economic terms: "Scarcity is the more general hunger of those who want more, without reference to what they already have."[26] Envy supposes that the God of love, the gifting God, is in fact the god of scarcity, so that if my neighbor gains more good, I have less. When we envy others, we have lost sight of what "good" truly is: participation in the infinite God who is infinite goodness and love. Cavanaugh invites us to see that envy is turned on its head in the Eucharist, by which Christ renews our ability to grieve for our neighbor's suffering and to rejoice in his or her good: "The abundance of the Eucharist is inseparable from the *kenosis*, the self-emptying, of the Cross. The consumer of the body and blood of Christ does not remain detached from what he or she consumes, but becomes part of the body. . . . The Eucharist effects a radical decentering of the individual by incorporating the person into a larger body."[27] This sacrificial decentering frees us from envy so as to love God's gifting in our neighbor, and thereby to love the true God whose gifts are not scarce or zero-sum.

Aquinas employs 1 John 3:14 particularly to depict envy's opposition to charity: "We know that we have passed out of death into life, because we love the brethren." When one reads 1 John 3:14 in context, one finds the story of Cain and Abel. Contrasting love with Cain's prototypical act of envy, 1 John states, "For this is the message which you have heard from the beginning, that we should love one another, and not be like Cain who was of the evil one and murdered his brother. And why did he murder him? Because his own deeds were evil and his brother's righteous" (1 John 3:11-12). Cain lives in a zero-sum world (that of Satan) rather than in attunement with the gifting God. As 1 John asks, "But if any one has the world's goods and sees his brother in need, yet closes his heart against him, how does God's love abide in him?" (1 John 3:17). The generosity of the gifting God is not mirrored by Cain, whose heart is enviously closed against his brother: "Any one who hates his brother is a murderer, and you know that no murderer has eternal life abiding in him" (1 John 3:15). By contrast, love gives up even one's own life for the good of others: "By this we know love, that he [Christ Jesus] laid down his life for us; and we ought to lay down our lives for the brethren" (1 John 3:16).

As Moberly suggests—and as the Lord confirms to Cain—Cain need not have remained with his "countenance fallen" (Gen 4:6). Cain could have been "lifted up" or "accepted" (Gen 4:7) if he had wished to enter into the pattern of the divine gifting, that is, the pattern of self-giving love. Unity among brethren cannot be monolithic; rather, it is a joyful unity in the abundance and diversity of God's gifting. Kass rightly comments that Genesis is concerned primarily with establishing a community "not founded in fratricide," a community founded instead in God's gifting.[28]

Sinning against the Holy Spirit

Examining the effects of envy in the human person and community, Aquinas endorses Gregory the Great's teaching that from envy sprout "hatred, tale-bearing, detraction, joy at our neighbor's misfortunes, and grief for his prosperity."[29] According to Gregory and Aquinas, envy for its part arises from pride and vainglory, which turn the person away from the gifting God.[30] In light of 1 John and of Wisdom 2:24—"through the devil's envy death entered the world, and those who belong to his party experience it"—Aquinas observes that although envy is not the greatest sin (the greatest sin is hatred of God), nonetheless "when the devil tempts us to envy, he is enticing us to that which has its chief place in his heart [*ipse principaliter in corde habet*]."[31] Envy craves the power that it associates with the good, and supposes that this power is ultimately something other than self-giving love. Thus the envious person sorrows when another person shares in God's goodness, because this sharing seems to threaten the status and power of the envious person.[32]

Aquinas points out that when this sharing has to do with a spiritual good, then the envious person sins against the Holy Spirit by sorrowing that grace is at work in another person. As Aquinas states, this deepest form of envy is, in a real sense, envy of the Holy Spirit, "who is glorified in His works."[33] Rather than praising the works of the Holy Spirit, the envious person sorrows over them. The Holy Spirit himself, who is Gift in Person, thereby becomes a cause of sorrow to the envious person. Willing that every good be added to oneself, so that one outshines all one's peers in every way, thus turns grotesquely into sorrow over the source of all goodness. Overweening desire to be gifted turns into sorrow, rather than joy, about the giver. The absurdity of envy is well depicted by Dante's vision of its purgatorial cure: "The eyelids of these shades had been sewn shut with iron threads," since they sorrowed to see others' good.[34] They have made painful what should be joyful, namely, the vision of God's good gifting.

Recall Rabbi Telushkin's gradual cures for the envy that we experience: helping others by contributing to their successes, observing how others' strengths make them worthy of the good things that come their way, praying for the success of those we envy, noting that the achievements of other people do not come without their own particular sufferings, and avoiding boasting (this last being emphasized also by Kass with regard to Joseph and his brothers). By contrast, the "daughters" of envy listed by Gregory and Aquinas contradict these injunctions. Rather than helping others, we secretly say negative things about them (tale-bearing). Rather than considering that others are worthy of successes, we openly attempt to lower their reputations (detraction). Rather than sympathizing with their sufferings, we take joy in fostering their misfortunes (by successfully defaming them). Rather than praying for their success, we sorrow at their prosperity (when we fail to defame them). Rather than seeking to avoid occasions of envy by not boasting, we frame our lives around a hatred for others that is produced by our sorrow at their successes.[35]

Telushkin suggests that religious persons will want to pray for others in order to reduce the envy that we feel. As he says with respect to our religious commitment, "If you are a religious person, be aware that envy will make it impossible for you to fulfill one of the most important biblical commands, 'Love your neighbor as yourself' (Lev 19:18). You can't both love someone and feel envy and hostility toward him."[36] But I wonder whether, absent belief in the gifting God who is the common good of all humans, envy can in fact be avoided—despite the excellent tips that Telushkin suggests for relieving the pressure of envy, and despite the fact that envy plagues some people more than others. Jesus significantly links Leviticus 19:18's commandment regarding love of neighbor (which requires freedom from envy) with Deuteronomy 6:5, "You shall love the Lord your God with all your heart, and with all your soul, and with all your might" (see Mark 12:29-31). DeYoung describes the way in which reliance upon God relieves us of envy: "A self secure in its unconditional worth, a worth based on God's love, is a self free to affirm others' gifts without feeling threatened or thereby made inferior."[37]

What Hobbes Teaches Us

Thomas Hobbes proposes that the concept of God as one, eternal, incorporeal, infinite, and omnipotent is a "just-so" story that arises from human ignorance of physical processes.[38] This evisceration of the Creator God has consequences for Hobbes' understanding of human loves. At best, says Hobbes, happiness consists in fulfilling one desire after another, in accord with our "perpetual and restless desire of power after power, that ceaseth only in death."[39] In Hobbes' view, far from signaling that we are ordered to a higher end (God), human restlessness comes from the fact that we cannot possess enough goods to secure our ease: even for the king, there is always a sense in which "he cannot assure the power and means to live well which he hath present, without the acquisition of more."[40]

Hobbes thus envisions life as a competition for scarce resources. No eternal goods are truly at stake, and so all that is left is the scarcity of temporal goods. The competition for these goods is fueled, Hobbes thinks, by the fact that humans are all basically the same as regards their natural powers, even though each person imagines himself to excel others. Each human therefore hopes to conquer all others, and since each is at the same level naturally, each envies all others: "For every man looketh that his companion should value him at the same rate he sets upon himself," that is, as superior to others.[41] Because no one person can claim anything as necessarily due to him or her from another person, it follows that were it not for the power of the state, a general condition of war would reign over human affairs, a condition in which no action could be declared unjust.[42]

Hobbes finds that the words "gift" and "grace" differ from a contractual relationship only because one party transfers his right to all-out war without requiring any transfer of right from the other party, "in hope to gain thereby friendship or service from another (or from his friends), or in hope to gain the reputation of charity or magnanimity, or to deliver his mind from the pain of compassion, or in hope of reward in heaven."[43] On this view, far from enacting divine selflessness, "gift" and "grace" are imbued with human self-interest.

Those who believe in the Creator God who freely loves all things into existence and moves them toward their ultimate end will not accept Hobbes' portrait of God or of humanity. Yet, considering only temporal goods, can we ever have enough? Are not resources in fact scarce? If we do not constantly care for the furtherance of our worldly reputation, will not others excel us so that we are forgotten and displaced? Do we not generally tend to consider ourselves at least the equal of our peers, and by nature the equal of all human beings? Why should others have more goods than we have?

It is true, as Telushkin and Aquinas both record, that envy crimps our enjoyment of life. We have self-interested reasons to moderate as much as possible not only our own experience of envy, but also our prompting of envy in others. Without faith in the Creator God, however, can we avoid envious sorrowing when we see our colleague and peer flush with temporal goods? Especially in light of the real insecurity that (as Hobbes so acutely sees) plagues each human life, so that we are constantly threatened with displacement and devaluation, can we avoiding envying our neighbor because of his or her greater goods?

In the passage from 1 John that is central for Aquinas, the movement from death to life—from Cain's murderous envy to eternal life in Christ—comes about through God's gift of charity. Similarly, in his four articles on envy, Aquinas twice quotes Job 5:2, where Eliphaz the Temanite (not otherwise noted for his wisdom) observes that "jealousy slays the simple."[44] In his response to Eliphaz, Job emphasizes that his suffering has overwhelmed him; his suffering goes beyond anything that he has done. Job displays the human person in a condition of radical displacement, the condition that, as Hobbes recognizes, we all fear. Could Job long avoid grieving over his friends' possession of goods that he himself so painfully lacks? Indeed, Job's protest against the radical displacement that he experiences subsides only with full recognition of God's presence and providence (Job 38–42). Like 1 John, the book of Job witnesses to the fact that charity, and the overcoming of envy as a sin against charity, requires faith.

Conclusion

The sins that arise from envy show all too well the importance of strategies against envy. Such strategies should include, as Telushkin and others observe, an avoidance of boasting and a focus on serving others. As William Cavanaugh suggests, furthermore, we should allow 1 John 3 to point us to the Eucharist. Aquinas observes that the Eucharist "works in man the effect which Christ's Passion wrought in the world," so that we are "as it were inebriated with the sweetness of the divine goodness."[45] The Eucharist sacramentally represents Christ's passion and thereby enables us to participate in his love for others. Recall 1 John 3:16, "By this we know love, that he laid down his life for us; and we ought to lay down our lives for the brethren." The effect of the Eucharist is the upbuilding of Christ's body, the church, in charity. For this reason, Aquinas (following Augustine) speaks of the Eucharist's twofold signification: "In the Sacrament of the Altar, two things are signified, viz. Christ's true body, and Christ's mystical body."[46]

Ralph Waldo Emerson, by contrast, points us away from the Eucharist. In his resignation sermon of 9 September 1832, titled "The Lord's Supper," Emerson argues that in the history of the church, the Eucharist has caused far more controversy than it has caused charitable communion. The disciples' common meal, in Emerson's view, was quickly converted into a "rite" by "half-converted Pagans and Jews" who were as "yet unable to comprehend the spiritual character of Christianity."[47] Emerson holds that to celebrate the outward form of the Eucharist is to remain in a religion of rites. As Emerson asks with an allusion to the forward march of history, "Is not this to make vain the gift of God? Is not this to turn back the hand on the dial?"[48] On this view, it would be ludicrous to propose that the seemingly divisive, outward rite of the Eucharist is the answer to the envy that sets us against each other.

In the Eucharist, however, we become one with Christ in his Holy Spirit so as to participate, as a visible community, in Christ's sacrificial love toward his Father and all human beings. We overcome envy not by self-reliance, but by receiving the Holy Spirit's healing power through our participation in Christ's changing of the world. Christ and the Holy Spirit can overcome our envy. Here we experience and bear witness (even if fragile witness, ever in need of renewal and growth) to the superabundant gifting, rather than scarcity, of the divine goodness. Insofar as we live in charity and free from envy, we do so as having "this treasure in earthen vessels, to show that the transcendent power belongs to God and not to us" (2 Cor 4:7).

CHAPTER 5

Discord, Contention, and Ecclesial Peace

Discussing discord as a sin against charity, Thomas Aquinas grants that discord need not always be sinful. When Paul and Barnabas disagree with each other in Acts 15:39, for example, their conflict does not rise to the level of discord because they continue to share the same aim. Similarly, when Paul provokes the Pharisees and Sadducees in Acts 23:6, he engages in praiseworthy discord by destroying an evil concord.[1] Yet Jesus condemns discord in Matthew 12:25, "Every kingdom divided against itself is laid waste, and no city or house divided against itself will stand," and Paul speaks out against discord or "dissension" in Galatians 5:20.[2] Aquinas notes that discord, which results from inordinate preference for one's own opinion, destroys the concord of charity that "directs many hearts together to one thing, which is chiefly the divine good, secondarily the good of our neighbor."[3] Contention brings discord to the level of speech, and can be good or bad depending on whether one is contending in an ordinate fashion for the truth.[4]

This chapter focuses on charity's effect of peace, not on discord and contention, which oppose peace. Yet it does so by exploring an often discordant and contentious question—namely, that of how to receive the Second Vatican Council. In the view of Karl Rahner, authentic reception of the council involves the church's "self-actualization *as* a world Church."[5] Rahner envisions the incultura-tion of the gospel in and by the world church as resulting in an "authentic pluralism," a "pluralism of proclamations" based upon the "hierarchy of truths" on which foundation "the whole of eccle-sial faith" must be formulated anew.[6] For Rahner, the reception of Vatican II—its actualization in and by the world church—requires attending more deeply to the "collegial constitutional principle in the Church," on the grounds that "a world Church simply cannot be ruled with the sort of Roman centralism that was customary in the period of the Piuses."[7] By means of this "collegial constitutional principle," which he finds in the documents of Vatican II, Rahner seeks to enhance the peace of the church against the corrosive power of discord and contention.

More recently, Joseph Chinnici has proposed that what is needed is a deeper reception of Vatican II's "turn toward the pastoral."[8] In the face of persistent discord among Catholics, he seeks a simulta-neously faithful and innovative dialogic process that responds to contemporary concerns while respecting the framework of "the inherited practices and interpretations already in place."[9] As a resource for the pastoral reception of Vatican II, he suggests the writings of the saints, especially those whose experience in religious orders (often as founders) enables them to frame "a way of being pastoral that addresses the gradualness of human transformation within the Church and society."[10]

These approaches to the ongoing reception of Vatican II build upon sociological interpretations of the causes of discord and con-tention in the church. By contrast, this chapter argues that the discord and contention noticeable in the reception of Vatican II require a theological interpretation and solution. I begin by sketch-ing John O'Malley's influential proposal for receiving the council. Proposing that the church has failed to receive the council's cues regarding change, collegiality, and style, O'Malley envisions the council as mandating a new understanding of the "ideal Christian." In light of O'Malley's proposal, I suggest that receiving the council means manifesting more fully the peace that comes through char-ity.[11] This peace is what the council seeks to foster in the church and the world; it is this peace that "ideal Christians" embody. By exploring what constitutes this peace, we gain insight into how the reception of the council should foster charity and remove discord and contention.

John W. O'Malley on Change, Collegiality, and Style: Envisioning the Council's "Ideal Christian"

In *What Happened at Vatican II*, John O'Malley emphasizes "three issues-under-the-issues."[12] For O'Malley, these "issues-under-the-issues" determine how we should understand the reception, or lack thereof, of the council. The three underlying issues are change, collegiality, and style. Although the council documents teach on various doctrinal and pastoral matters, O'Malley focuses attention on these three "more general and fundamental" issues.[13] The three issues are interconnected, and O'Malley suggests that the council's position on each of the three points has yet to be fully received or implemented in the church. He readily grants that "by their very nature the three issues do not in practice admit final and absolute resolution."[14] He points out, however, that the three "across-the-board issues" correspond to the council's portrait of what O'Malley calls the "ideal Christian."[15] The ideal Christian is "more inclined to reconciliation with human culture than to alienation from it, more inclined to see goodness than sin, more inclined to speaking words of friendship and encouragement than of indictment."[16]

The ideal Christian follows a "biblical and patristic" style, and thereby repudiates "other styles and . . . the model derived in the early Christian centuries from political institutions of the Roman Empire."[17] O'Malley contrasts the ideal Christian's "biblical and patristic" style with the "scholastic" style. By eschewing the "scholastic" style, O'Malley states, the council "moved from the dialectic of winning an argument to the dialogue of finding common ground. It moved from abstract metaphysics to interpersonal 'how to be.' It moved from grand conceptual schemes or *summae* with hundreds of logically interconnected parts to the humble acceptance of mystery."[18] In sum, breaking free of the "scholastic" style of the past nine centuries, the council envisions an ideal Christian who would be dialogic, seek common ground, appreciate lived experience, and humbly accept mystery. In this light, Christ Jesus appears primarily as "a friend of all people, especially the poor and victims of war and injustice."[19]

For pre–Vatican II Catholics, O'Malley finds, the "shift in style entails a shift in value-system" tantamount to a conversion.[20] As with learning a new language, embodying the more "biblical and patristic" style requires "an inner transformation" in which one not only discards the concepts undergirding the "scholastic" style but also works "to enter fully into the values and sensibilities of a culture different from one's own and to appropriate them."[21] This shift in value system is, according to O'Malley, what is meant by *ressourcement*. By studying the Fathers so as to understand change in the church, *ressourcement* as a theological movement provides "a style of discourse more closely resembling the style of the Fathers than the style used by previous councils."[22]

The personal attributes of the ideal Christian include the following. He or she focuses on "reconciliation" and "persuasion" rather than apodictic (legislative and judicial) statements.[23] He or she recognizes change as "legitimate and even good" and possesses a "keener sense of history" than earlier Christians possessed.[24] He or she knows that "the call to holiness is something more than external conformity to enforceable codes of conduct," and that holiness manifests itself specifically "in commitment to the service of the others in the world."[25] He or she moves away from "unilateral decision-making" and invites reciprocity.[26] He or she avoids "drawing firm lines of demarcation" or "social disciplining," and therefore relies less upon "a precise, technical vocabulary and the use of unambiguous definitions."[27] As examples of day-to-day practice, O'Malley points to changes in biblical interpretation, liturgical outreach, and ecumenical relations.[28]

In short, O'Malley holds that in seeking to receive the council today, we must ask ourselves whether we have truly opened ourselves to the systemic personal/ecclesiastical *change* and *collegiality* required by this *style* of Christian living, or whether we have remained entrenched in old modes.

Is O'Malley right to suggest that the council calls for a radical transformation in the ideal Christian's understanding of change, collegiality, and style—and therefore that the reception of the council's theological teachings can be discerned primarily in sociological/institutional terms? O'Malley grants that holiness is "one of the great themes running through the council" and that "holiness, the council thus said, is what the church is all about."[29] If holiness is so important for the council and its reception, what do Christians and the church need to do in order to receive more fully the council's call to embody the charity of Christ (and thus to become "ideal Christians")?[30] This question requires a deeper theological reflection on the personal and communal embodiment of charity. As a resource for such reflection I turn to Aquinas' theology of peace as an effect of charity (*Summa Theologiae* 2-2.29), with particular attention to his biblical quotations.

Aquinas on Peace

In his first article, Aquinas begins by distinguishing peace from concord. Concord, he points out, can exist between persons intent on executing a wicked project. Although concord is a union of wills, it need not be rooted in a shared commitment to truth and goodness. By contrast, peace requires concord but goes beyond it. This is so because peace requires an internal union in the person as well as an external union among persons. Whereas concord between persons is consistent with interior disorder within each person, peace builds its concord between persons upon an interior order within each person. In this way Aquinas affirms Augustine's definitions of peace in *De Civitate Dei* (29.13) as consisting in "well ordered concord" and "the tranquility of order."[31]

Peace, Unity, and Diversity: 1 Corinthians 14:33

Aquinas goes on to quote 1 Corinthians 14:33, "God is not a God of confusion [Vulgate: *dissensionis*] but of peace."[32] The context of this verse underscores its significance for Aquinas' theological exposition. First Corinthians 14 has to do with ecclesial peace, the peace of the "body of Christ" (1 Cor 12:27), which is built upon a diversity of gifts united by one Spirit (1 Cor 12) and thus upon charity (1 Cor 13). Paul's concern is the lack of charity in the Corinthian church. This lack of charity obstructs the proper effect of the Eucharist, namely, the upbuilding of the church in love. As Paul remarks, "When you assemble as a church, I hear that there are divisions among you; and I partly believe it, for there must be factions among you in order that those who are genuine among you may be recognized" (1 Cor 11:18-19). Paul emphasizes the unity-in-diversity of ecclesial peace: "Now there are varieties of gifts, but the same Spirit; and there are varieties of service, but the same Lord; and there are varieties of working, but it is the same God who inspires them all in every one. To each is given the manifestation of the Spirit for the common good" (1 Cor 12:4-7). As Paul's Trinitarian language (Spirit, Lord, God) suggests, peace arises not from the community itself but from the triune God's gifting. From this gifting arises the church's visible order or structure, which exists to serve the invisible order of charity. Paul notes that "God has appointed in the church first apostles, second prophets, third teachers, then workers of miracles, then healers, helpers, administrators, speakers in various kinds of tongues" (1 Cor 12:28). Members should not be jealous of other members who possess a higher role in the visible order, both because each member is necessary for the good of the whole, and because the "still more excellent way" (1 Cor 12:31) is the life of charity fostered by the church's public and visible confession of faith in Jesus: "Love never ends" (1 Cor 13:8).

Interior and Exterior Peace: Isaiah 48:22 and Galatians 5:17

Since there can be concord among wicked people, in the *sed contra* of article 1 Aquinas differentiates peace from concord by quoting Isaiah 48:22, "'There is no peace,' says the Lord, 'for the wicked.'" Aquinas has ecclesial peace in view, the peace of the people of God. Again the context of the verse is significant: Isaiah 48 delivers a warning against lack of holiness on the part of the people of God, a warning that for Aquinas addresses the church: "O that you had hearkened to my commandments! Then your peace would have been like a river, and your righteousness like the waves of the sea; your offspring would have been like the sand, and your descendants like its grains; their name would never be cut off or destroyed from before me" (Isa 48:18-19).

What does it mean when the people of God do not follow God's commandments? Such people "swear by the name of the Lord, and confess the God of Israel, but not in truth or right" (Isa 48:1). They lay claim to the covenantal inheritance of Israel, but they give the glory not to Israel's God but to idols. In Isaiah 48, God recalls the people to the truth that he alone is the source of peace and righteousness. But if peace requires that the people of God be focused on God and his Word, can weak human beings actually experience such peace?

In the *respondeo* of article 1, Aquinas identifies Galatians 5:17 as a succinct statement of the problem: "For the desires of the flesh are against the spirit, and the desires of the spirit are against the flesh." Following Augustine, Aquinas reads this verse as describing not the Holy Spirit but rather the fallen human person (flesh-spirit), in whom, as Aquinas puts it, "the sensitive appetite tends sometimes to that which is opposed to the rational appetite."[33] How can we experience peace if inwardly our appetites are at war? Charity, and its effect of peace, requires our appetites to be ordered toward the goal of union with the Trinity. This interior peace manifests itself in exterior peace, as Paul argues in Galatians 5. In this regard Paul condemns certain acts: "Now the works of the flesh are plain: immorality, impurity, licentiousness, idolatry, sorcery, enmity, strife, jealousy, anger, selfishness, dissension, party spirit, envy, drunkenness, carousing, and the like. I warn you, as I warned you before, that those who do such things shall not inherit the kingdom of God" (Gal 5:19-21). In this sense, interior peace requires "[crucifying] the flesh with its passions and desires" (Gal 5:24), so as "through love [to] be servants of one another" (Gal 5:13).

Peace and God: Wisdom 14:22

If peace is so difficult to attain, should the church aim instead merely at concord? Should a mutual toleration replace charitable peace as the church's goal with respect to the unity of the human race?[34] Drawing once again upon *De Civitate Dei* (19.13), Aquinas argues in the second article of his question on peace that "whoever desires anything desires peace, in so far as he who desires anything, desires to attain, with tranquility and without hindrance, to that which he desires."[35] Yet it might seem that concord suffices to provide this tranquility and lack of hindrance. In answer, Aquinas argues that only peace can give "calm and unity to the appetite," because peace involves the unified ordering of the appetites to a true good.[36] Only a true good calms and unites the appetites. This is so because "every evil, though it may appear good in a way, so as to calm the appetite in some respect, has nevertheless many defects, which cause the appetite to remain restless and disturbed."[37]

Is such peace attainable in this life? The temptation, as Aquinas recognizes, is to postpone the quest for peace, and to choose instead to live according to one's temporal desires, whatever they happen to be. In this regard Aquinas quotes Wisdom 14:22, "Afterward it was not enough for them to err about the knowledge of God, but they live in great strife due to ignorance, and they call such evils peace." What "evils" does Wisdom have in view with respect to this false "peace" that flows from idolatry? Wisdom points especially to sacralized killing of children, idolatrous worship, sexual immorality, murder, and lying:

> For whether they kill children in their initiations, or celebrate secret mysteries, or hold frenzied revels with strange customs, they no longer keep either their lives or their marriages pure, but they either treacherously kill one another, or grieve one another by adultery, and all is a raging riot of blood and murder, theft and deceit, corruption, faithlessness, tumult, perjury, confusion over what is good, forgetfulness of favors, pollution of souls, sex perversion, disorder in marriage, adultery, and debauchery (Wis 14:23-26).

Wisdom emphasizes that such deformities, rampant in idolatrous cultures, cannot be followed by the people of God. The people of God instead find their peace in God, who is merciful (see Wis

15:1-3). Union with God heals and fulfills our restless appetites and brings about ecclesial peace.

Peace and Jesus: Matthew 10:34 and Mark 9:49

In discussing whether all human beings desire peace, Aquinas takes up in the second article's objections two seemingly contradictory sayings of Jesus. In Matthew 10:34, Jesus says, "Do not think that I have come to bring peace on earth; I have not come to bring peace, but a sword." By contrast, in Mark 9:50) Jesus commands his disciples to manifest peace to the world: "Salt is good; but if the salt has lost its saltness, how will you season it? Have salt in yourselves, and be at peace with one another." In both cases, as Aquinas recognizes, Jesus is describing the difference between the people of God and those who follow the ways of the fallen world. The people of God have "peace" because they have "salt," that is, because they follow the path of self-giving love. Jesus makes this point through a set of apodictic images that prepare for the metaphor of salt:

> Whoever causes one of these little ones who believe in me to sin, it would be better for him if a great millstone were hung round his neck and he were thrown into the sea. And if your hand causes you to sin, cut it off; it is better for you to enter life maimed than with two hands to go to hell, to the unquenchable fire. And if your foot causes you to sin, cut it off; it is better for you to enter life lame than with two feet to be thrown into hell. And if your eye causes you to sin, pluck it out; it is better for you to enter the kingdom of God with one eye than with two eyes to be thrown into hell, where the worm does not die, and the fire is not quenched (Mark 9:42-48).

Jesus makes clear that to be a community of peace involves much more than concord or mutual toleration. Put positively, we must love God and our neighbor with self-giving love. Shortly before this discourse on "salt," Jesus calls together his disciples and instructs them, "If any one would be first, he must be last of all and servant of all" (Mark 9:35).

Given that peace only arises from charitable holiness, as Vatican II also affirms, does Jesus bring peace to the people of God? It seems that he himself answers in the negative: "I have not come to bring peace, but a sword" (Matt 10:34). As Aquinas knows, however, the "sword" that Jesus brings is the sword of self-giving love. This "sword" divides human beings because, as Jesus says, "he who does not take his cross and follow me is not worthy of me" (Matt 10:38). The way of the cross is the way of peace in the deepest sense: "He who finds his life will lose it, and he who loses his life for my sake will find it" (Matt 10:39). To find one's life by losing it for Jesus means to gain the fulfillment of all our desires through a participation in the triune life of God.

Perfect and Imperfect Peace: Psalms 147:14 and 119:65, Isaiah 32:17, and Acts 15

Is such peace possible now? In the third article of his question on peace, Aquinas observes that "there is a twofold true peace," perfect and imperfect.[38] The gift of the Holy Spirit in the body of Christ enables Jesus' followers to enjoy imperfect peace in this life. It is imperfect because "though the chief movement of the soul finds rest in God, yet there are certain things within and without which disturb the peace."[39] Our charity is not yet perfect, and so neither is our peace. To depict perfect peace, which "unites all one's desires" through union with God, Aquinas quotes Psalm 147:14 (Vulgate 147:3), "He makes peace in your borders; he fills you with the finest of the wheat." Aquinas applies to the heavenly New Jerusalem this description of what God does for Jerusalem and Zion. In this New Jerusalem, "The Lord builds up Jerusalem; he gathers the outcasts of Israel. He heals the brokenhearted, and binds up their wounds. He determines the number of the stars, he gives to all of them their names" (Ps 147:2-4).

Two issues arise at this point. First of all, if peace comes through charity, which follows upon faith in the Redeemer, then it would seem that only Christians have peace; but, as Aquinas points out in an objection, "heathens [*gentiles*] sometimes have peace."[40] Second, what about the divisions among Christians that the church has endured throughout the centuries? Such divisions are found already in the Fathers and even in the apostolic age: Aquinas cites the debate between Augustine and Jerome and the disagreement of Paul and Barnabas (Acts 15).[41] Even if Christians have charity, it seems that Christians often lack peace with each other, whereas non-Christians often live in peace. As Aquinas observes in an objection, it might be wiser to identify peace as the effect of justice rather than as the effect of supernatural charity. In this vein, Isaiah 32:17 appears to ascribe peace to justice: "The effect of righteousness [Vulgate: *opus justitiae*] will be peace, and the result of righteousness, quietness and trust for ever."

In response, Aquinas finds that "peace is the *work of justice* indirectly, in so far as justice removes obstacles to peace: but it is the work of charity directly, since charity, according to its very nature, causes peace."[42] Indeed, as Isaiah 32:15 teaches, the people of God enjoy peace only when "the Spirit is poured upon us from on high, and the wilderness becomes a fruitful field." Since peace requires an internal and external unity of appetites, it relies upon love of God and neighbor. This is ecclesial peace, rooted, as Vatican II underscores, in holiness. To this effect Aquinas quotes Psalm 119:165, "Great peace have those who love thy law; nothing can make them stumble."[43] Without holiness, peace has no firm foundation and is not real peace.

What about dissension among Christians? Ecclesial peace, Aquinas notes, is consistent with differences regarding matters of opinion. The peace that flows from charity does not require that Paul and Barnabas always agree about prudential matters; their "sharp contention" (Acts 15:39) about whether to take Mark does not destroy ecclesial peace because it does not overthrow their agreement about the God who reveals himself in Christ Jesus. When Christians divide about matters of faith, by contrast, their discord breaks ecclesial peace. Thus Paul and Barnabas both accept the teaching of the apostolic council of Jerusalem (Acts 15:6-35). As more than mere propositions, the church's doctrine directs believers to the eschatological fullness of peace, the "state of perfect peace, wherein the truth will be known fully, and every desire fulfilled."[44]

Peacemaking: Mark 9:50, Matthew 5:9, and Galatians 5:20

In the fourth and final article of his question on peace, Aquinas asks whether peace itself should be understood by Christians as a virtuous path toward the goal of peace. Does not peace result from peacemaking, rather than from charity? It would seem that Jesus recognizes peace as a virtue rather than simply as the effect of a virtue. For example, when Jesus commands his disciples to "be at peace with one another" (Mark 9:50), this command seems to require a virtue of peace.[45] Likewise, when Jesus affirms, "Blessed are the peacemakers" (Matt 5:9), he seems to have in view a distinct virtue.[46] And if "dissension" (Gal 5:20) is a vice, then its opposite, peace, should be a virtue.[47] In reply, Aquinas refuses to separate peace from the virtue of charity. No instrument other than charity causes peace. Charity does so because peace arises when our appetites are united to God and to each other through love. The Beatitudes are founded upon the charity or holiness of believers: as Jesus says, "unless your righteousness exceeds that of the scribes and Pharisees, you will never enter the kingdom of heaven" (Matt 5:20).

Conclusion

How should the church and her members receive the council's teachings so as to make manifest to the world the peace that is the fruit of the bond of charity? O'Malley emphasizes three points in this regard: the need for styles of discourse that focus on reconciliation and persuasion rather than condemnation, the need to be receptive to the ongoing change that historical existence requires, and the need to serve others in mutual reciprocity rather than acting in a unilateral fashion. For O'Malley, the church and her members can further receive and implement Vatican II by attending to style, change, and collegiality. These three points fit with commonly heard critiques of the exercise of papal teaching authority: it is overly insensitive to its own possible limitations and lapses and overly critical of the alleged errors of others (style); it denies that its teaching changes despite evidence to the contrary (change); and it is unilateral and often deaf to the experience of the laity (collegiality). In short, O'Malley suggests that the full reception of the council must begin with implementing sociological or institutional changes in the operational structures of the Catholic Church.

By contrast, Aquinas' discussion of peace suggests a different path for the reception of the Second Vatican Council in light of discord and contention. Exploring the relationship of unity and diversity in the church, Aquinas observes that the diversity of the gifts of the Holy Spirit, including the hierarchical diversity in ministry, serves rather than opposes the unity of the church. He examines how interior peace is required for exterior peace, and he shows why the church's peace must go beyond mere concord. He points out that the path of peace is worship of the true God, whereas conflict has its roots in idolatry. Since Jesus both gives his disciples peace and warns that he has not come to bring peace, Aquinas seeks to show how radical self-giving love unites and divides human beings. He explains how the peace of the church is consonant with certain kinds of discord and contention among believers (but not other kinds), and he identifies perfect peace as an eschatological reality. He insists that peacemaking has its roots in charity: love alone suffices. Only such peace can overcome discord and contention and enable the church to receive, in the deepest sense, the council's call to bear witness more fully to the gospel.

CHAPTER 6

Schism and Liturgical Mediation

In Numbers 16 Moses and Aaron defend their leadership of the people of God against a schism led by Korah, Dathan, and Abiram. In seeking to understand schism and its healing, this chapter first explores the role of (hierarchical) liturgical action in uniting the people of God. Since my sympathetic reading of Numbers 15–18 cuts against the grain of contemporary biblical exegesis, I briefly examine how Richard Elliott Friedman and Walter Brueggemann understand Numbers 16. In distinct ways, Friedman and Brueggemann suggest that the story and its historical underpinnings involve a sordid power struggle. In this light, I turn to Thomas Aquinas' study of schism as a sin against charity. Through his use of Numbers 16, Aquinas helps us to appreciate how liturgical action serves the unity in charity of the people of God.

The Liturgical Unity of the People of God: Numbers 15–18

After detailing the animal offerings, cereal offerings, and drink offerings that individual Israelites should regularly offer, Numbers 15 addresses three issues regarding the unity of the people of God. First, can non-Israelites fittingly be joined to the unity of Israel's liturgical life? YHWH teaches through Moses that the answer is yes: "If a stranger is sojourning with you, or any one is among you throughout your generations, and he wishes to offer an offering by fire, a pleasing odor to the Lord, he shall do as you do. For the assembly, there shall be one statute for you and for the stranger who sojourns with you. . . . As you are, so shall the sojourner be before the Lord" (Num 15:14-15). The liturgical life of Israel aims to draw in the stranger so as to enrich the unity of the people before God.

Second, YHWH, speaking through Moses, addresses unintentional failure to obey his commandments and offers a liturgical solution aimed at restoring unity. YHWH explains that if the lack of obedience "was done unwittingly without the knowledge of the congregation, all the congregation shall offer one young bull for a burnt offering, a pleasing odor to the Lord, with its cereal offering and its drink offering, according to the ordinance, and one male goat for a sin offering" (Num 15:24). The priest offers the sacrificial offerings on behalf of the whole congregation so that the congregation shares in the priestly action and receives forgiveness and renewed unity as a people before God. This forgiveness and unity extends to any non-Israelites who join the people in the liturgical action: "And all the congregation of the people of Israel shall be forgiven, and the stranger who sojourns among them, because the whole population was involved in the error" (Num 15:26). Liturgical action mediates the divine forgiveness that reunifies the participants.

Third, YHWH commands through Moses that Israel not countenance intentional disobedience. Deliberate rebellion separates a person from the community's liturgical unity: one cannot despise YHWH's commandments and worship YHWH at the same time. As an example of a person who "reviles the Lord" by despising "the word of the Lord" (Num 15:30-31), Numbers gives the instance of someone who violates the Sabbath rest. Because this person disregards the foundation of Israel's liturgical unity before God, there is no liturgical solution to his plight: "That person shall be utterly cut off; his iniquity shall be upon him" (Num 15:31). So as to remind all the people of their obligation to obey the commandments, YHWH also requires Moses to give the people a sign of their liturgical unity, namely, "tassels on the corners of their garments," with each tassel containing a blue cord (Num 15:37).

Rather than speaking to each member of the congregation separately, YHWH speaks through Moses, and the liturgical action is led by Aaron. But why should Moses and Aaron be privileged within the one people of God? Does not this privileging undermine the real unity of the people? Can a people truly be united before God if each member of the people does not possess the same prerogatives as every other member?

In light of Numbers 15's exposition of liturgical action as uniting the people of God, Numbers 16 examines whether liturgical action, undertaken hierarchically, truly fosters the people's unity. Koran, Dathan, and Abiram argue that the liturgical action of the people, which is supposed to unite the people before God, actually divides the people because of the privileged role of Moses and Aaron in proclaiming God's word and in offering sacrifices to God on behalf of the whole people. If the whole people is God's people, then the liturgical action (word and sacrificial offering) should be such as to embody the people's unity rather than to instantiate diversity among the people as regards their status before God.

Given this concern, Korah, Dathan, and Abiram—along with a less central figure named On—"rose up before Moses, with a number of the people of Israel, two hundred and fifty leaders of the congregation, chosen from the assembly, well-known men" (Num 16:2). These leaders insist that the equality of each member of the people of Israel be embodied liturgically. They say to Moses and Aaron, "You have gone too far! For all the congregation are holy, every one of them, and the Lord is among them; why then do you exalt yourselves above the assembly of the Lord?" (Num 16:3). Their position is that each member of the assembly of the Lord experiences the Lord's presence, and therefore each member is holy. In their view, liturgical action, as led by Moses and Aaron, rends the unity of the assembly of the Lord.

In response, Moses prays for a clear sign that YHWH has chosen Moses and Aaron as mediators of the people's liturgical unity. Moses also observes the hypocrisy behind the accusations. Korah, as a descendent of Levi, has already been set apart by YHWH for liturgical action. Korah's complaint may be an effort to take the place of Aaron. Similarly, Dathan and Abiram may wish to take the place of Moses. They complain against Moses: "Is it a small thing that you have brought us up out of a land flowing with milk and honey, to kill us in the wilderness, that you must also make yourself a prince over us?" (Num 16:13).

In defense of his authority, Moses calls for a liturgical test. He requests that YHWH disregard the liturgical offering of Korah, Dathan, and Abiram. At Moses' request, both Korah (along with his supporters) and Aaron bring their censers filled with burning incense before the Lord (Num 16:17). Moses and Aaron stand before the Tent of Meeting, and "Korah assembled all the congregation against them at the entrance of the tent of meeting" (Num 16:19). Whereas Korah, Dathan, and Abiram suggest that the unity of Israel depends upon overturning Moses and Aaron's liturgical pretensions, Moses responds to Korah that the real issue is what YHWH wants from his people: "It is against the Lord that you and all your company have gathered together; what is Aaron that you murmur against him?" (Num 16:11).

The scene is a full-blown schism: Korah and the congregation stand against Moses and Aaron at the Tent of Meeting. Moses and Aaron's opponents hope that YHWH will reject Moses' privileged status in proclaiming YHWH's word and Aaron's privileged status in sacrificing to YHWH on behalf of the people. But their hopes go unfulfilled. YHWH threatens to destroy all the congregation that stands with Korah, and he causes an earthquake to swallow up Korah, Dathan, and Abiram (with their families). Although YHWH spares the congregation, he does not spare the two hundred and fifty leaders who dare to worship YHWH outside of the liturgical mediation of Aaron: "Fire came forth from the Lord, and consumed the two hundred and fifty men offering the incense" (Num 16:35). Yet when YHWH threatens to consume the whole congregation, Moses and Aaron "fell on their faces, and said, 'O God, the God of the spirits of all flesh, shall one man sin, and wilt thou be angry with all the congregation?'" (Num 16:22).

Because of the intercession of Moses and Aaron, YHWH spares the congregation. In liturgical unity with Moses and Aaron, who minister on behalf of the people by God's will, the people find life. The unity of the people of Israel before God is dependent upon, rather than negated by, Moses and Aaron's ministry. So as to remind the people of this reality, YHWH commands Aaron's son Eleazar to collect the censers of Korah, Dathan, Abiram, and the two hundred and fifty leaders, and to meld these censers together into a sign of liturgical unity, "a covering for the altar, to be a reminder to the people of Israel, so that no one who is not a priest, who is not of the descendants of Aaron, should draw near to burn incense before the Lord" (Num 16:40).

On the day after the destruction of Korah's movement, however, the people of Israel blame Moses and Aaron for the destructive results of the schism: "The people of Israel murmured against Moses and against Aaron, saying, 'You have killed the people of the Lord'" (Num 16:41). YHWH again encounters the people of Israel at the Tent of Meeting and threatens to consume them; once again Moses and Aaron's intercession brings life for the rebellious people. The incense from Aaron's censer, as he makes "atonement for the people" (Num 16:47), stops the spread of the plague, which nonetheless kills "fourteen thousand seven hundred" (Num 16:49)—a number whose sevens are filled with liturgical significance.

YHWH also delivers a miraculous sign through the rods deposited in the Tent of Meeting by ensuring that only Aaron's "sprouted and put forth buds, and produced blossoms, and . . . bore ripe almonds" (Num 17:8). Aaron's rod of authority is life-giving. This is the answer that YHWH gives to the people of Israel who complain to Moses, "Behold, we perish, we are undone, we are all undone. Every one who comes near, who comes near to the tabernacle of the Lord, shall die. Are we all to perish?" (Num 17:12-13). The people of Israel will not perish—they will retain their life-giving unity before the Lord—so long as they embody that unity through the liturgical differentiation willed by the Lord. YHWH promises Aaron, "I give your priesthood as a gift, and any one else who comes near shall be put to death" (Num 18:7).

Numbers 15–18 as a Power Struggle

If we take this story from Numbers at face value, it would appear that God wills for the unity of the people of God to include diverse roles, so that unity in charity is fostered, not negated, by divinely ordained distinctions within the people of God. Yet many contemporary scholars would not agree with the reading that I have given above. Based in part upon the fact that the challengers of Moses are Reubenites, whereas the challengers of Aaron are Levites, scholars identify diverse strands within the story. Richard Elliott Friedman suggests that the details about Aaron were written by the priestly author P, and that P's purpose is to make clear that no forgiveness is possible for the people of Israel except through the mediation of priests. As Friedman says, "Over and over, P develops this point that the Aaronid priest at the sacrificial altar is the people's proper channel to the deity. If you have sinned and want to be forgiven, the thing to do is bring a sacrifice to a priest at the Tabernacle."[1] According to Friedman, P's God is one of strict justice, a juridical God: "In the P text, there is not a single reference to God as *merciful*. The very words 'mercy,' 'grace,' 'faithfulness,' and 'repent' never occur."[2] The offering of divine forgiveness belongs not to God, but to the priests. Only through the set of rules put forward by the priests can there be any hope for the people.

Not surprisingly, Friedman does not imagine P's motives in writing to be particularly pure; P's writing is theopolitical propaganda at a time of competing priestly families. As Friedman reconstructs the context, P "had to deal with challenges from other priests and other religious centers. He had to defend his group's legitimacy and to protect their authority. And he had to ensure their livelihood. He also had to fight the insult to his ancestor Aaron."[3] Since other biblical writers had presented Aaron as the molder of the Golden Calf, P had to highlight Aaron's rightful authority. In seeking to understand the place of P's narratives within the Torah, Friedman goes on to argue that P's perspective, in the hands of a later Aaronid priest who redacted the Torah, provides "the governing structure of the work."[4] This later Aaronid priest, whom Friedman suggests may well have been Ezra, opposed the "Shiloh Levite priests who had produced E and D" even while retaining these Shilonite strands in the final redaction of the Torah.[5]

From a more explicitly theological perspective, Walter Brueggemann argues that "Torah has within it more that is dynamic, open, and elusive than is conveyed in the usual Western, gentile notion of Jewish law."[6] But Brueggemann does not extend this praise of the Torah as "dynamic, open, and elusive" to Numbers 16. Discussing the "Mosaic Torah mediation of Yahweh to Israel," Brueggemann remarks (based upon Numbers 16 as well as Exodus 32 and Numbers 12) that "we may locate in the person and office of Moses a zeal for leadership that smacks of authoritarianism and that is a harbinger of the authoritarianism that pervades Israel's testimony that is now marked as patriarchalism."[7] In Numbers 16, Moses plays a rigidly patriarchal and authoritarian role. The malign influence of Numbers 16, Brueggemann holds, appears in the long history of religious "intolerance of rivals."[8] Such intolerance "eventuates, in the Christian tradition, in various claims of infallibility and in the sanctions of the Inquisition, and eagerly identifies as 'heresy' whatever deviates from the interpretive hegemony of the moment."[9]

For Brueggemann, then, Moses in Numbers 16 represents the human will to power. Far from confirming the value of divinely ordained liturgical mediation for the unity in charity of the people of God, Numbers 16's presentation of Moses and Aaron anticipates the worst moments of Christianity, from bishops' endless fights over "orthodoxy" (whose violence reveals itself paradigmatically in the Inquisition) to Vatican I's solemn declaration of papal infallibility. Like Friedman, Brueggemann finds Numbers 16 to be an expression of a priestly group's desire to consolidate its own religious, political, and economic position against that of its rivals within the people of God.

Schism and the Liturgy: A Thomistic Account

Does Numbers 16 merely record the effort of priests to gain power, or does it have permanent significance in showing the relationship of hierarchical liturgical action to the unity in charity of the people of God? In seeking to answer this question (without entering into historical controversies regarding separations among Christians), I wish to examine Thomas Aquinas' exposition of the sin of schism, with particular attention to his use of Numbers 16. Does his account of schism advance our understanding of the church's liturgical action in Christ, who is the new Moses and new Aaron?

Aquinas on Schism

Numbers 16 appears twice in Aquinas' treatment of schism, which he places among the sins against charity. Aquinas takes his definition of "schism" from Augustine.[10] Unlike heretics, schismatics do not differ from the church on faith or worship. Instead, while affirming the faith and worship of the church, schismatics aim at the disunion of the people of God: "The schismatic intends to sever himself from that unity which is the effect of charity: because charity unites not only one person to another with the bond of spiritual love, but also the whole Church in unity of spirit."[11] Thus schism seeks to break not merely any unity, but the church's unity. Aquinas notes that "this is the chief unity, and the particular unity of several individuals among themselves is subordinate to the unity of the Church."[12]

The church's unity is constituted in two ways. First, unity arises through the "mutual connection or communion of the members of the Church" in charity.[13] In this regard the schismatic acts directly against charity, because "the schismatic intends to sever himself from that unity which is the effect of charity: because charity unites not only one person to another with the bond of spiritual love, but also the whole Church in unity of spirit."[14] Yet according to Aquinas, the church's "unity of spirit," while consisting in the invisible bond of charity between the members of the church, nonetheless also has a divinely willed visible dimension, an apostolic structure of sacramental mediation of Christ's gifting in the Holy Spirit.

Second, therefore, the schismatic makes himself or herself known by challenging this visible apostolic unity, ordained by Christ. In so doing, the schismatic rejects "the subordination of all the members of the Church to the one head," who is Christ Jesus.[15] Aquinas applies here St. Paul's warning about the person who is "puffed up without reason by his sensuous mind" and who does not hold "fast to the Head, from whom the whole body, nourished and knit together through its joints and ligaments, grows with a growth that is from God" (Col 2:18-19). Christ makes his headship visible through the apostolic structure of the church, which is led by the successor of Peter. While Aquinas distinguishes clearly between subordination to Christ and subordination to the pope, nonetheless the pope plays a role in mediating the visible reign of Christ among believers.[16] Schismatics "refuse to submit to the Sovereign Pontiff [*Summus Pontifex*], and to hold communion with those members of the Church who acknowledge his supremacy."[17]

Aquinas notes that unbelief and hatred of God are more grievous sins than schism, because unbelief and hatred reject God directly, whereas schism rejects "ecclesiastical unity, which is a participated good, and a lesser good than God himself."[18] Yet Aquinas adds that "of all sins committed by man against his neighbor, the sin of schism would seem to be the greatest, because it is opposed to the spiritual good of the multitude."[19] While schism might appear to affect only the external unity of the church—the church's visible structure—in fact schism cuts to the deepest reality of the church, unity in charity. It does not destroy that unity, because unity in charity is God's gift to his church in the Holy Spirit. But it wounds the church's unity by dividing persons who otherwise would be visibly united in charity, and it thereby strikes at the purpose for which God created and redeemed human beings—in Jesus' words, "that they may all be one; even as thou, Father, art in me, and I in thee, that they also may be in us" (John 17:21).

In Aquinas' view, Numbers 16 justifies excommunication as the punishment of schism: "It is written (Numbers 16:26): 'Depart from the tents of these wicked men,' those, to wit, who had caused the schism, 'and touch nothing of theirs, lest you be involved in their sins.' "[20] The unique punishment that God brings about in Numbers 16 reflects the fact that unity in charity is the very thing for which God gathers his people.[21] While expressing the hope that excommunication will suffice to heal the wound to unity, Aquinas accepts the position of medieval canon law regarding "the compulsion of the secular arm" (*coercionem brachii saecularis*).[22] Without agreeing with Aquinas in this regard, one can agree with his appreciation for the value of true unity in charity. As Aquinas states, "Charity unites not only one person to another with the bond of spiritual love, but also the whole Church in unity of spirit."[23] When believers are at odds with each other, Christ's peace does not reign. How then to strengthen unity in charity?

Aquinas on Sacramental Liturgy as an Instrument of Unity

Quoting Augustine, Aquinas observes with regard to the liturgical life of both Israel and the church: "'It is impossible to keep men together in one religious denomination, whether true or false, except they be united by means of visible signs or sacraments.' But it is necessary for salvation that men be united together in the name of the one true religion. Therefore sacraments are necessary for man's salvation."[24] Since humans apprehend invisible truths by means of reflection upon sensible things, "visible signs or sacraments" enable humans to unite in the knowledge and love of God—"just as in the divine Scriptures spiritual things are set before us under the guise of things sensible."[25]

The ability of "visible signs or sacraments" to promote human unity vis-à-vis God recalls Numbers 15. There YHWH instructs Israel about the regular sacrificial offerings that Israel will need to make "when you come into the land you are to inhabit, which I give you" (Num 15:2). The members of the people of Israel will be united to each other and to those who sojourn among them by observing together the same sacrificial liturgy. By contrast, those who reject the foundation of the sacrificial liturgy (the Sabbath) will be cut off from the people. Not only does liturgical worship ("visible signs or sacraments") unify the people of God, but also, as Numbers 16 emphasizes, this unifying worship takes place through the divinely ordained ministry of certain members of the people. In the case of the Eucharist, Aquinas notes that "the power of consecrating this sacrament on Christ's behalf is bestowed upon the priest at his ordination: for thereby he is put upon a level with them to whom the Lord said (Luke 22:19): 'Do this for a commemoration of me.'"[26]

Aquinas makes clear that the priest's exalted "power of consecrating this sacrament" does not undermine the Eucharist's ability to signify the unity of believers in Christ. As he states, "In the sacrament of the altar, two things are signified, viz. Christ's true body and Christ's mystical body."[27] Through the Eucharist, the people of God become the one "mystical body" that the Eucharist signifies. Following Augustine again, Aquinas states that the Eucharist both signifies and causes the grace of unity: "'Our Lord betokened his body and blood in things which out of many units are made into some one whole: for out of many grains is one thing made,' viz. bread; 'and many grapes flow into one thing,' viz. wine."[28] By participating in the sacrament of the Eucharist, believers are inflamed with charity and become more deeply united.[29]

What role does priestly mediation of the Eucharist play? As Korah says, "All the congregation are holy, every one of them" (Num 16:3), but they are holy in union with divinely ordained leaders. The priestly office reminds the community of believers that they cannot give themselves unity in charity. Only God gives this gift; as Moses warns Korah and his followers, "It is against the Lord that you and all your company have gathered together; what is Aaron that you murmur against him?" (Num 16:11). By virtue of baptism, all members of the church share in the "spiritual priesthood for offering spiritual sacrifices."[30] But in receiving Christ from ordained priests, members of the "spiritual priesthood" are configured in the Holy Spirit to Christ's receptive obedience.

Thus the church's unity in charity arises from worshiping in and through the new Moses/Aaron, Jesus Christ. Aquinas notes regarding the Eucharist, "Such is the dignity of this sacrament that it is performed only as in the person of Christ. Now whoever performs any act in another's stead, must do so by the power bestowed by such a one."[31] Christ bestows this power to consecrate the Eucharist not on every member of his body, but only on those who receive the sacrament of orders. The liturgical action by which the church deepens her unity in charity does not embody a unity of undifferentiated equality. Rather, the people of God practice embodied receptivity even in the action that most constitutes the people's unity in Christ. In this way Christ configures his body to his own kenotic love, and in the eucharistic liturgy we "are truly made partakers of the fruit of our Lord's Passion."[32]

Describing at some length the roles of the priest and the people in the eucharistic liturgy, Aquinas portrays the joining of the prayers of the priest and the people in "the sacrament of unity and peace."[33] As Aquinas emphasizes elsewhere, Jesus alone is the head of his body in the sense that "the interior influx of grace is from no one save Christ, whose manhood, through its union with the God-head, has the power of justifying."[34] Yet Jesus enables his ordained ministers to participate in the "exterior guidance" of the church.[35] As regards liturgical action, this means that "the dispensing of the sacraments belongs to the Church's ministers; but their [the sacra-ments'] consecration is from God himself."[36] The unity in charity of the members of the church comes from the consecration of the sacraments, by which the sacraments contain and cause the grace of the Holy Spirit.[37]

But is not the church continuously afflicted by schism and other power struggles? As I hope to have shown, Numbers 16 suggests that it need not be so. Moses and Aaron serve the unity of the peo-ple before God by means of liturgical signs and intercessory prayers. The people's need for these signs and prayers reminds us that unity before God, unity in charity, comes through embodied liturgical action that cannot have its source in us, but rather must have its source in God. If we are to be the people of God, we must receive this unity as a gift, as we learn to do in and through our differenti-ated participation in the liturgy of the Eucharist. In the words of Henri de Lubac, following the patristic and medieval tradition, "The Church and the Eucharist are formed by one another day by day."[38]

Conclusion

Interpreting Numbers 15–18, I argued that God's gift of unity depends upon liturgical mediation, so that the people of God prac-tice embodied receptivity in their liturgical action; otherwise each person in the congregation lays claim to a self-sufficient relationship to God. Does this exegesis retain its value even if power struggles between priestly families in Israel lie behind the text of Numbers 15–18? In answer, I inquired theologically into the nature of schism and its antidotes. Schism may appear to wound the church's unity only as regards its visible external form, without threatening the internal unity that depends solely upon Christ's gift of the grace of the Holy Spirit. On this view, Numbers 15–18 would seem to rep-resent a sordid, strictly external episode in Moses and Aaron's (and Israel's) career. However, such a view underestimates the unity of the internal and the external, the visible and the invisible. It does so because it does not sufficiently appreciate how liturgical action fosters the church's inner unity in charity. Liturgical action cannot be separated from the church's external structure because true unity in charity requires embodied practice in kenotic receptivity.

From this Thomistic reading of Numbers 15–18, I would draw three points. First, true unity is not impeded by the presence of an ordained priesthood in addition to the priesthood of all believers, because the ordained priesthood assists the priesthood of all believers in embodying a unity rooted in cruciform charity. Second, liturgical action remains the privileged locus for overcoming the divisive effects that power struggles inevitably have in the church. Third, liturgical action depends upon a theocentric understanding of reality: in and through Christ and the Holy Spirit, the Father accomplishes the unity in charity that humans seek. We cannot give it to ourselves.

CHAPTER 7

War and the Interpretation of Scripture

Among the sins against charity, Thomas Aquinas includes war, strife, and sedition. He distinguishes strife from legitimate self-defense and argues that "strife is always sinful" because it is "inspired by vengeance and hatred."[1] A favorite source for Aquinas' theology of strife is the book of Proverbs: "A hot-tempered man stirs up strife" (Prov 15:18); "A fool's lips bring strife" (Prov 18:6); "A greedy man stirs up strife" (Prov 28:25).[2] Unlike strife, sedition includes not only aggression but also preparation for aggression. Sedition differs from war because war involves an external enemy, whereas sedition involves civil conflict, and sedition differs from strife because sedition involves groups rather than individuals.[3]

All instances of strife and sedition are sinful. Does the same hold for war? The Letter of James condemns war in clear terms: "What causes wars, and what causes fightings among you? Is it not your passions that are at war in your members? You desire and do not have; so you kill. And you covet and cannot obtain; so you fight and wage war" (Jas 4:1-2). Likewise, the Second Vatican Council's Pastoral Constitution on the Church in the Modern World, *Gaudium et Spes*, praises those "who renounce violence in claiming their rights, and who have recourse to means of defence which are otherwise available only to weaker parties, provided this can be done without harm to the rights and obligations of others or of the community."[4] While not as clear as the Letter of James, *Gaudium et Spes* encourages Christians to govern our passions and "renounce violence."

In light of the community's obligation to protect its members from unjust violence, however, *Gaudium et Spes* has more to say about war. According to *Gaudium et Spes*, "so long as the danger of war is present, and there is no competent international authority with appropriate powers, then, once all means of peaceful negotiation are exhausted, the right of legitimate defense cannot be denied to governments."[5] Indeed, governments have a "duty" (*officium*) to defend the populace by means of military force if other options have been exhausted.[6] Although recent popes have generally opposed particular wars, the *Catechism of the Catholic Church* reaffirms the teaching of *Gaudium et Spes* on just war.[7] While war always involves an unjust aggressor, and thus belongs among the sins against charity, engaging in warfare can be just.

Does Catholic moral teaching thereby compromise its witness to Christ Jesus, the "prince of peace" who "has reunited all of us to God through his cross" and has put "hatred to death in his own flesh"?[8] Suggesting that the answer is yes, Hannah Arendt argues that the only way for the Catholic Church to follow Jesus' teachings faithfully would have been to "turn away from politics" by prescribing "a manner of life in which human affairs were withdrawn entirely from the public arena and transferred to a personal realm between one man and another."[9] According to Arendt, this manner of life was possible until the fourth century, when the church, inspired by Constantine, adopted "the Roman political conception of religion" and thereby (for better or worse) renounced "the strong anti-institutional tendency of the Christian creed that is so manifest in the New Testament."[10]

Is Arendt correct? This chapter examines two influential Christian theologies of war. John Howard Yoder, followed by leading exegetes such as Richard B. Hays, influentially argues that Christian charity requires nonviolence.[11] By contrast, Thomas Aquinas, like *Gaudium et Spes*, holds that waging war does not always violate charity, even though all war is a sin against charity arising from one or more unjust aggressors.[12] I focus on how Yoder and Aquinas interpret Scripture in their theologies of war.[13]

John Howard Yoder: Pacifism as a Biblical Mandate

For John Howard Yoder, Jeremiah's urging of the Jews of his time not to side with Egypt against Babylon, but instead to submit peacefully to Babylon's rule and then to exile in Babylon, provides the paradigm for "the politics of Jesus."[14] Drawing upon the Jewish playwright Stefan Zweig, Yoder argues that "the move to Babylon was not a two-generation parenthesis, after which the Davidic or Solomonic project was supposed to take up again where it had left off. It was rather the beginning, under a firm, fresh prophetic mandate, of a new phase of the Mosaic project."[15] This new phase, Yoder suggests, is defined by Jeremiah 29, especially verses 7 and 10: "But seek the welfare of the city where I have sent you into exile, and pray to the Lord on its behalf, for in its welfare you will find your welfare. . . . For thus says the Lord: When seventy years are completed for Babylon, I will visit you, and I will fulfill to you my promise and bring you back to this place." God's visitation occurs in the Messiah; until then, the Jews are to "seek the welfare of the city where I have sent you into exile" in the ways that are open to them. These ways are necessarily nonviolent, because the Jews cannot possess any military or political power in the dispersion. Instead, the Jews of the dispersion bear witness to their God by manifesting a life of wisdom, rooted in proclamation of the true God's "sovereignty over creation and history,"[16] that provides an alternative to history's multiple failed (and failing) efforts to build human culture upon regimes of violence.

Yoder therefore finds military or political efforts to revive the independence of Judea and Jerusalem to be false paths, even when such paths present themselves as the fulfillment of Jeremiah's prophecy, as do the books of Ezra and Nehemiah. The Maccabees and Bar Kochba embody the worst failures of all. Although Jesus stands as an alternative to such political messianism, nonetheless to see Jesus in opposition to his fellow Jews would be to ignore the living tradition of the Judaism that flows through Jeremiah and continues for centuries after Jesus. Not only does the apparent Old Testament approval of "holy war" actually remove war from the royal sphere, as in the book of Joshua,[17] but also the failure of the Jewish kings reveals the failure of violence. In the Sermon on the Mount, Jesus presents nonviolence and love of enemy as the intensification and fulfillment, not the negation, of the Torah. By consciously living out "the fate of the suffering Servant of JHWH [*sic*] in Isaiah 40-53," Jesus makes clear "the linkage of non-violence with martyrdom, and the linkage of suffering with salvation, which one finds as well among the early Christians, the later Jews, and the (much later) pacifist minority Christians."[18] Yoder notes that in fact "it was in the process of becoming non-Jewish that Christianity also became non-pacifist."[19]

According to Yoder, Constantinian Christians abandoned the path of Jesus in much the same way that the Maccabees abandoned the path of Jeremiah. Rather than obeying and trusting God and thereby embodying nonviolent forgiveness,[20] Constantinian Christians chose "a morality of 'utility' or of 'prosperity'"—that is to say, they shifted from "a moral life founded transcendently to one rendered serviceable to the present power structure."[21] In so doing, Yoder argues, Constantinian Christians veered away from Jesus' teachings, which correspond with those of Jeremiah and with God's rejection of the Davidic kings' unrighteousness. Christianity became a tool of the state's politics rather than an alternative to the state's politics. Aware of the argument that Christians could do no other once they became the majority religion, Yoder replies that following Jesus' path could never lead to a majority "religion," precisely because the path of Jesus stands as an alternative to the state's politics. As Yoder remarks,

> If then we trust God for the defence not only of his large concerns but also of our own authentic welfare, we shall not be enticed by the kinds of reasoning recently called 'realism' or 'responsibility'. We shall not usually ask 'what would happen if everyone acted the way we think we must?' because being a disarmed minority we know they never will. Our action should

be paradigmatic for the coming kingdom, not for how unbeliev-
ing majorities can act.[22]

Is Jesus' path then fundamentally antisocial, destructive of or coun-
terproductive to the societies in which his followers (like the Jews
of the Diaspora[23]) exist on the margins? On the contrary, Yoder
suggests that the truly energizing and lasting contribution to these
societies, which insofar as they rely on violence will inevitably fail,
consists in displaying "the concrete shape of the culture of faithfulness," namely, love of enemy as God loves his enemies.[24]

Does Yoder's portrait of Jesus' and early Christianity's pacifism
square with the New Testament's witness? In *The Politics of Jesus*,
originally published in 1972, Yoder sets forth in full his understanding of Jesus as "a model of radical political action."[25] Rejecting the
temptation of being king, Jesus nonetheless preaches the good news
of the kingdom of God. In announcing the fulfillment of Isaiah
61:1-2, Jesus brings about "the acceptable year of the Lord" (Luke
4:19), the jubilee that challenges all worldly values.[26] Jesus aims to
form a community of disciples that "is marked by an alternative
to accepted patterns of leadership. The alternative to how the kings
of the earth rule is not 'spirituality' but servanthood."[27] This is the
meaning of Jesus' repeated refusal to claim the worldly prerogatives
of Davidic kingship, which the multitude—and Peter when he drew
his sword in the garden of Gethsemane—wanted him to claim.

Jesus' utter rejection of "messianic violence"[28] indicates the true
radicality of his politics. As Yoder says, "Here at the cross is the
man who loves his enemies, the man whose righteousness is greater
than that of the Pharisees, who being rich became poor, who gives
his robe to those who took his cloak. . . . The cross is not a detour
or a hurdle on the way to the kingdom, nor is it even the way
to the kingdom; it is the kingdom come."[29] At the cross we find
not a mere ideal or a mere victim. Instead we find Jesus' concrete
way of life, which bears true witness to the God of Israel and in
which Jesus asks us to follow him. Jesus threatens the powers that
be precisely as "the bearer of a new possibility of human, social,
and therefore political relationships" whose identifying mark is the

cross, on which Jesus forgives and redeems his enemies and reveals himself to be a king unlike any worldly king.[30] As Jesus makes clear, followed by Paul, Jesus' followers must share in his cross by participating in his "social nonconformity," his insistence upon forgiveness, and his refusal to accept the norms of worldly violence.[31]

Yoder's interpretation faces a challenge from Paul's injunction, "Let every person be subject to the governing authorities. For there is no authority except from God, and those that exist have been instituted by God. . . . But if you do wrong, be afraid, for he [who is in authority] does not bear the sword in vain; he is the servant of God to execute his wrath on the wrongdoer" (Rom 13:1, 4). In response, Yoder notes that other New Testament texts present "secular government as the province of the sovereignty of Satan," over which Jesus triumphs.[32] Furthermore, he points out that Romans 12 and 13 focus on praising love that is "patient in tribulation" (Rom 12:12), that obeys the command to "bless those who persecute you" (Rom 12:14), and that recognizes that vengeance belongs solely to the Lord (Rom 12:19). Can it be, then, that Paul means for the governing authorities to take vengeance? At the very least, Yoder says, it is "clear that the function exercised by government is not the function to be exercised by Christians," since subject peoples and slaves in the Roman Empire could not belong to the military or police.[33]

In Yoder's view, furthermore, Paul is discussing the governing authorities' judicial rather than war-making power, and so Paul at most has police (not soldiers) in mind. Insofar as Paul requires of Christians subjection to and respect for the governing authorities, he does so, Yoder suggests, as part of Christian subordination and "willingness to suffer," a participation in Christ's "victorious patience with the rebellious powers of his creation."[34] Yoder concludes by pairing Romans 12–13 with Matthew 5 and arguing that Paul and Jesus are saying the same thing: "They *both* instruct Christians to be nonresistant in all their relationships, including the social. They *both* call on the disciples of Jesus to renounce participation in the interplay of egoisms which this world calls 'vengeance' or 'justice.' "[35] Christians are to undertake their ministry of reconciliation while being in, but not of, the violent world.

Summa Theologiae *2-2.40: Aquinas' Biblical Exegesis in His* Quaestio *on War*

Thomas Aquinas argues that waging war is not always sinful, even though war indicates a sinful break, resulting from aggression, in the unity of charity. In treating war among the sins against charity in *Summa Theologiae* 2-2, question 40,[36] Aquinas draws upon the Gospels and Paul's epistles from the New Testament, as well as Exodus, Deuteronomy, Joshua, Psalms, Isaiah, and 1 Maccabees from the Old. How do these biblical passages shape Aquinas' view of war?[37] Rather than following the order of the biblical texts' appearance in the four articles of question 40—which would concentrate attention upon the argumentation of question 40—I seek to focus on the biblical texts themselves, first by surveying the role of the Old Testament texts and then by exploring the role of the New Testament texts.

Exodus 20:8, Isaiah 58:3, and 1 Maccabees 2:41 appear in Aquinas' discussion in question 40, article 4, regarding whether fighting battles on holy days, such as the Sabbath or the feasts, is morally permissible.[38] How could it be permissible to fight and kill fellow human beings on, for instance, the joyous and solemn celebrations of Christmas and Easter? The Sabbath commandment poses this dilemma in particularly striking terms: "Remember the sabbath day, to keep it holy. Six days you shall labor, and do all your work; but the seventh day is a sabbath to the Lord your God; in it you shall not do any work, you, or your son, or your daughter, your manservant, or your maidservant, or your cattle, or the sojourner who is within your gates" (Exod 20:8-10). Not only Israelites, but even cattle and sojourners, must not work in Israel on the Sabbath. If this is so, then it certainly seems that Israelite soldiers (or foreign mercenaries on behalf of Israel) cannot do their work of fighting on the Sabbath. Moreover, the rationale for this commandment bears strongly against the work of fighting: "For in six days the Lord made heaven and earth, the sea, and all that is in them, and rested the seventh day; therefore the Lord blessed the sabbath day and hallowed it" (Exod 20:11). The Sabbath is "hallowed," and so it would seem that war has no place within the Sabbath, a day that God makes holy, a day that embodies the blessings of unity and peace. As Aquinas puts it in his first objection in article 4, "*Sabbath* is interpreted *rest*. But wars are full of unrest."

Unrest, Aquinas notes in the second objection in article 4, is condemned by Isaiah as making a mockery of Israel's fast days. Isaiah 58 begins with a dialogue between Israel and God. God grants that Israel seeks God: "They seek me daily, and delight to know my ways . . . they ask of me righteous judgments, they delight to draw near to God" (Isa 58:2). Nonetheless God describes Israel as an unrighteous nation that forsakes his ways. Israel pleads its cause: " 'Why have we fasted, and thou seest it not? Why have we humbled ourselves, and thou takest no knowledge of it?' " (Isa 58:3). The answer is that Israel observes the fast days, but does not do so with care for the poor among the people. Those who can afford it fast, while the poor laborers are required to work. Far from bearing spiritual fruit, therefore, Israel's fasting produces contention among religious parties: "Behold, you fast only to quarrel and to fight and to hit with wicked fist. Fasting like yours this day will not make your voice to be heard on high. Is such the fast that I choose, a day for a man to humble himself?" (Isa 58:4-5). Israel might keep the outward form of fasting, but the goal of fasting, human humility before God and each other, is absent. God calls upon Israel to recognize the true marks of a humble fast: "Is not this the fast that I choose: to loose the bonds of wickedness, to undo the thongs of the yoke, to let the oppressed go free, and to break every yoke? Is it not to share your bread with the hungry, and bring the homeless poor into your house; when you see the naked, to cover him, and not to hide yourself from your own flesh?" (Isa 58:5-7). Only such justice would make possible a true and spiritually fruitful (covenantal) dialogue between Israel and God.

In the second objection of article 4, Aquinas focuses on God's warning through Isaiah that "you fast only to quarrel and to fight and to hit with wicked fist" (Isa 58:4). As Aquinas remarks, if God condemns Israel for quarrels and fisticuffs on fast days, far less would it be permissible for Israel actually to wage war on the Sabbath and other holy days.

With these objections in view, Aquinas appeals to 1 Maccabees in the *sed contra* of article 4. Whereas Yoder finds 1 Maccabees to be a false path that continues Israel's rebellion against God's word through Jeremiah, Aquinas reads 1 Maccabees as depicting a morally just defense of the lives of Jews who sought to observe Torah and to worship God in the Temple. Recall the violence that Antiochus Epiphanes employed to compel all Israelites to renounce the Torah: "Where the book of the covenant was found in the possession of any one, or if any one adhered to the law, the decree of the king condemned him to death. . . . According to the decree, they put to death the women who had their children circumcised, and their families and those who circumcised them; and they hung the infants from their mothers' necks" (1 Macc 1:57, 60-61). Although many Israelites abandoned the Torah and worshiped idols (cf. 1 Macc 1:43), many others refused to follow Antiochus' decree. Their nonviolent resistance was met by violence: "They chose to die rather than to be defiled by food or to profane the holy covenant; and they did die. And very great wrath came upon Israel" (1 Macc 1:63-64).

Should the Israelites have stopped here, with martyrdom rather than with violent resistance? As it happened, the priest and community leader Mattathias turned to violent resistance when he saw a fellow Jew offering the idolatrous sacrifice commanded by Antiochus. Explicitly comparing Mattathias to Phinehas the grandson of Aaron (see Num 25), 1 Maccabees notes that Mattathias "gave vent to righteous anger; he ran and killed him upon the altar. At the same time he killed the king's officer who was forcing them to sacrifice, and he tore down the altar" (1 Macc 2:24-25). He and his sons then fled to the hills and prepared to mount military resistance against Antiochus along with other groups of Israelites who were also hiding in the hills.

Some of these groups refused to fight on the Sabbath, since God's commandment states that on the Sabbath "you shall not do any work" (Exod 20:10) in order that the day might be kept holy. For this reason, Antiochus chose the Sabbath as the day to attack one group of Israelites, whose decision not to fight resulted in slaughter: "But they did not answer them or hurl a stone at them or block up their hiding places, for they said, 'Let us all die in our innocence; heaven and earth testify for us that you are killing us unjustly.' So they attacked them on the sabbath, and they died, with their wives and children and cattle, to the number of a thousand persons" (1 Macc 2:36-38). Reasoning that otherwise Antiochus' forces "will quickly destroy us from the earth" (1 Macc 2:40), Mattathias and his followers determined that the use of military force in self-defense was acceptable on the Sabbath. Aquinas quotes this text as authoritative in his *sed contra*: "So they made this decision that day: 'Let us fight against every man who comes to attack us on the sabbath day; let us not all die as our brethren died in their hiding places'" (1 Macc 2:41).

First Maccabees does not give further justification for this decision regarding military violence on the Sabbath, other than by showing that the Israelites under Mattathias' command enjoyed military successes that enabled them to reinstitute Torah observance in Israel. Aquinas aims to give further justification for the Maccabees' decision. He quotes Jesus' words in John 7:23, "If on the sabbath a man receives circumcision, so that the law of Moses may not be broken, are you angry with me because on the sabbath I made a man's whole body well?" But what does Jesus' healing on the Sabbath have to do with the Maccabees' military violence on the Sabbath? On the surface, the biblical text that Aquinas has chosen seems only to highlight the difference between healing and killing, and thereby further to cast into doubt whether the Maccabees took seriously enough God's commandment to keep the Sabbath day holy.

In this regard, Aquinas argues that a physician's attending to the bodily health of an individual is analogous to the Maccabees' attending to the health of the body politic (*salus reipublicae*). Through the military violence of the Maccabees, "many are saved from being slain, and innumerable evils both temporal and spiritual are prevented."[39] In 1 Maccabees 2:20-21, Judas Maccabeus describes the health of the body politic that the Maccabees seek to serve: "They come against us in great pride and lawlessness to destroy us and our wives and our children, and to despoil us; but we fight for our lives and our laws." The Jews' lives and laws, ordered to union with God, constitute the health of their body politic.[40] Military violence on the Sabbath is licit only when absolutely necessary to preserve the health of the body politic: "As soon as the need ceases, it is no longer lawful to fight on a holy day."[41]

What about Aquinas' use of the book of Joshua? Does Aquinas appreciate how the book of Joshua, according to Yoder, undermines the king's role in sanctioning war? The answer is both yes and no. Since Aquinas thinks a war can be just if lawful authority undertakes it to preserve the health of the body politic, he suggests that Joshua's description of the role of priests in war still applies. He comments, "Prelates and clerics may, by the authority of their superiors, take part in wars, not indeed by taking up arms themselves, but by affording spiritual help to those who fight justly, by exhorting and absolving them, and by other like spiritual helps."[42] This affirmation, which allows priests to serve in the military as chaplains, refuses to grant to the king sole responsibility for the sanction of war. Aquinas notes that the true end even of war should be a charitable peace that manifests union with God: "Among the faithful, carnal wars should be considered as having for their end the divine spiritual good to which clerics are deputed."[43] The health of the body politic is not abstracted from the "divine spiritual good" of the body of Christ.

Aquinas also uses Joshua to reflect upon how military stratagems comport with Jesus' injunction, "So whatever you wish that men would do to you, do so to them; for this is the law and the prophets" (Matt 7:12).[44] Moses similarly teaches in the Torah, "Justice, and only justice, you shall follow, that you may live and inherit the land which the Lord your God gives you" (Deut 16:20).[45] Do not duplicitous stratagems violate justice and the golden rule? Aquinas supposes that each person would want others to protect him or her from unjust violence; on these grounds just war seems plausible. No one, however, wishes others to deceive them. The question, then, is what constitutes deceit. As Aquinas notes, God commands Joshua to defeat the soldiers of Ai by means of an ambush: "I have given into your hand the king of Ai, and his people, his city, and his land; and you shall do to Ai and its king as you did to Jericho and its king; only its spoil and its cattle you shall take as booty for yourselves; lay an ambush against the city, behind it" (Josh 8:1-2).

Does God thereby legitimize deceit on behalf of military violence and plunder?

Aquinas notes that Joshua does not trick the king of Ai by lying or through "the breaking of a promise," which would be unjust.[46] Instead the king of Ai was fooled by what appeared to be Israel's weakness. Holding back the full truth differs from deceit, since we are not always required to reveal to others everything that we know. As Aquinas puts it, "A man may be deceived by what we say or do, because we do not declare our purpose or meaning to him."[47] Soldiers thus need not reveal their plans to their enemies. Do not soldiers wish for their enemies to reveal their plans to them, however? Does Jesus' injunction, "Whatever you wish that men would do to you, do so to them," apply here? Aquinas points out that no one could rightly wish that others reveal everything they know. He recalls in this respect what Jesus says earlier regarding sacred teaching: "Do not give to dogs what is holy; and do not throw your pearls before swine, lest they trample them under foot and turn to attack you" (Matt 7:6).[48] If sacred teaching does not always need to be shared with all, then neither do military plans.

If we hold something back from someone to his or her harm, however, is this truly treating the other person as we would wish to be treated? According to Aquinas, the actions of soldiers in war must intend the health of body politic (peace). When other persons attack the body politic, soldiers can seek to defend the body politic by inflicting harm upon the attackers. In so doing, the defenders must not violate Jesus' golden rule. Aware of how prevalent such violations are, Aquinas emphasizes (following St. Ambrose's *De officiis*) that "there are certain 'rights of war and covenants [*iura bellorum et foedera*], which ought to be observed even among enemies.'"[49] Throughout his discussion of war, Aquinas keeps at the forefront God's commandment in Psalm 82:4, "Rescue the weak and the needy; deliver them from the hand of the wicked."[50]

If this is how Aquinas employs the Old Testament in his examination of war, how does he employ the New Testament? We have already discussed his use of Matthew 7:6 and 7:12, as well as of John 7:23. The other gospel passages that he quotes in the four articles of the question on war are Matthew 5:39, 10:34, and 26:52

(twice), and Luke 3:14. Matthew 5:39 appears to rule out war along with all other violent acts: "Do not resist one who is evil. But if any one strikes you on the right cheek, turn to him the other also." Matthew 10:34 indicates, in metaphorical language, that Jesus' coming will not end conflicts between human beings: "Do not think that I have come to bring peace on earth; I have not come to bring peace, but a sword." Matthew 26:52 contains Jesus' warning (to Peter, and by extension to the whole church) against seeking to defend him by military force, a warning that sounds a cautionary note against every use of military force: "Put your sword back into its place; for all who take the sword will perish by the sword." Lastly, Luke 3:14 contains John the Baptist's response to Roman soldiers who ask him how they should live their lives in holiness. John the Baptist replies, "Rob no one by violence or by false accusation, and be content with your wages."

Two of these passages appear to reject military violence (Matt 5:39 and Matt 26:52) while two appear at least to allow for military violence in some circumstances (Matt 10:34 and Luke 3:14). Aquinas' reference to Luke 3:14 comes in the *sed contra* of the first article, in which Aquinas seeks to show that it is not always sinful to wage war. Since the context of this discussion is war's place among the sins against charity, the objections in the first article have particular importance. The first objection flows from Matthew 26:52, and the second objection from Matthew 5:39. Aquinas considers these two biblical texts to be the most powerful arguments for the view that waging war is *always* a sin. If the sword inevitably brings not life but death (Matt 26:52), then Jesus' commandment not to defend oneself against an attacker (Matt 5:39) makes sense.

The quotation of Luke 3:14 is embedded within a larger text from Augustine, who cites John the Baptist's words to the Roman soldier in order to show that Jesus does not condemn soldiering in itself (Augustine also has in view Jesus' dealings with the centurion in Luke 7/Matthew 8). Augustine's view that John the Baptist and Jesus condemn abuses that occur within soldiering, not war or soldiering in every instance, guides Aquinas' interpretation of Matthew 5:39 and 26:52. Like the *sed contra*, Aquinas' replies to the first two objections depend upon texts from Augustine. Augustine and Aquinas agree with Yoder that Jesus requires the actions of his followers to be "paradigmatic for the coming kingdom," but they do not agree that this means that Christians must be "a disarmed minority."[51]

Regarding Matthew 26:52, Aquinas, following Augustine, distinguishes between ways in which a person may be said to "take the sword." His point is that there is a difference between taking up weapons as a bandit or murderer on one's own authority and taking up weapons when commissioned by a lawful authority to defend the lives of innocent people who are under attack. Peter does not "take the sword" under lawful authority; rather, he simply pulls out his sword and strikes off the ear of the high priest's slave. Jesus, who possesses lawful authority, strongly reprimands Peter and points out that if Jesus wished a military defense, he would immediately receive "more than twelve legions of angels" from the Father (Matt 26:53). What constitutes taking the sword under lawful authority? Aquinas gives three criteria: the command of those entrusted with the care of the body politic, a just cause, and a rightful intention, namely, "the advancement of good, or the avoidance of evil."[52]

But if Jesus, possessing lawful authority, tells Peter to sheathe his sword, why would Aquinas (and Augustine) suppose that Christian members of the body politic could have warrant to "take the sword"? Even given the three criteria, could resorting to military violence be a Christian act, "paradigmatic for the coming kingdom"? Quoting Augustine, Aquinas rejects " 'the passion for inflicting harm, the cruel thirst for vengeance, an unpacific and relentless spirit, the fever of revolt, the lust of power, and such like things.' "[53] Aquinas holds, however, that those in authority may resort to waging war if they do so in order to obey God's command in Psalm 82:4, "Rescue the weak and the needy; deliver them from the hand of the wicked."[54] When "the weak and the needy" are under attack, their defense may be an act "paradigmatic for the coming kingdom," so long as their defense is lawfully authorized and intends not harm or vengeance but the health of the body politic.

What about Jesus' command in Matthew 5:39 not to "resist one who is evil," but instead to turn the other cheek? Even granting Aquinas' claim that Jesus' words to Peter do not rule out lawful taking of the sword in defense of the body politic, Jesus' command against resisting evildoers appears to require Christians to be "a disarmed minority," as Yoder says. Following Augustine, Aquinas holds that Jesus' command should be interpreted with reference to the spiritual and bodily good of others.[55] If only one's own good is at stake, then, as Jesus says, "if any one strikes you on the right cheek, turn to him the other also; and if any one would sue you and take your coat, let him have your cloak as well; and if any one forces you to go one mile, go with him two miles. Give to him who begs from you, and do not refuse him who would borrow from you" (Matt 5:39-42). But if the good of others is also involved, then one may not be free to accept abuse and give all one's possessions away. Aquinas adds that one must take into account the good of the attacker, who would benefit spiritually from being thwarted.[56] John the Baptist is therefore correct when he does not condemn soldiering as such, but rather condemns abuses of power and desire for booty: "Rob no one by violence or by false accusation, and be content with your wages" (Luke 3:14).

In this vein Aquinas interprets Matthew 10:34, where Jesus says, "Do not think that I have come to bring peace on earth; I have not come to bring peace, but a sword." Aquinas points out that Jesus here makes a distinction between kinds of peace. Jesus brings spiritual peace, found in the forgiveness of sins and the life of charity through the indwelling of the Holy Spirit. Otherwise Jesus' words in the gospel of John would make no sense: "Peace I leave with you; my peace I give to you; not as the world gives do I give to you" (John 14:27). How then can Jesus also say that he has "not come to bring peace, but a sword"? Aquinas explains that Jesus teaches here that he has not come to bring "evil peace," which is rooted in injustice.[57] Because evil peace is not of the Lord, it is possible, where evil peace reigns, to seek true peace by waging war. Yet since bishops and priests are ordained so as to consecrate the Eucharist, which is the sacramental sign of the perfect peace accomplished by Christ's passion, Aquinas holds that bishops and priests may not be soldiers. Thus Jesus tells Peter, when he seeks to defend Jesus by means of the sword, "Put your sword back into its place" (Matt 26:52).[58]

To this point, we have focused with regard to the New Testament on the Gospels. What role do texts from St. Paul's epistles play in Aquinas' theology of war? He quotes six texts from the Pauline epistles, including three from Romans, two from the Corinthian correspondence, and one from 2 Timothy. Like Yoder, Aquinas recognizes that Romans 13 needs to be read in the context of Romans 12. For this reason, the second objection in the first article raises the point that "whatever is contrary to a divine precept is a sin" and "war is contrary to a divine precept," namely, Romans 12:19: "Beloved, never avenge yourselves, but leave it to the wrath of God; for it is written, 'Vengeance is mine, I will repay, says the Lord.'"[59]

The immediate context of Romans 12:19 both deepens Paul's warning against vengeance and provides some leeway for self-defense. Romans 12:18 offers the leeway: "If possible, so far as it depends upon you, live peaceably with all." Paul implies that there may be situations in which living peaceably will not be possible, although he does not describe further what this means.[60] Yet Romans 12:20 deepens Paul's warning against vengeance, by quoting and commenting upon Proverbs 25:21-22: "No, 'If your enemy is hungry, feed him; if he is thirsty, give him drink; for by so doing you will heap burning coals upon his head.' Do not be overcome by evil, but overcome evil with good."[61]

Aquinas readily grants that at times Christians are called "to refrain from resistance or self-defense."[62] Members of the body of Christ must treat enemies with love. As we have seen, Aquinas holds that such love includes love for the health of the body politic and for the true good of one's enemy. With regard to lawful authority's concern for the body politic, Aquinas quotes Romans 13:4: "But if you do wrong, be afraid, for he does not bear the sword in vain; he is the servant of God to execute his wrath on the wrong-doer."[63] If lawful authority is indeed "the servant of God" in bearing the sword, it follows that bearing the sword can be licit for human beings, including Christians, so long as they "aim at peace."[64] As Augustine says (quoted by Aquinas), "True religion looks upon as peaceful those wars that are waged not for motives of aggrandizement, or cruelty, but with the object of securing peace, of punishing evil-doers, and of uplifting the good."[65] In this way, Aquinas brings together Romans 12:19 and Romans 13:4: since lawful authority can "bear the sword" justly, Paul's injunction not to act vengefully does not require nonviolence.

If Christians can in appropriate cases "bear the sword" justly, can bishops and priests "bear the sword"? Quoting Romans 1:32, where Paul remarks that both those who do wicked deeds and those who approve them are guilty, Aquinas observes (in an objection) that because approving a deed is tantamount to doing the deed, it would seem that clergy can "bear the sword" in just wars.[66] In reply to this view, Aquinas puts forward another Pauline text, 2 Timothy 2:4, which argues that just as soldiers please their superiors by soldiering, so Timothy, as "a good soldier of Christ Jesus" (2 Tim 2:3), should focus on tending his spiritual flock. Aquinas argues that 2 Timothy 2:4 applies to all bishops and priests, who are called to be spiritual soldiers of Christ Jesus rather than to become "entangled in civilian pursuits" (2 Tim 2:4).

The ordained priesthood revolves for Aquinas around the sacrament of the Eucharist. He describes the "ministry of the altar" as originating at the Last Supper, when Jesus told the Twelve, "For as often as you eat this bread and drink the cup, you proclaim the Lord's death until he comes" (1 Cor 12:26).[67] Since the "ministry of the altar" has as its special focus the sacramental representation of Christ's passion, Aquinas concludes that "it is unbecoming for them [the clergy] to slay or shed blood, and it is more fitting that they should be ready to shed their own blood for Christ, so as to imitate in deed what they portray in their ministry."[68] He comments that just as the marriage act is meritorious but unlawful for those vowed to virginity, so also fighting in a just war is meritorious but unlawful to those who, like bishops and priests, are "deputed to works more meritorious still."[69] When enemies threaten a bishop's or priest's flock both spiritually and bodily, the bishop or priest must respond solely with spiritual weapons, due to the character of his ministry. In confirmation of this point, Aquinas quotes 2 Corinthians 10:4, where Paul affirms with regard to his apostolic ministry that "the weapons of our warfare are not worldly but have divine power to destroy strongholds."[70]

But does not every Christian "eat this bread and drink the cup" and thereby "proclaim the Lord's death until he comes" (1 Cor 11:26)? Why should only bishops and priests specially represent Christ's passion? Should not *all* Christians "be ready to shed their own blood for Christ, so as to imitate in deed what they portray"? If bishops and priests cannot wage war on the grounds that war goes against what they represent eucharistically, then why do not these same grounds (and the same prohibition) apply to every Christian who partakes of the eucharistic banquet, as Yoder holds?

Aquinas affirms that all Christians should be ready "to shed their own blood for Christ": charity inclines the believer who is persecuted because of Christ to hold fast "to faith and justice notwithstanding the threatening danger of death."[71] All Christians must be prepared for martyrdom, but relatively few instances of oppression invite martyrdom. This is so because wicked persons may seek to harm the good of the individual and/or the good of the body politic without directly aiming at the body of Christ. Similarly, members of the body of Christ represent Christ not only by directly serving the church, but also by serving the good of individuals and/or the good of the body politic, in which the protection of the weak and the needy fosters the ordering of the whole community to God.[72]

Aquinas suggests that the work of bishops and priests is "more meritorious" because of their sacramental ministry and because of their focus on "the contemplation of divine things, the praise of God, and prayers for the people."[73] A bishop or priest who engages in commerce or war thereby neglects the greater good for which he was ordained. Even so, businessmen and soldiers are called to build up human society in charity and to represent Christ in their mode of life. As Aquinas puts it, "Several things are requisite for the good of a human society."[74]

Conclusion

Yoder argues that Jesus and Paul "*both* instruct Christians to be non-resistant in all their relationships, including the social. They *both* call on the disciples of Jesus to renounce participation in the interplay of egoisms which this world calls 'vengeance' or 'justice.'"[75]

While agreeing that Christians cannot participate in an "interplay of egoisms," nonetheless Aquinas holds on the basis of the Old and New Testaments that Christians do not need "to be nonresistant in all their relationships." Does the health of the body politic thereby trump the health of the body of Christ?

Aquinas' understanding of the body politic arises from Psalm 82:4, "Rescue the weak and the needy; deliver them from the hand of the wicked." This view of the body politic interprets the human city in light of the heavenly city. The obligations of justice that humans owe to each other, obligations that charity intensifies, require leaders to oppose, at times by military force, those who would gravely harm the body politic. In Aquinas' reading of Scripture as a unified *sacra doctrina*, Jesus' teachings are consistent with John the Baptist's words about soldiering; given the command to "rescue the weak and the needy," Jesus' followers can "bear the sword" (Rom 13:4) justly. On this basis Aquinas likewise interprets Joshua and 1 Maccabees. Even though the New Testament re-envisions Israel around Christ Jesus, so that soldiers fight on behalf of the body politic rather than on behalf of the Israel of God,[76] Aquinas' exegesis ensures that the Old Testament is not cut off from the New and that the New Testament teaching does not contain internal contradiction. Incorporated into Christ's eschatological kingdom through the Eucharist, believers embody Christ's peace in the world—a witness that includes defending the body politic against unjust efforts to wound and rend it by oppressing the weak and needy.[77]

Depending on their vocation, Christians bear witness to Jesus' self-giving love in distinct manners. In the celebration of the holy Eucharist, bishops and priests sacramentally represent (*in persona Christi*) Jesus' Paschal sacrifice. The sacrament of holy orders enables bishops and priests to communicate to others the power of Christ's passion, preeminently in the Eucharist.[78] In defending the health of the body politic (as ordered to the health of the body of Christ), soldiers embody Jesus' self-giving love in a lesser way, but one that is also needed in a fallen world. The upbuilding of the body of Christ is distinct but not separable from the upbuilding of the body politic. "The weak and the needy" are delivered "from the hand of the wicked" in diverse ways. The justice of repelling threats to the body politic by limited military force does not deny that God's peace in Christ Jesus is eucharistically at work in the world.

Yoder holds that Christ's refusal to participate in violence indicates a radical rejection of the norms of worldly power, and that Christians in the world must embody Christ's alternative to worldly power. By contrast, Aquinas reads Scripture as showing that military violence, when called forth by the need to "rescue the weak and needy" (and thus by a sin against charity), can embody the witness of Christians to an order not dominated by unjust worldly power.[79] This exegetical tradition, which Aquinas inherits and develops, continues to ground the Catholic Church's teaching on war in *Gaudium et Spes* and the *Catechism of the Catholic Church*.[80]

CHAPTER 8

Scandal, Scapegoats, and Spiritual Downfall

According to Thomas Aquinas, scandal contradicts charity's outward act of beneficence. The beneficent person does good to his or her friends; charity extends this friendship to all humans. In this regard, Aquinas cites the words of Paul: "So then, as we have opportunity, let us do good to all men, especially to those who are of the household of faith" (Gal 6:10).[1] We must pray for all people and be prepared to do good to all, while first doing good to those closest to us (for example, our parents and our children, who have most claim upon us).[2] Those closest to us do not have an exclusive claim to our beneficence: as Aquinas says, "one ought, for instance, to succor a stranger, in extreme necessity, rather than one's own father, if he is not in such urgent need."[3]

Causing scandal is the opposite of doing "good to all men." But since there are many ways that we can harm others, in what does the vice of scandal specifically consist? This chapter compares Aquinas' view with that of René Girard. Although Girard does not write as a theologian, Girard and Aquinas both interpret scandal in light of Scripture and the life of charity. Their distinct approaches provide ample material not only for more profoundly conceiving of scandal, but also—by God's grace—for avoiding it.

René Girard on Scandal

Treating two early works by René Girard, *Violence and the Sacred* and *Things Hidden Since the Foundation of the World*, Hans Urs von Balthasar identifies Girard's approach as a high point, even if a somewhat problematic one, "in the field of soteriology and in theology generally."[4] Indebted to Nietzsche but taking the side of Christ, Girard argues that Christ unveils a mechanism behind all human violence.[5] This mechanism is that of the sacrificial scapegoat, which Girard envisions as constituting the basis of all human institutions. For Girard, human desire is imitative, focusing on what others desire, and so rivalries (power struggles) are endemic to human life. These rivalries threaten to destroy the possibility of human community, and "the accumulated tension can only be dispersed by being discharged, quasi-fortuitously, onto a victim common to both sides, a 'scapegoat.'"[6] By destroying the scapegoat, the rivals cathartically release the pent-up violence and regain, at least for a short period, the ability to live together in peace. The scapegoat or sacrificial victim thus is at the same time accursed (bearing sin) and sacred (establishing peace). The "gods" are invented by humans in the image of this violence. The gods thirst for bloody sacrifice and in return deliver peace to human communities. According to Girard, civilization is built upon the scapegoat-sacrifice, although at the same time civilized institutions seek to veil and to moderate the rivalries that produce the scapegoat-sacrifice.

Girard conceives of the Old Testament as being in the process of unveiling the sacrificial mechanism. The Old Testament takes the side of Abel, the scapegoat, rather than the side of Cain; this is particularly important because Cain is the founder of cities and of culture. For Girard, the prophets likewise undermine the mechanism of sacrificial worship and take the side of the victims. Jesus then fulfills the prophets by entering into the scapegoat-sacrifice role and unmasking it: violent action, and above all the ritual victimizing that Jesus endures, is shown to be radically sinful. The kingdom that Jesus inaugurates is unique in being grounded upon love and reconciliation rather than violence and victimization. However, the history of the church, for Girard, manifests a return to the scapegoat-sacrifice in various ways (even within the New Testament, where Hebrews envisions Jesus' death in sacrificial terms). But now that sacrifice has been unmasked by God in Jesus, its horrific violence can no longer be hidden and so civilization can no longer be built upon it.

In his *I See Satan Fall Like Lightning*, Girard explains, "What Jesus invites us to imitate is his own *desire*, the spirit that directs him toward the goal on which his intention is fixed: to resemble God the Father as much as possible."[7] In the Gospels, Girard argues, our violent mimetic rivalry is described by "the noun *skandalon* and the verb *skandalizein*."[8] According to Girard, a "scandal" (*skandalon*) is an obstacle that at the same time repels and attracts us. This obstacle is the fact that we imitatively desire the same object that others desire. No matter how much we are thwarted, we continue to seek violently to obtain the object. We multiply obstacles, multiply scandal, in this spiral of mimetic violence. The innocent are "scandalized" by being mimetically drawn into this violent rivalry of desire, what Girard calls a "mimetic contagion."[9] Thus Jesus recognizes that Peter, for instance, is "the puppet of his own mimetic desire, incapable of resisting pressures that work upon him from moment to moment."[10] All the disciples deny Jesus and flee from the cross, and we would have done the same in their place. The pressure of the crowd is too powerful: the crowd desires a scapegoat, a victim, to release cathartically the pressure of mimetic rivalry, so that the Hobbesian war of all against all can be once more concealed.

A "scandal" begins with two rivals seeking the same object, and is caught up into other such scandals until "the most polarizing scandal remains alone on the stage."[11] This most polarizing scandal involves not two individual rivals, but the whole community against one victim. Girard notes that "Jesus resorts to the vocabulary of scandal to designate himself as everyone's victim and to designate all those who are polarized against him. He exclaims, 'Happy is the one who is not scandalized by me.' "[12] In Girard's view, Jesus is the "universal scandal," and his cross, with its polarized beams, symbolizes "scandal par excellence."[13] The disciples are "scandalized" by Jesus insofar as they come, with the crowd, to treat him as an obstacle who must be gotten rid of in order to restore the community's unity. Jesus becomes the supreme "scandal," or the locus of all mimetic rivalry in the community, and all are "scandalized" by him. All share in persecuting him as the chosen cathartic or substitutionary victim. Girard comments in this regard, "It is clearly mimetic contagion that explains the hatred of the masses for exceptional persons."[14] Resulting from the multiple "scandals" or mimetic rivalries that threaten to overwhelm the community, the "collective lynching" of Jesus constitutes the scandal that unmasks mimetic violence once and for all.[15]

Jesus desires God the Father rather than desiring a worldly object. For this reason, Jesus can thwart Satan's effort to involve him in a mimetic rivalry.[16] Peter, who sees Jesus as a king who stands above suffering, seeks to draw Jesus into a rivalry that ultimately would end with Jesus and Peter fighting over worldly power; to this appeal, Jesus answers (as Girard translates it), "Get behind me, Satan, for you are a scandal to me" (Matt 16:23). According to Girard's interpretation of Mark 3:23-26, furthermore, Satan leads human beings to try to resolve "scandals" by means of "the violent expulsion of scapegoats," a temporary restoration of a modicum of order that, by victimizing a single person ("the single victim mechanism"), ultimately increases the violence and enhances Satan's effectiveness in sowing disorder and destruction.[17] As Girard summarizes the process: "In us and about us scandals proliferate; sooner or later they carry us along toward mimetic snowballing and the single victim mechanism."[18] As the crucified Son of God, Jesus rejects "rivalistic desire" and instead shows humans another path: imitation of the God who chooses to be powerless.[19] Girard comments, "By depriving the victim mechanism of the darkness that must conceal it so it can continue to control human culture, the Cross shakes up the world."[20] The cross, powerfully vindicated by Jesus' resurrection, overcomes the mythology of bloodthirsty gods who demand victims. As Girard explains, "The Resurrection empowers Peter and Paul, as well as all believers after them, to understand that all imprisonment in sacred violence is violence done to Christ."[21]

Thomas Aquinas on Scandal

Does Aquinas' understanding of "scandal" have parallels to Girard's? As we have seen, Girard interprets the Gospels' references to scandal in light of his theory of mimetic rivalry, in which desire for the same object produces an obstacle to human community that eventually leads to a scandal intense enough to be resolved by the bloody sacrifice of a victim. In its deepest sense, for Girard, scandal signifies the way in which human desire ends up in bloodshed. Jesus offers a path beyond scandal because he refuses to get involved in the competition of desire for this-worldly objects; instead, he focuses his desire upon God the Father. His resurrection exposes the falsity and futility of the violence that scandal, at its peak, brings about. Not violence but nonviolence truly unites humans, who thereby are freed from the "rivalistic desire" that leads to the ever-worsening obstacles to communion that are "scandals."

Scandal and Spiritual Downfall

Following Jerome, Aquinas defines scandal as "something less rightly [*minus rectum*] said or done that occasions spiritual downfall."[22] As Aquinas understands it, then, "scandal" involves moving someone else to sin. Scandal is when one person says or does something that disposes another (or others) to stumble on the spiritual path; in this way Aquinas takes account of the Greek *skandalon*, rendered by Jerome as "offense, downfall, or a stumbling against something."[23] When we say or do the right thing, we assist others in spiritual uprightness, whereas when we say or do "something less rightly," we can occasion the spiritual downfall of the other person and thus bring about scandal.

Aquinas points out that only one's own will, by freely consenting, can cause one to do evil. In the strict sense, one cannot cause another person's spiritual fall. Scandal only provides the stimulus for the spiritual fall of another person. Here Aquinas distinguishes between active scandal and passive scandal. Active scandal describes the one who seeks to lead the other into evil. Passive scandal describes the condition of the one who is scandalized. At times one can be scandalized or led into sin ("passive" scandal) without any active scandal on another's part; this is strictly the fault of the one who is scandalized. As an example, Aquinas gives the case of one who "through being ill-disposed, is led into sin, for instance, into envy of another's good."[24] At other times one undergoes passive scandal and is led into sin due to the active scandal of another person who seeks by word or deed to lead one into sin. There are also instances of active scandal, the attempt to lead others into sin, that fail; in such instances there is obviously no passive scandal.

In accord with Romans 14, Aquinas notes that some persons are "weak," that is, prone to the falling into sin that is "passive" scandal. Such persons are easily influenced toward sin by their relationships with others, whether or not these other persons intend active scandal. Girard sees desire as necessarily conflictual or rivalry-producing due to how desire arises when we see someone else desiring a particular object. He has a strong sense of how our desires are profoundly influenced by the environments in which we find ourselves. For his part, Aquinas recognizes that some persons are "weak," but Aquinas leaves more room for the active intention of leading another person into sin. Such evil intention plays little role (despite being personified by the metaphor of "Satan") in Girard, because he assumes that whatever this-worldly desire we have will be imitated in a competitive fashion by others, thus automatically leading to scandal and violence. Indeed, in a certain sense all scandal is purely "passive" for Girard. An active agent of scandal is hardly needed, because scandal will arise simply due to the fact that our worldly desire will focus on the same objects.

Girard's account of desire depicts a structure of sin, or a structure of scandal, that is inescapable. He depicts a world in which, at least prior to the ameliorating influence of Christianity, the contagion of the *libido dominandi* overwhelms free choice. Only Jesus, through his cross and resurrection, shows humans another way. Aquinas' portrait of scandal suggests much more control over whether one gets caught up in scandal (because scandal, whether passive or active, requires that one freely sin). From this perspective, Girard may underestimate the fact that scandal involves a free decision to sin. Given his rather mechanistic account of the effects of this-worldly desire, he does not seem to leave much room for freedom.

Scandal as Contagion?

In an objection to his own position, however, Aquinas proposes that scandal is not a sin because scandal is not voluntary. In support of this position, he cites Matthew 18:7, where Jesus says, "Woe to the world for temptations to sin! For it is necessary that temptations come, but woe to the man by whom the temptation comes!" If it is "necessary that temptations come," then it would seem that active scandal (even if not passive scandal) is necessary. If so, then Girard's presentation of scandal as arising necessarily from our competing this-worldly desires, desires that are aroused by imitation of each other in pursuing particular objects, fits better with Jesus' view of scandal than does Aquinas' emphasis on freedom.

In replying to the objection, Aquinas recognizes the limits of his emphasis on freedom with respect to active scandal. He observes that "it must be that scandals come, so long as men fail to change their evil mode of living."[25] Only the grace of the Holy Spirit can accomplish such a change in our mode of living. This is not because of inevitable rivalries arising from mimetic desire, but because our wills are disordered and our sensual desires hold sway. From this perspective, Aquinas interprets Jesus' words in Matthew 18:7 as meaning that "scandals must occur, seeing the condition of man who fails to shield himself from sin. Thus a physician on seeing a man partaking of unsuitable food might say that such a man must injure his health, which is to be understood on the condition that he does not change his diet."[26] Human freedom is built into this way of understanding Jesus' words. Such freedom seems presumed by the context of Jesus' words in Matthew 18, especially Jesus' warning that "whoever causes one of these little ones who believe in me to sin, it would be better for him to have a great millstone fastened round his neck and to be drowned in the depth of the sea."[27] Aquinas adds that while God does not will scandal, nonetheless God turns the evil of scandal to good: as Paul tells the Corinthians, "there must be factions among you in order that those who are genuine among you may be recognized" (1 Cor 11:19).[28]

In Girard, it does not seem that "scandal" denotes what Aquinas would call a "special sin." If every sin involves scandal, then scandal is not a specific kind of sin, but rather an aspect of every sin. All scandal involves "something less rightly said or done," and in this respect Aquinas grants that scandal is not a specific sin, since this definition encompasses all sins.[29] But Jerome's full definition includes the phrase "that occasions spiritual downfall." Active scandal intends the spiritual fall of another person. This intention makes scandal a specific kind of sin, namely, the effort to harm one's neighbor spiritually.

Why is this a sin against *charity* in particular? Scandal is the opposite of fraternal correction, which is an outward act of charity.[30] Whereas fraternal correction seeks the spiritual good of the neighbor, active scandal seeks the spiritual harm of the neighbor. The sin of active scandal can accomplish this goal even without committing another sin, "as when a man scandalizes his neighbor by a deed which is not a sin in itself, but has an appearance of evil."[31] Active scandal thereby eats away at the communion of charity. As opposed to Girard's view that all this-worldly desire leads to scandal, Aquinas holds that scandal arises only from the intentional desire to harm another person spiritually.

Even if one has no intentional desire to harm a person spiritually, however, what happens if by pursuing one's desires, one necessarily harms another person spiritually (by creating the conditions for mimetic rivalry, scandal, and violence)? For Aquinas, this-worldly desires are not in themselves the problem. The problem is the intention with which (and the circumstances in which) we pursue them. In other words, are they disordered desires, or are they rightly ordered (yet still this-worldly) desires? If the latter, then in Aquinas' view they are not "rivalistic." They can be this-worldly desires that build up, rather than tear down, the common good.

Scandalizing the Weak

Girard's emphasis on how actions that are not per se sinful lead to scandal is in accord with the witness of much human experience, and Aquinas recognizes this fact. After all, the spiritual life itself, as embodied by a holy person or by the church, can cause passive scandal in the weak (those who are already inclined toward sin). From Augustine, Aquinas gives two examples of cases in which holy persons should avoid actions regarding spiritual goods that might lead to scandal in the weak. The first example is excommunication, which risks causing a schism if the excommunication scandalizes others by leading them to join themselves to the false beliefs and practices of the excommunicates. The second example is fraternal correction, which can backfire by increasing the sinfulness of the person being corrected.[32] With regard to spiritual gifts backfiring, Aquinas also cites Jesus' warning: "Do not give dogs what is holy; and do not throw your pearls before swine, lest they trample them under foot and turn to attack you" (Matt 7:6).[33]

If actions intended to bestow spiritual goods can cause scandal in the weak by turning them away from God and thus occasioning their spiritual downfall, the same can easily happen with regard to actions that have only to do with temporal goods. A person who possesses much wealth, for example, often unintentionally inspires envy, thereby scandalizing his or her neighbor—a case of passive scandal without active scandal. Should Christians therefore avoid possessing wealth? Similarly, even our eating certain foods can be an occasion of sin for others. Aquinas cites Paul's remark (which relates both to Old Testament food laws and to pagan offerings of meat to idols), "If your brother is being injured by what you eat, you are no longer walking in love. Do not let what you eat cause the ruin of one for whom Christ died" (Rom 14:15).[34] Should Christians therefore not eat meat?

In the same vein, Aquinas observes that Christians often go to court as contending parties in order to adjudicate matters pertaining to temporal goods. Legal action, by seeming to make a mockery of the unity of charity, can be an occasion for the spiritual downfall of the weak by leading them to scoff at Christian claims. Paul offers strong words in this regard: "To have lawsuits at all with one another is a defeat for you. Why not rather suffer wrong? Why not rather be defrauded?" (1 Cor 6:7). As a final example, Aquinas quotes Paul's willingness to do without payment from his churches in order to avoid giving the impression that he preaches for temporal gain: "If others share this rightful claim upon you, do not we still more? Nevertheless, we have not made use of this right, but we endure anything rather than put an obstacle in the way of the gospel of Christ" (1 Cor 9:12).

These instances of passive scandal show that Girard and Aquinas are not so far apart as regards their sense of the prevalence of scandal in the world. Yet Aquinas thinks that his distinction between active scandal and passive scandal remains crucial for understanding our experience of sinful conflict and social disorder. Although active scandal can never be countenanced, Christians and the church must risk passive scandal if "things that are necessary for salvation" are at stake.[35] This is the case even with temporal goods. In this regard Aquinas observes that "Blessed Thomas of Canterbury demanded the restitution of Church property, notwithstanding that the king took scandal from his doing so."[36]

Thomas à Becket and the English king desired the same object, the same temporal good, namely the property of the church. But Girard's emphasis on renunciation of this-worldly desire in order to avoid the inevitable scandalous conflict would not, in Aquinas' view, work as regards Thomas à Becket. The reason is the defense of the common good. As Aquinas says, "If it were permissible for wicked men to rob other people of their property, this would tend to the detriment of the truth of life and justice."[37] In other words, it would tend to further scandal. Becket was right to stand up to the king even with respect to the church's temporal goods. The temporal goods of the church serve the salvation of humans and therefore cannot simply be given up by those entrusted with their care.

On the other hand, Archbishop Becket would not have needed to defend his own possessions in the same way. Aquinas notes that when we are dealing with our own temporal goods, we are obliged to give them up rather than cause scandal. Yet, in the case of unjust requests, we should first see whether scandal can be avoided by fraternal correction of the unjust request. We should also recognize that out of desire for our temporal goods, malicious people can stir up scandal (for instance, envy of the wealth of particular persons). The common good calls upon us to refuse to give way to such malice, which would both "give wicked men an opportunity of plunder, and would be injurious to the plunderers themselves, who would remain in sin as long as they were in possession of another's property."[38]

This insistence upon not giving way to malicious promoters of scandal (for example, those who foment envy and greed as regards the church's property) differs significantly from Girard's assumption that scandal is inevitable because of "rivalistic desire," even though like Girard, Aquinas assumes that society will be plagued by much scandal due to human weakness (passive scandal) and human malice (active scandal).

Jesus and the Pharisees

Aquinas' understanding of the relationship of spiritual goods to scandal is shaped by Jesus' conflict with the Pharisees. In Girard's reading, Jesus' conflicts are instances of his opposition to the spread of the social contagion of violent scandal, which in the end will require a bloody victim. Whether this interpretation suffices for the complexity of Jesus' engagement with the Pharisees is doubtful. Jesus critiques the Pharisees on doctrinal matters, arguing that in claiming to observe the Torah meticulously, they actually abandon the true meaning of the Torah (see, e.g., Matt 15:1-9). In his conflict with the Pharisees as described in the Gospels, Jesus is presented as scandalizing them in the sense that they turn decisively away from him. Arguably, however, these Pharisees sought Jesus' death not because of the necessarily violent mechanism of "rivalistic desire" but because of his appropriation to himself of the divine identity.

In Matthew 15:14, which is cited by Aquinas in his discussion of scandal, Jesus teaches about the Pharisees: "Let them alone; they are blind guides. And if a blind man leads a blind man, both will fall into a pit."[39] As leaders of the community, the Pharisees use their influence to lead people away from Jesus, and Jesus accuses them of both blindness and hypocrisy (see Matt 15:7). Aquinas treats the Pharisees' being scandalized as evidence of their malice: turning away from the truth conveyed by Jesus' teaching, they maliciously sought to turn others away from the truth. He differentiates such malicious scandal from the scandal of the broader Jewish populace, which proceeded from weakness and ignorance and which could in principle be alleviated through good teaching.

Both these examples of "passive" scandal arise from Jesus' teaching. Aquinas insists that no teacher should ever "suppress the truth and teach error in order to avoid any scandal that might ensue." Even so, teaching, like other works of mercy, can sometimes be postponed or hidden for a time so as to avoid passive scandal on the part of the weak or ignorant.[40] But Jesus' teaching could not be postponed or hidden, because of his mission to bring salvation to all humankind. The possibility of scandal must be weighed against the spiritual good that is to be communicated. Aquinas distinguishes the spiritual goods that are necessary for salvation from those not necessary for salvation. Were all spiritual goods absolutely necessary for salvation, there could be no excuse for postponing them, no matter what the risk of scandal. Yet charity does not require communicating spiritual goods openly in each and every circumstance; sometimes this communication can be postponed or hidden.

All active scandal sins against charity by intending spiritual harm to others. By contrast, Jesus speaks to the Pharisees for their good rather than with the intention of harming them spiritually, even though he knows that the Pharisees will stumble on his teaching and scandalize others, including the weak and ignorant. The highly conflictual doctrinal debates between Jesus and the Pharisees underscore the need for distinguishing kinds of scandal. Inquiring into whether scandal is always a mortal sin, Aquinas takes note of Jesus' warning that "whoever causes one of these little ones who believe in me to sin, it would be better for him to have a great millstone fastened round his neck and to be drowned in the depth of the sea" (Matt 18:6). Paul makes a similar point in 1 Corinthians 8:12 regarding scandal caused by eating food offered to idols: "Thus, sinning against your brethren and wounding their conscience when it is weak, you sin against Christ." These texts suggest that scandal, in all forms, is a mortal sin (deadly to the life of charity).[41]

In his reply, Aquinas lays out the distinctions that we have seen above. Jesus was justified in his doctrinal confrontations with the Pharisees, despite the scandal thereby caused, because his mission of salvation made it necessary to teach openly and because he intended not the spiritual harm but rather the spiritual healing of his audience, including the weak and ignorant who were scandalized against him by the Pharisees. Active scandal intends spiritual harm and thus is always a mortal sin, and teaching in an inappropriate mode or circumstances can be a venial sin. But Jesus' confrontations with the Pharisees were neither of these. Jesus is subject neither to active scandal nor to passive scandal, because both involve a sinful falling away from the good. Recall that after Jesus rebuked the Pharisees for their understanding of vows regarding temple offerings and for their interpretation of the Torah's food laws, the disciples came to Jesus and said, "Do you know that the Pharisees were offended when they heard this saying?" (Matt 15:12).[42] As Aquinas explains, the blame for the Pharisees' being scandalized lies not in Jesus' teaching itself, but in the Pharisees' reception of that teaching: in this way the Pharisees scandalized themselves.[43]

Scandal and the Saints

What about Jesus' followers, those who live in faith and charity in the Holy Spirit? Can they be scandalized or actively cause scandal? Aquinas cites two consoling passages from Psalms: "Those who trust in the Lord are like Mount Zion, which cannot be moved, but abides for ever" (Ps 125:1); and "Great peace have those who love thy law; nothing can make them stumble" (Ps 119:165). So long as we have charity, we cannot intend to lead someone else into spiritual harm (active scandal) or be dislodged from our own attachment to spiritual good (passive scandal).

This is a point of connection between Aquinas and Girard. For Girard, so long as we desire God the Father and take the side of the victim rather than engaging in the violence of mimetic power struggles, we can avoid the contagion of scandal. Likewise, although Aquinas' account of charity and this-worldly desire is more complex, Aquinas too argues that we can avoid scandal (active or passive) insofar as we cleave, in Christ and the Holy Spirit, to God and his law of self-giving love.

Does this mean that the saints never sin? No, but the saints' venial sins are "insufficient in themselves to give scandal."[44] In this respect Aquinas cites another psalm, "But as for me, my feet had almost stumbled, my steps had well nigh slipped" (Ps 73:2). Charitable people may "almost stumble," but thanks to the grace of the Holy Spirit they do not fall—that is, actively scandalize others or become scandalized themselves—while they have charity. Aquinas quotes Paul's encomium to the power of charity: "For I am sure that neither death, nor life, nor angels, nor principalities, nor things present, nor things to come, nor powers, nor height, nor depth, nor anything else in all creation, will be able to separate us from the love of God in Christ Jesus our Lord" (Rom 8:38-39).[45]

But how then to interpret the turbulent life of Peter, both before and after Christ's pasch? Aquinas notes that it would seem that Peter scandalized the Gentiles by refusing, in accordance with Jewish Torah observance, to eat with them. He has in view Paul's recollections in Galatians 2:14, "But when I saw that they were not straightforward about the truth of the gospel, I said to Cephas before them all, 'If you, though a Jew, live like a Gentile and not like a Jew, how can you compel the Gentiles to live like Jews?'" Following Augustine and Paul, Aquinas affirms that Peter sinned in his behavior toward the Gentiles. Peter's behavior, however, was a venial sin whose intent was not to lead anyone into spiritual harm; he sought simply to avoid scandalizing Jewish converts in Jerusalem. His sin gave no one real reason to be scandalized.[46]

More difficult perhaps is Peter's tense exchange with Jesus after Peter had proclaimed Jesus to be "the Christ, the Son of the living God" (Matt 16:16), and Jesus had responded by blessing Peter as "the rock" on which "I will build my church" (Matt 16:18). When Jesus then sought to prepare his disciples for his approaching passion, Peter "began to rebuke him, saying, 'God forbid, Lord! This shall never happen to you'" (Matt 16:22).[47] Does Peter have a sinful motive in trying to persuade Jesus not to undergo his passion, so that Peter's words are active scandal (even if Jesus is not scandalized)? Neither Girard nor Aquinas states that Peter is actively trying to cause Jesus to fall, but Girard does attribute to Peter the desire of "worldly ambition," from which Jesus is pure.[48] It is unclear whether Girard considers "worldly ambition" to be in itself sinful, or whether worldly ambition is simply one of the this-worldly desires that inevitably lead to mimetic rivalry and thus to scandal and violence. Certainly "worldly ambition" is not for Girard a desire that we should have: instead of having this-worldly desires, we should desire God the Father and share in Jesus' renunciation of this-worldly power in favor of the victims.

For Aquinas, following Jerome, Peter's "sense of piety" led him to deny that such things as crucifixion could happen to "the Christ, the Son of the living God." Because Peter's intention was not to cause Jesus' downfall and because Jesus was not scandalized, Aquinas interprets Jesus' calling Peter a "scandal" (Matt 16:23) to mean that Peter's words make him a hindrance, an obstacle to Jesus' mission.[49] In Aquinas' view, Jesus is not here condemning Peter for the sin of active scandal, even though Peter's counsel would have led Jesus astray. Jesus is not thereby scandalized, of course, because "passive" scandal (that is, being scandalized) requires falling into sin.

Concluding Reflections

Girard paints a broad portrait of disordered desire leading inevitably to bloodshed, in which the blood of victims serves as to "unify," in a grotesque manner, the conflicting members of the society. Scandal in this sense is the contagion of bloodshed-producing conflict as people compete for the same goods. Girard mounts a plausible case that such competition, fueled by mimetic lust and rivalry, shapes the desires and the patterns of unification that mark fallen human societies. Girard's key insight is that biblical faith sides with the victims rather than with the power-hungry.

Von Balthasar insightfully offers three criticisms of Girard's scapegoat theory. First, since Girard holds that religion is a covert system of scapegoating, he has no concept of "natural religion"; outside of biblical faith, God is completely subsumed by the idols.[50] Second, Girard focuses on power and violence, but neglects justice. Third, Girard's account of "the 'omnipresence of violence'" endangers our freedom either to sin or to do good.[51] Von Balthasar finds, however, that Girard's focus on turning our desire toward the God who renounces both worldly power and the blood of victims stands as a powerful call for spiritual renewal. Likewise, although Girard proposes a reordering of desire that does not so much heal our this-worldly desires as overcome them completely, his basic goal accords with the need to refashion our this-worldly desires through the grace of the Holy Spirit.

When Aquinas addresses the sin of scandal, he brings to the fore the aspects identified by von Balthasar as needing further emphasis in Girard's theory of the scapegoat: God, justice, and freedom. Scandal is not merely a violent contagion arising necessarily from rivalistic/mimetic desire; rather, scandal consists specifically in the injustice of freely seeking our neighbor's aversion to God. Given his emphasis on the agent's freedom and the justice or injustice of the agent's acts, Aquinas pays particular attention to the relationship of Jesus and the Pharisees, who contended with each other over matters of truth and religious practice. He therefore examines closely how one should act in order to avoid scandalizing the weak and the ignorant, even while recognizing that sometimes charity requires that one risk unintended scandal. Similarly, the centrality of God in his thought leads Aquinas to inquire into whether Jesus' followers, transformed by the Holy Spirit, can actively scandalize others or be scandalized themselves.

Both Aquinas and Girard, then, can be read profitably on scandal. Although they use the term in different senses, they have similar views of the human situation. Girard helps us to see the societal dimensions of scandal, what might be called the structures of sin. Aquinas helps us to appreciate the way in which particular people freely cause scandal and consent to be scandalized, and he also allows us to recognize the goodness of this-worldly desire despite the prevalence of disordered desire. How can we help others move closer to God rather than moving them further away from God? The answer, for both Aquinas and Girard, is Jesus Christ. "In this is love, not that we loved God but that he loved us and sent his Son to be the expiation for our sins. Beloved, if God so loved us, we also ought to love one another" (1 John 4:10-11).

Conclusion

Quoting Étienne Gilson's remark that "the most marvelous of all things a being can do is to be," Josef Pieper attempts to describe the basis of love: "For what the lover gazing upon his beloved says and means is *not*: How good that you are *so* (so clever, useful, capable, skillful), but: It's good that you are; how wonderful that you exist!"[1] God's creative act, pouring forth the goodness of finite being, is sheer love. God loves us into existence and rejoices in created goodness: "And God saw everything that he had made, and behold, it was very good" (Gen 1:31). When by God's gift we experience the joy of loving God in himself—his Trinitarian communion—our joy involves peace. Our rational appetite finds its fulfillment in loving the infinite goodness of God (and the participated goodness of our neighbors).[2]

Faced with evils or defects in goodness, the charitable person's response is mercy. God has mercy upon us by bountifully healing our defects through his causal love, and in light of our defects we have mercy on each other by seeking to do good to each other. As regards outward acts, this manifests itself as beneficence—the bestowal of gifts—and the works of mercy, among which Aquinas numbers "to feed the hungry, to give drink to the thirsty, to clothe

the naked, to harbor the harborless, to visit the sick, to ransom the captive, to bury the dead," as well as "to instruct the ignorant, to counsel the doubtful, to comfort the sorrowful, to reprove the sinner, to forgive injuries, to bear with those who trouble and annoy us, and to pray for all."[3] The works of mercy also include fraternal correction, to which Aquinas gives special place because of its difficult but necessary role in sustaining the communion of the people of God.

In all these ways, we say to the beloved, whether God or our neighbor: "It's good that you are; how wonderful that you exist!" We say this not merely on the natural level, but in light of God's gift of a participation in his own Trinitarian life, eternal life with the Father, Son, and Holy Spirit. With the Father, Son, and Spirit we proclaim, "It's good that you are; how wonderful that you exist!" In this proclamation is the joy and peace of charity.[4]

By contrast, the sins against charity bespeak the opposite of this joy and wonder in another's existence. Far from rejoicing in God or neighbor, hatred sees the existence of God or neighbor as opposed to our own good. The freshness of joy and wonder is lost in sloth, which sorrows rather than exults about God's gifting, with the result that the slothful person falls into despair, cowardice, sluggishness, spite, malice, and unlawful bodily pleasures. In its selfish joylessness, envy cries out, "How sad it is that you exist more perfectly than I do!" rather than "How wonderful that you exist!" Discord and contention, rooted in pride, set up one's own opinion over against the gift of communion with God and neighbor; joy and wonder are squelched by the desire to dominate others. Schism severs the visible unity of the people of God, the body of Christ to which we should rather respond, with ever greater praise, "How wonderful that you exist!" War, as unjust slaughter driven by the desire to dominate, distorts and destroys human life, and strife and sedition aggressively seek to harm human communion. Scandal actually seeks the eternal spiritual harm of others. How profoundly opposed these actions are to joy and wonder in another's being!

It is one thing to urge others to understand these sins and avoid them; it is another thing to avoid them oneself. If we imagine ourselves as the primary agent of our charitable formation, we lose contact with the giver and become graspers—with the predictable result of joyless and restless hatred, envy, sloth, discord, contention, schism, war, strife, sedition, and scandal. What happens, however, when we know that God can heal us and elevate us into charitable communion with God and neighbor, and yet we freely sin against charity anyway?

Consider the justification offered by Peter Bamm, a German army physician in World War II who knew but did nothing about the killing of the Jews in Sevastopol by S.S. units, as quoted by Hannah Arendt:

> The totalitarian state lets its opponents disappear in silent anonymity. It is certain that anyone who had dared to suffer death rather than silently tolerate the crime would have sacrificed his life in vain. This is not to say that such a sacrifice would have been morally meaningless. It would only have been practically useless. None of us had a conviction so deeply rooted that we could have taken upon ourselves a practically useless sacrifice for the sake of a higher moral meaning.[5]

Jesus teaches that the life of charity means taking up one's cross and following him, even to the point of death (Matt 16:24-26). As he puts it in the gospel of John, "If the world hates you, know that it has hated me before it hated you" (John 15:18). When we suppose that charity is not difficult for fallen people in a fallen world, we can slip into the sins against charity almost unconsciously, out of concern for our own lives and for our families who depend on us: in our jobs, our communities, our culture, why undertake "a practically useless sacrifice for the sake of a higher moral meaning"? This is what Arendt puts her finger on through her phrase "the banality of evil."

On the other hand, sins against charity often do not slip up upon us; we may act against charity in a more obviously direct manner. After King David has sexual intercourse with Uriah's wife Bathsheba, David calls back Uriah from the siege at Rabbah in order to entice Uriah to have intercourse with Bathsheba so that he will suppose that Bathsheba's child is his own. David is unsuccessful, and he then conceives a hatred toward Uriah's existence. He instructs his general, Joab, to orchestrate the siege in a manner that will result in Uriah's death, and Joab carries out these orders.

The prophet Nathan informs David of the violence that will come upon David's family as a result of his sin. Speaking on behalf of God, Nathan says, "Why have you despised the word of the Lord, to do what is evil in his sight? You have struck down Uriah the Hittite with the sword, and have taken his wife to be your wife, and have slain him with the sword of the Ammonites. Now therefore the sword shall never depart from your house" (2 Sam 12:9-10). How can we respond to such crushing awareness that we, knowing better and filled with God's gifts, have deliberately sinned against charity and caused irredeemable harm?

David's response to the prophet Nathan, who risked his own life to correct David on behalf of God, is instructive. David says simply, "I have sinned against the Lord" (2 Sam 12:13). He repents. He does not thereby avoid punishment, but he avoids the deadly punishment of separating himself from God, the giver of all goodness. As Jesus exhorts us, "Repent, and believe in the Gospel" (Mark 1:14). God wants to give us his gifts, beginning with the gift of repentance. To repent we must acknowledge, terrible though it be, that "I have sinned against the Lord."[6]

As Walter Brueggemann writes in commenting upon 2 Samuel 12, "Passive verbs are wonderful. They describe the action but without suggesting there is an agent who must answer. Kings, presidents, and prime ministers love to speak with passive verbs: 'At 1100 hours the bomb was dropped.'"[7] Brueggemann is right to express surprise that David managed, at this critical juncture in his life, to avoid passive verbs. As Brueggemann observes, "Who would have thought him capable of that?"[8] The answer is God. Discussing Aquinas' moral theology, Paul Wadell states, "A God of perfect love wants what is best for us, but only a God of such stunning goodness can make it possible for us. Our radical need is never overcome. From first to last we depend on God to offer us what we cannot give ourselves."[9]

David Bentley Hart, in drawing attention to the violence of pagan culture and the change that Christianity wrought, argues that

"Christians brought something new into the ancient world: a vision of the good without precedent in pagan society, a creed that pre-scribed charitable service to others as a *religious* obligation, a story about a God of self-outpouring love."[10] In studying the sins against charity, we have in a roundabout way been studying this God of self-outpouring love. It is his triune love that enables humans to overcome the reality of Hobbesian scarcity and the desire for domi-nation and to seek to live a life of God-reliance based upon God's gifting. Hart identifies the joy and wonder, the freshness, of this way of life despite the ever-present sins against charity: "Over the course of many centuries, Christianity displaced the reigning values of a civilization with its own values, and for a time its rather extraor-dinary idea of the human, illumined by the unearthly radiance of charity, became the shining sun around which other values were made to revolve, and in the light of which the good or evil of any act had to be judged."[11] He draws attention to the figure of Peter weeping over his sin of denying Jesus three times, and points out that in Peter we find the human person in full greatness as a moral agent called to a supreme destiny while being, in worldly terms, not a king or an eminent man but a Galilean peasant.[12] Hart calls this "the face of the faceless."[13]

In the repentant Peter, we see the weeping of charity—a renewed charity that ensures that the sins against charity do not have the last word, but instead are markers for a new life. Jesus, too, wept (John 11:35). The sins against charity, and their deadly fruit, demand our weeping. But joy and peace, not weeping, are the last word: "The hour is coming, indeed it has come, when you will be scattered, every man to his home, and will leave me alone; yet I am not alone, for the Father is with me. I have said this to you, that in me you may have peace. In the world you have tribulation; but be of good cheer, I have overcome the world" (John 16:32-33).

Notes

Introduction

1 Richard B. Hays, *First Corinthians* (Louisville, Ky.: John Knox, 1997), 226.

2 William T. Cavanaugh, *Theopolitical Imagination: Discovering the Liturgy as a Political Act in an Age of Global Consumerism* (New York: T&T Clark, 2002), 9. Cavanaugh is indebted to Henri de Lubac, *Catholicism: Christ and the Common Destiny of Man*, trans. Lancelot C. Sheppard and Elizabeth Englund (San Francisco: Ignatius, 1988).

3 Hays, *First Corinthians*, 227–28.

4 Hays, *First Corinthians*, 222.

5 Richard B. Hays, *The Moral Vision of the New Testament: Community, Cross, New Creation; A Contemporary Introduction to New Testament Ethics* (New York: HarperCollins, 1996), 202.

6 Throughout this volume, for all biblical quotations I use the Revised Standard Version, Catholic Edition (©1965 NT and 1966 OT) (San Francisco: Ignatius Press, 1995 [reprint]).

7 Pope Benedict XVI, *Deus Caritas Est* (encyclical), Vatican translation (Boston: Pauline, 2006), §18. See also Manfred Lütz, "The Church, Love, and Power," in *Where Are the Helpers? Charity and Spirituality*, ed. Paul Josef Cordes, trans. Anthony J. Figueiredo and James D. Mixson (Notre Dame, Ind.: University of Notre Dame Press, 2010), 139–62.

8   Thomas Aquinas, *Summa Theologiae*, 2-2.23.1. I use the 1920 translation done by the Fathers of the English Dominican Province (Westminster, Md.: Christian Classics, 1981).

9   Alasdair MacIntyre, *Three Rival Versions of Moral Enquiry: Encyclopaedia, Genealogy, and Tradition* (Notre Dame, Ind.: University of Notre Dame Press, 1990), 191; cf. 80: "In moral enquiry we are always concerned with the question: what *type* of enacted narrative would be the embodiment, in the actions and transactions of actual social life, of this particular theory?" (Here and throughout this book, emphasis is in original.)

10   My summary is drawn from the *Summa Theologiae*. See also Thomas Aquinas, *On Love and Charity: Readings from the "Commentary on the Sentences of Peter Lombard,"* trans. Peter A. Kwasniewski, Thomas Bolin, and Joseph Bolin (Washington, D.C.: Catholic University of America Press, 2008); Thomas Aquinas, *On Charity (De Caritate)*, trans. Lottie H. Kendzierski (Milwaukee, Wis.: Marquette University Press, 1984). For the development of Aquinas' view of the nature of love from his *Commentary on the Sentences* to his *Summa Theologiae*, see Michael Sherwin, *By Knowledge and By Love: Charity and Knowledge in the Moral Theology of St. Thomas Aquinas* (Washington, D.C.: Catholic University of America Press, 2005), 64–81; and Christopher J. Malloy, "Thomas on the Order of Love and Desire: A Development of Doctrine," *Thomist* 71 (2007): 65–87.

11   For medieval background to Aquinas' discussion of charity, see Michael Sherwin, "Aquinas, Augustine, and the Medieval Scholastic Crisis concerning Charity," in *Aquinas the Augustinian*, ed. Michael Dauphinais and Matthew Levering (Washington, D.C.: Catholic University of America Press, 2007), 181–204; Robert Wielockx, *La discussion scholastique sur l'amour d'Anselme de Laon à Pierre Lombard d'après les imprimés et les inédits* (Ph.D. dissertation, Catholic University of Louvain, 1981). See also William of St. Thierry, *The Nature and Dignity of Love*, trans. Thomas X. Davis (Kalamazoo, Mich.: Cistercian, 1981).

12   Plato, *Symposium*, trans. Michael Joyce, in *The Collected Dialogues of Plato Including the Letters*, ed. Edith Hamilton and Huntington Cairns (Princeton, N.J.: Princeton University Press, 1961), 206a (p. 558) and 211a (p. 562); cf. 201b (p. 553).

13   Plato, *Symposium*, 211c (pp. 562–63). For discussion, see L. A. Kosman, "Platonic Love," in *Eros, Agape, and Philia*, ed. Alan Soble (St. Paul, Minn.: Paragon House, 1989), 149–64; Robert E. Wagoner, *The Meanings of Love: An Introduction to Philosophy of Love* (Westport, Conn.: Praeger, 1997), chap. 2.

14 See Anders Nygren, *Agape and Eros*, trans. Philip S. Watson (Philadelphia: Westminster, 1953); Ceslaus Spicq, *Agape in the New Testament*, 3 vols. (St. Louis, Mo.: B. Herder, 1963); C. S. Lewis, *The Four Loves* (New York: Harcourt Brace, 1960); Martin D'Arcy, *The Mind and Heart of Love* (New York: Henry Holt, 1947); Josef Pieper, *Faith, Hope, Love*, trans. Richard Winston and Clara Winston (San Francisco: Ignatius, 1997); Paul Tillich, *Love, Power, and Justice: Ontological Analyses and Ethical Applications* (Oxford: Oxford University Press, 1954); Gene Outka, *Agape: An Ethical Analysis* (New Haven, Conn.: Yale University Press, 1972); Edward Collins Vacek, *Love, Human and Divine: The Heart of Christian Ethics* (Washington, D.C.: Georgetown University Press, 1994). See also Søren Kierkegaard, *Works of Love: Some Christian Reflections in the Form of Discourses*, trans. Howard Hong and Edna Hong (New York: Harper & Row, 1962), for a radical rejection of *eros* and *philia*.

15 See Aquinas, *Summa*, 1-2.25.2.

16 Aquinas, *Summa*, 1-2.26.3.

17 See Aquinas, *Summa*, 1-2.28.1–2.

18 See Aquinas, *Summa*, 1-2.28.3. See Peter A. Kwasniewski, "St. Thomas, *Extasis* and Union with the Beloved," *Thomist* 61 (1997): 587–603. For a theology shaped by this insight, see G. J. McAleer, *Ecstatic Morality and Sexual Politics: A Catholic and Antitotalitarian Theory of the Body* (New York: Fordham University Press, 2005).

19 For discussion, see Christopher J. Malloy, *Love of God for His Own Sake and Love of Beatitude: Heavenly Charity According to Thomas Aquinas* (Ph.D. dissertation, Catholic University of America, 2001).

20 See Sherwin, *By Knowledge*, esp. 152–63. Sherwin's book demonstrates the inaccuracy of James Keenan's view of the will's autonomy in Aquinas: see Keenan, *Goodness and Rightness in Thomas Aquinas's "Summa Theologiae"* (Washington, D.C.: Georgetown University Press, 1992).

21 Aquinas, *Summa*, 2-2.4.1. See Romanus Cessario, *Christian Faith and the Theological Life* (Washington, D.C.: Catholic University of America Press, 1996).

22 Aquinas, *Summa*, 2-2.2.7.

23 See Aquinas, *Summa*, 2-2.2.7, ad 3 and elsewhere.

24 Aquinas, *Summa*, 2-2.2.8, ad 3.

25 Aquinas, *Summa*, 2-2.4.3.

26 Aquinas, *Summa*, 2-2.17.2.

27 See Aquinas, *Summa*, 2-2.23.1, including the *sed contra*.

28 Guy Mansini, "*Similitudo, Communicatio*, and the Friendship of Charity in Aquinas," in *Recherches de théologie ancienne et médiévale, Supplementa* 1, *Thomistica*, ed. E. Manning (Leuven: Peeters, 1995), 5. Mansini draws

upon Joseph Bobik, "Aquinas on Friendship with God," *New Scholasticism* 60 (1986): 257–71. See also Jean-Pierre Torrell, "La charité comme amitié chez saint Thomas d'Aquin," *La Vie Spirituelle* 155 (2001): 265–83; Joseph Bobik, "Aquinas on *Communicatio*: The Foundation of Friendship and Caritas," *Modern Schoolman* 64 (1986): 1–18; Guy Mansini, "Aristotle on Needing Friends," *American Catholic Philosophical Quarterly* 72 (1998): 405–17; Anthony W. Keaty, "Thomas's Authority for Identifying Charity as Friendship: Aristotle or John 15?" *Thomist* 62 (1998): 581–601.

29 Aquinas, *Summa*, 2-2.23.3, ad 1; see also 2-2.24.2.

30 On this theme, see Augustine, *City of God*, trans. Henry Bettenson (New York: Penguin, 1984), 14.28 and elsewhere. See also Mansini, "*Similitudo, Communicatio*," 10–11; Bobik, "Aquinas on Friendship with God," 269–70; L. Gregory Jones, "The Theological Transformation of Aristotelian Friendship in the Thought of St. Thomas Aquinas," *New Scholasticism* 61 (1987): 385.

31 See Michael Sherwin, "St. Thomas and the Common Good: The Theological Perspective; An Invitation to Dialogue," *Angelicum* 70 (1993): 307–28, esp. 310–13; Jeanne Heffernan Schindler, "A Companionship of *Caritas*: Friendship in St. Thomas Aquinas," in *Friendship and Politics: Essays in Political Thought*, ed. John von Heyking and Richard Avramenko (Notre Dame, Ind.: University of Notre Dame Press, 2008), 139–62, esp. 151–56; Romanus Cessario, *The Moral Virtues and Theological Ethics* (Notre Dame, Ind.: University of Notre Dame Press, 1991). See also Thomas M. Osborne's discussions of the limitations of pagan virtue: "The Augustinianism of Thomas Aquinas's Moral Theory," *Thomist* 67 (2003): 279–305; Thomas M. Osborne, "Perfect and Imperfect Virtues in Aquinas," *Thomist* 71 (2007): 39–64.

32 Aquinas, *Summa*, 2-2.23.1, ad 1. See esp. Malloy, *Love of God*, 286–363; Edgardo A. Colón-Emeric, *Wesley, Aquinas, and Christian Perfection: An Ecumenical Dialogue* (Waco, Tex.: Baylor University Press, 2009), 108–11.

33 Aquinas, *Summa*, 2-2.24.12. This paragraph briefly summarizes question 24. For related discussion, see Lawrence Dewan, "St. Thomas, James Keenan, and the Will," chap. 9 in *Wisdom, Law, and Virtue: Essays in Thomistic Ethics* (New York: Fordham University Press, 2007).

34 Servais Pinckaers, *The Sources of Christian Ethics*, trans. Mary Thomas Noble (Washington, D.C.: Catholic University of America Press, 1995), 30. See also Gerald W. Schlabach, *For the Joy Set Before Us: Augustine and Self-Denying Love* (Notre Dame, Ind.: University of Notre Dame Press, 2001), esp. 59–91 on "The Grammar of Augustinian Continence."

35 Aquinas, *Summa*, 2-2.25.1.

36 See Aquinas, *Summa*, 2-2.25.4–5; see also Malloy, *Love of God*, 238–43, 269–71. For the possibility of a natural love of God over self, see Thomas M. Osborne, *Love of Self and Love of God in Thirteenth-Century Ethics* (Notre Dame, Ind.: University of Notre Dame Press, 2005). For further background to *Summa* 2-2.25–26, see Kevin Corrigan, "Love of God, Love of Self, and Love of Neighbor: Augustine's Critical Dialogue with Platonism," *Augustinian Studies* 34 (2003): 97–106.

37 See Romanus Cessario, *Introduction to Moral Theology* (Washington, D.C.: Catholic University of America Press, 2001), 205–12; Pinckaers, *Sources of Christian Ethics*, 152–55, 224–31.

38 Quoted by Aquinas in *Summa*, 2-2.45.1, *sed contra*.

39 Aquinas, *Summa*, 2-2.45.2.

40 See Aquinas, *Summa*, 2-2.45.6.

41 Aquinas, *Summa*, 2-2.33.1.

42 Cf. Servais Pinckaers, "The Body of Christ: The Eucharistic and Ecclesial Context of Aquinas's Ethics," in Pinckaers, *The Pinckaers Reader: Renewing Thomistic Moral Theology*, ed. John Berkman and Craig Steven Titus, trans. Mary Thomas Noble, Craig Steven Titus, Michael Sherwin, and Hugh Connolly (Washington, D.C.: Catholic University of America Press, 2005), 26–45, esp. 32, 42–43.

43 See Michael Sherwin, *By Knowledge*; Timothy P. Jackson, *Love Disconsoled: Meditations on Christian Charity* (Cambridge: Cambridge University Press, 1999); Timothy P. Jackson, *The Priority of Love: Christian Charity and Social Justice* (Princeton, N.J.: Princeton University Press, 2003); Stephen J. Pope, *The Evolution of Altruism and the Ordering of Love* (Washington, D.C.: Georgetown University Press, 1994); Paul J. Wadell, *Friendship and the Moral Life* (Notre Dame, Ind.: University of Notre Dame Press, 1989); Eric J. Silverman, *The Prudence of Love: How Possessing the Virtue of Love Benefits the Lover* (Lanham, Md.: Lexington, 2010); Pope Benedict XVI, *Deus Caritas Est*. See also Jean-Luc Marion, *Prolegomena to Charity*, trans. Stephen Lewis (New York: Fordham University Press, 2002); Amy Laura Hall, *Kierkegaard and the Treachery of Love* (Cambridge: Cambridge University Press, 2002); Oliver O'Donovan, *The Problem of Self-Love in St. Augustine* (New Haven, Conn.: Yale University Press, 1980); Martha C. Nussbaum, *Upheavals of Thought: The Intelligence of Emotions* (Cambridge: Cambridge University Press, 2001); M. Jamie Ferreira, *Love's Grateful Striving* (Oxford: Oxford University Press, 2001).

44 Joseph Telushkin, *A Code of Jewish Ethics*, vol. 2, *Love Your Neighbor as Yourself* (New York: Random House, 2009), 3.

45 Telushkin, *A Code of Jewish Ethics*, vol. 1, *You Shall Be Holy* (New York: Random House, 2006), 481.

46 Pope Benedict XVI, *Caritas in Veritate*. Translation (Vatican City: Libreria Editrice Vaticana, 2009).

47 See Leonard Boyle, *The Setting of the "Summa Theologiae" of Saint Thomas* (Toronto: Pontifical Institute of Mediaeval Studies, 1982).

48 Rebecca Konyndyk DeYoung, *Glittering Vices: A New Look at the Seven Deadly Sins and Their Remedies* (Grand Rapids: Brazos, 2009), 11. She adds, all too accurately, "By contrast, many voices in contemporary culture, unfortunately, dismiss, redefine, psychologize, or trivialize them" (11).

49 Markus Bockmuehl, *Jewish Law in Gentile Churches: Halakhah and the Beginning of Christian Public Ethics* (Grand Rapids: Baker Academic, 2000), 3.

50 Aafke E. Komter, *Social Solidarity and the Gift* (Cambridge: Cambridge University Press, 2005), 1 and 207. See also Pope Benedict XVI, *Deus Caritas Est*, §§31, 37; Benedict XVI, *Caritas in Veritate*, §78.

51 See Aquinas, *Summa*, 1.85.7, including ad 3.

52 Hans Reinders, *Receiving the Gift of Friendship: Profound Disability, Theological Anthropology, and Ethics* (Grand Rapids: Eerdmans, 2008).

53 Nancey Murphy, *Bodies and Souls, or Spirited Bodies?* (Cambridge: Cambridge University Press, 2006); Joel B. Green, *Body, Soul, and Human Life: The Nature of Humanity in the Bible* (Grand Rapids: Baker Academic, 2008).

54 See Green, *Body, Soul*, 85, 105, 116, and elsewhere.

55 Green, *Body, Soul*, 62–65. See also David Novak's similar position, and my response, in Levering, *Jewish-Christian Dialogue and the Life of Wisdom: Engagements with the Theology of David Novak* (London: Continuum, 2010).

56 Aquinas, *Summa*, 3.68.12, ad 2. For philosophical accounts of the spiritual soul see, e.g., Eleonore Stump, *Aquinas* (London: Routledge, 2003), 191–216; Ric Machuga, *In Defense of the Soul: What It Means to Be Human* (Grand Rapids: Brazos, 2002); W. Norris Clarke, "The Immediate Creation of the Human Soul by God and Some Contemporary Challenges," in *The Creative Retrieval of St. Thomas Aquinas: Essays in Thomistic Philosophy, New and Old* (New York: Fordham University Press, 2009), 173–90.

57 Thomas Lewis, Fari Amini, and Richard Lannon, *A General Theory of Love* (New York: Random House, 2000), 218.

58 Aquinas, *Summa*, 2-2.45.5, ad 3.

59 Green, *Body, Soul*, 45.

60 Green, *Body, Soul*, 179.

61 On participation, see most recently John Rziha, *Perfecting Human Actions: St. Thomas Aquinas on Human Participation in Eternal Law*

(Washington, D.C.: Catholic University of America Press, 2009), esp.
6–28.

62 Cessario, *Introduction to Moral Theology*, 204.

Chapter 1

1 I should note at the outset that the concern that charity is exclusionary
and "violent" differs from the concern that "religion" is violent, since
scholars such as Schwartz and Schneider suggest that non-monotheistic
religious commitments have at least the potential to be nonviolent. For
a critique of the view that "religion" is violent, see William T. Cavanaugh, *The Myth of Religious Violence: Secular Ideology and the Roots of
Modern Conflict* (Oxford: Oxford University Press, 2009). Cavanaugh
argues that "the attempt to create a transhistorical and transcultural
concept of religion that is essentially prone to violence is one of the
foundational legitimating myths of the liberal nation-state. The myth of
religious violence helps to construct and marginalize a religious Other,
prone to fanaticism, to contrast with the rational, peace-making, secular
subject. . . . [R]eligion-and-violence arguments serve a particular need
for their consumers in the West. These arguments are part of a broader
Enlightenment narrative that has invented a dichotomy between the
religious and the secular and constructed the former as an irrational
and dangerous impulse that must give way in public to rational, secular
forms of power" (4; cf. 135, 142).

2 Rémi Brague, *The Law of God: The Philosophical History of an Idea*, trans.
Lydia G. Cochrane (Chicago: University of Chicago Press, 2007), 128.
See Lewis Ayres, *Nicaea and Its Legacy: An Approach to Fourth-Century
Trinitarian Theology* (Oxford: Oxford University Press, 2004), 97–99,
for the complexity of the period.

3 See Robert Louis Wilken, "A Constantinian Bishop: St. Ambrose of
Milan," in *God, Truth, and Witness: Engaging Stanley Hauerwas*, ed. L.
Gregory Jones, Reinhard Hütter, and C. Rosalee Velloso Ewell (Grand
Rapids: Brazos, 2005), 73–87; cf. H. A. Drake, *Constantine and the Bish-
ops: The Politics of Intolerance* (Baltimore, Md.: The Johns Hopkins Uni-
versity Press, 2000), esp. 441–83.

4 Basil the Great, *On the Holy Spirit*, 40, trans. by David Anderson (Crest-
wood, N.Y.: St. Vladimir's Seminary Press, 1997), §40, p. 67.

5 Robert Louis Wilken, *The Spirit of Early Christian Thought: Seeking the
Face of God* (New Haven, Conn.: Yale University Press, 2003), 105.

6 Wilken, *Early Christian Thought*, 106. Wilken emphasizes that although
Augustine seeks to understand the unity and Trinity of God, his conceptual labor aims at union with the living God, not merely at conceptual

clarification (109). See also Gerald W. Schlabach, *For the Joy Set before Us: Augustine and Self-Denying Love* (Notre Dame, Ind.: University of Notre Dame Press, 2001), esp. 27–58.

7   Guy G. Stroumsa, *The End of Sacrifice: Religious Transformations in Late Antiquity*, trans. Susan Emanuel (Chicago: University of Chicago Press, 2009), 24–25.

8   Stroumsa, *End of Sacrifice*, 25. Stroumsa notes his debt here to Emmanuel Lévinas. The point that Stroumsa makes is also central in David Bentley Hart's discussion of the "Christian difference" in his *Atheist Delusions: The Christian Revolution and Its Fashionable Enemies* (New Haven, Conn.: Yale University Press, 2009), esp. 111–82.

9   Stroumsa, *End of Sacrifice*, 103, 104, 107; cf. 95–100. On this topic Stroumsa is in dialogue with Jan Assmann's view that the claim to truth in religion inevitably provokes violence, as well as with Peter Brown's argument that the Christianization of the pagan world should not be attributed to violent intolerance. See Assmann, *Moses the Egyptian: The Memory of Egypt in Western Monotheism* (Cambridge, Mass.: Harvard University Press, 1997); Peter Brown, *Authority and the Sacred: Aspects of the Christianisation of the Roman World* (Cambridge: Cambridge University Press, 1995), 29–54.

10 Regina M. Schwartz, *The Curse of Cain: The Violent Legacy of Monotheism* (Chicago: University of Chicago Press, 1997). She draws upon Erik Peterson, *Der Monotheismus als politische Problem. Ein Beitrag zur Geschichte der politischen Theologie im Imperium Romanum* (Leipzig: Jacob Hegner, 1935); cf. Edward Gibbon's *The Decline and Fall of the Roman Empire*, 6 vols. (New York: Random House, 1994). For Christian responses to Schwartz's argument, see Alan Jacobs, "Afterword," in *Must Christianity Be Violent? Reflections on History, Practice, and Theology*, ed. Kenneth R. Chase and Alan Jacobs (Grand Rapids: Brazos, 2003), 224–35; Hans Boersma, *Violence, Hospitality, and the Cross: Reappropriating the Atonement Tradition* (Grand Rapids: Baker Academic, 2004), 82–95; Miroslav Volf, "Christianity and Violence," in *War in the Bible and Terrorism in the Twenty-First Century*, ed. Richard S. Hess and Elmer A. Martens (Winona Lake, Ind.: Eisenbrauns, 2008), 7–8; Elmer A. Martens, "Toward Shalom: Absorbing the Violence," in Hess and Martens, *War in the Bible*, 33–57; and R. W. L. Moberly, "Genesis 4: Cain and Abel," chap. 5 in *The Theology of the Book of Genesis* (Cambridge: Cambridge University Press, 2009), which draws upon his "Is Monotheism Bad for You? Some Reflections on God, the Bible, and Life in the Light of Regina Schwartz's *The Curse of Cain*," in *The God of Israel*, ed. Robert P. Gordon (Cambridge: Cambridge University Press, 2007), 94–112.

11 Schwartz, *Curse of Cain*, x.

12 Schwartz, *Curse of Cain*, 4.

13 Schwartz, *Curse of Cain*, 109–10. Schwartz's reading, which contrasts scarcity and plenitude, relies upon Sigmund Freud's psychoanalysis.

14 Schwartz, *Curse of Cain*, 10; cf. 118–19 for Schwartz's view of what could have been. Schwartz also connects the rise of modern historical-critical scholarship with the rise of German nationalism: "With the archeologist's spade and the philologist's verb ending, miracles gave way to science, mythic origins to history, and the once sacred understanding of collective identity—as a people forged by the Deity—gave way to secular understandings of collective identity, including modern nationalism" (11).

15 Schwartz, *Curse of Cain*, 15, 33.

16 Laurel C. Schneider, *Beyond Monotheism: A Theology of Multiplicity* (London: Routledge, 2008), 4. See also Schneider's *Re-imagining the Divine: Confronting the Backlash Against Feminist Theology* (Cleveland, Ohio: Pilgrim, 1999).

17 Schneider, *Beyond Monotheism*, 67. She reads Tertullian in light of A. O. Ogbonnaya's *On Communitarian Divinity: An African Interpretation of the Trinity* (New York: Paragon House, 1994). Ogbonnaya argues, in Schneider's words, that Tertullian's "innovation of 'trinity' makes the most sense in terms of African cultural presuppositions of communal (which is not to say polytheistic) divinity in general" (Schneider, *Beyond Monotheism*, 66).

18 Schneider, *Beyond Monotheism*, 67–68.

19 Schneider, *Beyond Monotheism*, 68.

20 Schneider, *Beyond Monotheism*, 71. She adds: "This means, as Moltmann, Jennings, and others have pointed out, that what came to be the Christian Trinity could not sustain the communality originally given it against the pressure to accommodate it to the hierarchical rules of empire and of imperial church. Nor could it sustain that openness to world implied in Tertullian's organic images against the pressure to maintain individual agency (such as the mind) that can dissociate itself from the disappointments and traumas of life on earth. . . . Eminently useful in the administration of imperial power, the logic of the One survived the fall of the Roman Empire, the splintering of the Greek and Roman Churches, and the convulsions of the Reformations" (71–72). Compare Ayres, *Nicaea and Its Legacy*, 364–83, which treats Augustine's Trinitarian theology and shows that Augustine does not collapse the three into the one. See also Ayres, " 'Remember That You Are Catholic' (*serm.* 52.2): Augustine on the Unity of the Triune God," *Journal of Early Christian Studies* 8 (2000): 39–82; and Michel Barnes, "Augustine in Contemporary Trinitarian Theology," *Theological Studies* 56 (1995): 237–50.

21 Schneider, *Beyond Monotheism*, 5.

22 Schneider, *Beyond Monotheism*, 5.

23 Schneider, *Beyond Monotheism*, 5.

24 Schneider, *Beyond Monotheism*, 200.

25 Schwartz, *Curse of Cain*, 119.

26 Schwartz, *Curse of Cain*, 33, 119. Compare David Bentley Hart, *The Beauty of the Infinite: The Aesthetics of Christian Truth* (Grand Rapids: Eerdmans, 2003), 233, 244–58. Hart notes that "the analogy of being is an emancipation from the tragedy of identity, which is the inmost truth of every metaphysics or theology (whether dialectical and dualist or idealist and monist) that fails to think being analogically. Because the analogy subsists not between discrete substances sheltered alike under the canopy of being—between 'my' essence, to which existence is somehow superadded, and God's essence, which possesses existence simply as a necessary attribute—but between the entire act of my being and the transcendent act of being in which it participates, the event of my existence, in its totality, is revealed as good and true and beautiful in its very particularity" (245).

27 Schwartz, *Curse of Cain*, 176.

28 Schneider, *Beyond Monotheism*, 203.

29 Schneider, *Beyond Monotheism*, 204.

30 Schneider, *Beyond Monotheism*, 205. She goes on to explain, with striking agnosticism: "Divine multiplicity, like any construct, is just a concept, metaphor. It is not divinity. 'Divinity is, if nothing else, free. And this means that it is also free of theology and doctrine.' The stories we tell of it, however, form the fabric of imagination about what is possible for us in this world that God so loves" (207). (The interior quotation here is taken from Schneider's earlier book, *Re-imagining the Divine*.)

31 Schneider, *Beyond Monotheism*, 205.

32 In a similar vein, Mario Costa, Catherine Keller, and Anna Mercedes write: "When our agape is infused with eros, the coalescing of our differences becomes fecund: we pulse with vital energy, expanding, opening, and generating new being and new energy. Such erotic fecundity, we suspect, drives the biopolitical production of the multitude. . . . Secure within the trustworthy persistence of agapeic love, we can risk an insistence on bright hope and pleasure all around. Engaged in such an erotic insistence, we might nurture the fecundity of diverse coalitions in ways both arduous and ardent, slipping between self and other such that loving the other as the self is our daily labor and our daily delight." Costa, Keller, and Mercedes, "Love in Times of Empire: Theopolitics Today," in *Evangelicals and Empire: Christian Alternatives to the Political Status Quo*, ed. Bruce Ellis Benson and Peter Goodwin Heltzel

(Grand Rapids: Brazos, 2008), 304. For Catherine Keller's perspective, see her *Face of the Deep: A Theology of Becoming* (New York: Routledge, 2003), and my review of this book in *Theological Studies* 66 (2005): 905–7.

33 Aristotle, *Nicomachean Ethics*, trans. H. Rackham, Loeb Classical Library, vol. 73 (Cambridge, Mass.: Harvard University Press, 1934), 8.8.1 (p. 481); quoted by Aquinas in *Summa*, 2-2.27.1, obj. 2.

34 Aristotle, *Nicomachean Ethics*, 8.8.1.

35 Aristotle, *Nicomachean Ethics*, 8.8.3 (p. 483); quoted by Aquinas in *Summa*, 2-2.27.1. Aquinas comments that a mother's "love is the greatest" (*maxime amant*). For Aristotle's view of friendship, see Lorraine Smith Pangle, *Aristotle and the Philosophy of Friendship* (Cambridge: Cambridge University Press, 2003). Aristotle's modeling of love on maternal love continues in *Nicomachean Ethics*, 9.4.1 (p. 533), where he describes a friend as one who, among other things, "wishes, and promotes by action, the real or apparent good of another for that other's sake" and "one who shares his friend's joys and sorrows." He attributes both characteristics paradigmatically to mothers.

36 Aquinas, *Summa*, 2-2.23.1.

37 Quoted by Aquinas in *Summa*, 2-2.23.1, *sed contra*.

38 Aquinas, *Summa*, 2-2.27.1, ad 2. Aquinas' way of putting this shows the influence of Augustine. For Augustine, as Gerald Schlabach writes, "When we love friends or neighbors rightly, the value they lose is their value as a tool of our own egocentric self-interest; the value we then recognize in them is their value insofar as God, the source of all things, creates and secures them." Schlabach, *For the Joy*, 37.

39 Aquinas, *Summa*, 2-2.27.1, ad 2: "Amare autem quaerunt caritatem habentes secundum se, quasi ipsum sit bonum caritatis: sicut et quilibet actus virtutis est bonum virtutis illius."

40 Aquinas, *Summa*, 2-2.27.2.

41 Aquinas, *Summa*, 2-2.27.2.

42 Aristotle, *Nicomachean Ethics*, 9.4.1 (p. 533); quoted by Aquinas in *Summa*, 2-2.27.2, obj. 2.

43 Aristotle, *Nicomachean Ethics*, 9.5.1 (p. 539); quoted by Aquinas in *Summa*, 2-2.27.2, *sed contra*.

44 Aquinas, *Summa*, 2-2.27.3, obj. 1.

45 Aquinas, *Summa*, 2-2.27.3.

46 Aquinas cites Romans 1:20, "Ever since the creation of the world his invisible nature, namely, his eternal power and deity, has been clearly perceived in the things that have been made." *Summa*, 2-2.27.3, obj. 2.

47 Quoted by Aquinas in *Summa*, 2-2.27.4, obj. 1. See also Schlabach on Augustine: "Augustine's abiding conviction was that we must not first

love the creature but must first love God. Still, what 'first' means here was difficult even for Augustine to say, since humans cannot actually see God. Clearly love of God was *ontologically* prior—first in ultimate importance according to both logic and God's creative intention. It was also *authoritatively* prior, according to Jesus' statement of the greatest commandments. Yet in what sense should it come first *chronologically* as a person grows in love? This was the puzzle." Schlabach, *For the Joy*, 37; cf. 39.

48 See F. Russell Hittinger, "When It Is More Excellent to Love than to Know: The Other Side of Thomistic 'Realism,'" *Proceedings of the American Catholic Philosophical Association* 57 (1983): 171–79.

49 Aquinas, *Summa*, 2-2.27.4. Aquinas observes that once we come to know God, our knowledge inaugurates a personal communion with him. As an example, Aquinas points to the people converted by the words of the Samaritan woman who met Jesus at the well. Their knowledge of God begins with her words and ends in personal experience of communion with the living God revealed in Christ: "It is no longer because of your words that we believe, for we have heard for ourselves, and we know that this is indeed the Savior of the world" (John 4:42). Quoted by Aquinas in *Summa*, 2-2.27.3, ad 2.

50 Aquinas, *Summa*, 2-2.27.4.

51 Quoted by Aquinas in *Summa*, 2-2.27.4, *sed contra*.

52 See Denis J. M. Bradley, "Thomas Aquinas on Weakness of the Will," in *Weakness of Will from Plato to the Present*, ed. Tobias Hoffman (Washington, D.C.: Catholic University of America Press, 2008), 82–114, esp. 99, 112. See also Alasdair MacIntyre, "Conflicts of Desire," in Hoffman, *Weakness of Will*, 276–92, esp. 286 and 291–92.

53 Aquinas, *Summa*, 2-2.27.4, ad 3. See my *Christ's Fulfillment of Torah and Temple: Salvation according to Thomas Aquinas* (Notre Dame, Ind.: University of Notre Dame Press, 2002).

54 Quoted by Aquinas in *Summa*, 2-2.27.4, obj. 3.

55 For this concern, see especially Peter Abelard, *Exposition of the Epistle to the Romans*, trans. Gerald E. Moffatt, in *A Scholastic Miscellany: Anselm to Ockham*, ed. Eugene R. Fairweather (Philadelphia: Westminster, 1956), 283. See also the response by Bernard of Clairvaux [to Peter Abelard] in his "Letter CXC," in *Life and Works of Saint Bernard*, ed. John Mabillon, trans. and ed. Samuel J. Eales (London: Burns & Oates, 1896), 2:576–91.

56 Aquinas, *Summa*, 2-2.27.5, *sed contra* and *responsio*.

57 Recalling a "Captain G." who brutally interrogated him in Communist Yugoslavia, Miroslav Volf calls for communal Eucharistic participation in the forgiveness wrought by Christ's passion: "The whole community

would be celebrating my transformed memory of his wrongdoing—a memory that allows me to name the Captain's offenses as wrongdoing but that does not elicit in me only condemnation and disgust; a memory through which I, in receiving Christ in the sacrament of his body and blood, also receive myself as a new creature, made in the image of the God who loves the ungodly, with an identity that transcends anything anyone could ever do to me; a memory that frees me from the hold of my suffered wrong and motivates me to extend a reconciling hand to the Captain, whom Christ has already embraced with open arms on the cross; a memory that I ponder in the hope of the final reconciliation." Volf, *The End of Memory: Remembering Rightly in a Violent World* (Grand Rapids: Eerdmans, 2006), 127–28.

58 Aquinas, *Summa*, 2-2.27.5.
59 Aquinas, *Summa*, 2-2.27.5.
60 Aquinas, *Summa*, 1.11.4; cf. 1.11.1.
61 Aristotle, *Nicomachean Ethics*, 2.6.10 (p. 93).
62 Aquinas, *Summa*, 1.27.6, ad 3.
63 Aquinas, *Summa*, 2-2.27.6.
64 Aquinas, *Summa*, 2-2.27.6, obj. 1.
65 Aquinas, *Summa*, 2-2.27.6, ad 3.
66 Aquinas, *Summa*, 2-2.25.1.
67 Aquinas, *Summa*, 2-2.25.1.
68 Aquinas, *Summa*, 2-2.27.7, obj. 1.
69 Aquinas, *Summa*, 2-2.27.7, obj. 3. See Schlabach, *For the Joy*, 40–42. Although Schlabach criticizes Augustine's practice toward the Donatists, he appreciates the theological account of love of enemy that Augustine provides and that Aquinas follows here.
70 Aquinas, *Summa*, 2-2.27.7, *sed contra*.
71 Aquinas, *Summa*, 2-2.27.7. For discussion, see Daniel M. Bell Jr., *Just War as Christian Discipleship: Recentering the Tradition in the Church Rather Than the State* (Grand Rapids: Brazos, 2009), 160–62.
72 Quoted by Aquinas in *Summa*, 2-2.27.8, obj. 2. In Aquinas, as in Augustine, love for God receives its concrete content through the incarnation. As Schlabach says, "Precisely because *caritas Dei* is mutual love, any love for God and for creatures 'in God' must be a grateful and fitting response to God's prior self-giving in Jesus Christ, which God's gift of self now made possible through 'the love of God poured into our hearts by the Holy Spirit which is given to us.' As Augustine said again and again (often at some critical juncture in his critiques of Platonism), we need a mediator, a true mediator who has taken up our clay and taken on the form of a servant in humility." Schlabach, *For the Joy*, 50. The friendship of God

in Christ frees us to love others rather than constraining us in a sectarian fashion, because Christ shows us God's supreme love.

73 Aquinas, *Summa*, 2-2.27.7; cf. 2-2.27.8, ad 2: "A man's love for his friends is sometimes less meritorious in so far as he loves them for their sake, so as to fall short of the true reason for the friendship of charity, which is God."

74 Aquinas, *Summa*, 2-2.27.7.

75 Aquinas, *Summa*, 2-2.27.8.

76 Aquinas, *Summa*, 2-2.27.8.

77 Quoted by Aquinas in *Summa*, 2-2.27.8.

78 Cf. Schlabach, *For the Joy*, 53, as well as his discussion of Augustine and Donatism on 124–42.

79 See Kelly S. Johnson, *The Fear of Beggars: Stewardship and Poverty in Christian Ethics* (Grand Rapids: Eerdmans, 2007). As Pope Benedict XVI puts it, "Openness to God makes us open towards our brothers and sisters and towards an understanding of life as a joyful task to be accomplished in a spirit of solidarity." *Caritas in Veritate*, §78. On the importance of spiritual begging, see Paul J. Griffiths, *Intellectual Appetite: A Theological Grammar* (Washington, D.C.: Catholic University of America Press, 2009), 47. See also Guy Mansini, "Mercy 'Twice Blest,'" in *John Paul II and St. Thomas Aquinas*, ed. Michael Dauphinais and Matthew Levering (Naples, Fla.: Sapientia, 2006), 75–100.

80 Aquinas, *Summa*, 2-2.23.1, *sed contra*.

81 Aquinas, *Summa*, 2-2.24.2, *sed contra*. Cf. Pope John Paul II, *Ecclesia de Eucharistia* (encyclical), Vatican translation (Boston: Pauline, 2003).

82 Aquinas, *Summa*, 2-2.161.1; 2-2.161.2, ad 3.

83 For further discussion, see, e.g., Joseph Ratzinger, *Faith and the Future* (San Francisco: Ignatius, 2009); Matthew Levering, *Christ and the Catholic Priesthood: Ecclesial Hierarchy and the Pattern of the Trinity* (Chicago: Hillenbrand, 2010).

Chapter 2

1 Aquinas, *Summa*, 2-2.34.1.

2 Aquinas, *Summa*, 2-2.34.1. See also Max Scheler's reflections on hatred, envy, and the desire for revenge, which he argues produces a psychological malaise (even in entire cultures) that he terms *ressentiment*. See Scheler, *Ressentiment*, trans. Lewis B. Coser and William W. Holdheim (Milwaukee, Wis.: Marquette University Press, 2003).

3 Aquinas, *Summa*, 2-2.34.1.

4 Aquinas, *Summa*, 2-2.34.1, *sed contra*.

5 Aquinas, *Summa*, 2-2.34.2, ad 1.

6   Aquinas, *Summa*, 2-2.34.3, *sed contra*.

7   Aquinas, *Summa*, 2-2.34.4.

8   Aquinas, *Summa*, 2-2.34.5, ad 2.

9   Quoted by Aquinas in *Summa*, 2-2.34.5, obj. 2.

10 Aquinas, *Summa*, 2-2.34.6, ad 2. On envy as the cause of hatred, see Joseph Epstein, *Envy* (New York: Oxford University Press, 2003), 48; DeYoung, *Glittering Vices*, 51.

11 Bloom, *Jesus and Yahweh: The Names Divine* (New York: Riverhead, 2005), 99.

12 Bloom, *Jesus and Yahweh*, 108; cf., for the same point, 172. In Bloom's view it is axiomatic that "Greek theological formulations and Hebraic experiential memories simply are antithetical to each other" (234).

13 Bloom, *Jesus and Yahweh*, 117. The result, says Bloom, is that we "always remain puzzled as to his character. Perhaps he was puzzled too, before he named himself Yahweh. After all, he had absorbed several other gods and godlings, and a certain dyspepsia is one of the consequences" (117).

14 Bloom, *Jesus and Yahweh*, 117.

15 Bloom, *Jesus and Yahweh*, 119.

16 Bloom, *Jesus and Yahweh*, 120.

17 Bloom, *Jesus and Yahweh*, 119, 121, 132. Bloom goes on to say, "If Yahweh is uncanny, he also is as canny as Jacob, who wins the new name of Israel. Mischievous, inquisitive, jealous, and turbulent, Yahweh is fully as personal as a god can be. . . . Shall we say that Yahweh is overambitious and therefore overworked?" (138–39).

18 Bloom, *Jesus and Yahweh*, 173.

19 Bloom, *Jesus and Yahweh*, 118.

20 Bloom, *Jesus and Yahweh*, 228.

21 Bloom, *Jesus and Yahweh*, 185. Bloom traces his own Gnosticism back to the rabbinic period: "Jewish Gnosticism, in my judgment, took its inception from the initial Roman Holocaust" (185).

22 Bloom, *Jesus and Yahweh*, 167. Bloom fears that Yahweh (the literary character) may be back in Israel, with disastrous consequences as usual.

23 Bloom, *Jesus and Yahweh*, 170. Bloom comments, "Loving Jesus is an American fashion, but loving Yahweh is a quixotic enterprise, misdirected because it refuses to know all the facts" (170). Compare the observations of Richard Dawkins, who considers Yahweh to be the "most unlovely instantiation" of the "God Hypothesis" (Dawkins, *The God Delusion* [Boston: Houghton Mifflin, 2006], 31). Dawkins' invective goes a good deal further than does Bloom's: "The God of the Old Testament is arguably the most unpleasant character in all fiction: jealous and proud of it; a petty, unjust, unforgiving control-freak; a vindictive, bloodthirsty ethnic cleanser; a misogynistic, homophobic, racist,

infanticidal, genocidal, filicidal, pestilential, megalomaniacal, sadomas-
ochistic, capriciously malevolent bully" (31). Not surprisingly, Dawkins
has a particular dislike of Judaism: "The oldest of the three Abrahamic
religions, and the clear ancestor of the other two, is Judaism: originally
a tribal cult of a single fiercely unpleasant God, morbidly obsessed
with sexual restrictions, with the smell of charred flesh, with his own
superiority over rival gods and with the exclusiveness of his chosen
desert tribe" (37). For Dawkins, Yahweh is quite simply a "psychotic
delinquent," an "evil monster," and a "cruel ogre" (38, 248, 250). See
also Simon Blackburn's caricature of the Old Testament in *Being Good*
(Oxford: Oxford University Press, 2001). These books, like Bloom's,
unconsciously echo eighteenth- and nineteenth-century Enlightenment critiques of the God of Israel and of Judaism. For this context,
see William I. Brustein, *Roots of Hate: Anti-Semitism in Europe before
the Holocaust* (Cambridge: Cambridge University Press, 2003), 77–94;
Michael Mack, *German Idealism and the Jew: The Inner Anti-Semitism of
Philosophy and German Jewish Responses* (Chicago: University of Chicago Press, 2003); Jonathan M. Hess, *Germans, Jews and the Claims of
Modernity* (New Haven, Conn.: Yale University Press, 2002).

24 Bloom, *Jesus and Yahweh*, 236.

25 Bloom, *Jesus and Yahweh*, 237.

26 Bloom, *Jesus and Yahweh*, 172. Cf. James L. Kugel, *The God of Old: Inside
the Lost World of the Bible* (New York: Free Press, 2003). Bloom admits
that "Jews who continue to trust in the Covenant do not encounter the
ambivalent Yahweh I describe, just as Christians who believe that Jesus
was the Christ behold a very different figure from the one I regard.
Perspective governs our response to everything, but most crucially with
the Bible." Bloom, *Jesus and Yahweh*, 173.

27 In this vein Bloom warns against the Christian misreading, filled in his
view with obvious contradictions, of the Tanakh as the "Old Testament":
"Christian theologians are (happily) no longer allied to state power, yet
their adherence to the shibboleth of 'Judeo-Christian tradition' needs
more clarification than some are willing to give to it. If the two traditions were not radically different, the remnants of Jewry, endlessly
assaulted, would now have dissolved." Bloom, *Jesus and Yahweh*, 116.
Later Bloom comments, "All gods age, Yahweh included, though *his*
dying may not prove to be final, since Islam could yet prevail. Gods
ebb with continental economies, and Europe's augmenting godless-
ness could be a symptom of its final decline in relation to globalization.
The Jesus Christ of evangelical Protestantism and of Mormonism is the
not-so-hidden God of the corporate world in the United States" (184).

Cf. Bloom's *The American Religion: The Emergence of the Post-Christian Nation* (New York: Simon & Schuster, 1992), esp. 45–128, 256–65.

28 Bloom, *Jesus and Yahweh*, 102, 149, and elsewhere. Bloom points out, "No text fulfills another, yet there are revisions and revisions: the Talmud adumbrates, which is one mode; St. John instead inflicts an Orphic *sparagmos*, or rending apart, upon the Torah, scattering Yahweh's limbs as though the Master of Presence was another Osiris, or a contemporary Israeli blown apart in a bus by a Palestinian suicide/homicide bomber. St. John, for Yahweh, is bad news" (149).

29 Bloom, *Jesus and Yahweh*, 151.

30 Bloom, *Jesus and Yahweh*, 141. On Bloom's reading Jesus was simply a false prophet.

31 Bloom, *Jesus and Yahweh*, 99. For the classic expression of this concern, see Abelard, *Exposition of the Epistle*, 283. For a recent response, see Miroslav Volf, *Free of Charge: Giving and Forgiving in a Culture Stripped of Grace* (Grand Rapids: Zondervan, 2005), 143–45.

32 Bloom, *Jesus and Yahweh*, 99.

33 Bloom, *Jesus and Yahweh*, 148. Like Bloom, Dawkins regards Christians as polytheists, without granting that polytheism is worse than monotheism. But Dawkins finds Jesus to be a "huge improvement" over Yahweh, precisely because Jesus "was not content to derive his ethics from the scriptures of his upbringing" (Dawkins, *God Delusion*, 250). Even so, Dawkins agrees with Thomas Jefferson that "'the Christian God is a being of terrific character—cruel, vindictive, capricious and unjust'" (31). This is largely due to the doctrine that Jesus' death on the cross reconciled humans to God. Dawkins again places a large amount of blame on the Old Testament, in particular the stories of God exiling Adam and Eve (and all their descendents) from Eden after they disobeyed his command and of God commanding Abraham to sacrifice his son Isaac. As Dawkins puts it, "So far, so vindictive: par for the Old Testament course. New Testament theology adds a new injustice, topped off by a new sado-masochism whose viciousness even the Old Testament barely exceeds" (251). This sado-masochism is constitutive of the Christian idea of God, because God designed a redemption from "sin" based on the gruesome violence of the cross. Not only is this doctrine "vicious, sado-masochistic and repellent," it is also, Dawkins suggests, "barking mad" (253). For Dawkins, the doctrine boils down to the notion that "in order to impress himself, Jesus had himself tortured and executed" (253). As Dawkins remarks, "If God wanted to forgive our sins, why not just forgive them, without having himself tortured and executed in payment"? (253). Not surprisingly, Dawkins blames this "repellent" doctrine on the Jewish religion, as mediated by Paul.

The idea of God suffering with us, so as to conquer unjust power from within by love, is foreign to Dawkins.

34 Bloom cites Jon D. Levenson's *The Death and Resurrection of the Beloved Son: The Transformation of Child Sacrifice in Judaism and Christianity* (New Haven, Conn.: Yale University Press, 1993), but without including Levenson's nuances.

35 Bloom, *Jesus and Yahweh*, 231.

36 Michael Mack points out regarding the progression of Enlightenment religious and political thought: "The Kantian and Hegelian body politic is one in which heaven takes the place of a contingent and imperfect earth. The Jews, however, represent this earthly remainder of incompleteness, of imperfection. The anti-Semitic stereotypes thus no longer fill the space of apocalypse. Instead, they now embody all that which hinders the construction of a perfect body politic in the here and now." Michael Mack, *German Idealism and the Jew: The Inner Anti-Semitism of Philosophy and German Jewish Responses* (Chicago: University of Chicago Press, 2003), 4. For his part, Bloom dreads that Yahweh, persisting in the Jewish imagination as well as in his Christian and Muslim variations, will "return" and cause a violent cataclysm.

37 See Romanus Cessario, *The Godly Image: Christ and Salvation in Catholic Thought from Anselm to Aquinas* (Petersham, Mass.: St. Bede's, 1990).

Chapter 3

1 DeYoung, *Glittering Vices*, 21. For sloth as mere laziness, see Wendy Wasserstein, *Sloth* (New York: Oxford University Press, 2005). See also DeYoung's account of how the notion of sloth as laziness arose from the Reformers' understanding of vocation: DeYoung, "Resistance to the Demands of Love: Aquinas on the Vice of *Acedia*," *Thomist* 68 (2004): 173–204, at 176–77. For further historical background, see S. Wenzel, *The Sin of Sloth: Acedia in Medieval Thought and Literature* (Chapel Hill: University of North Carolina Press, 1967).

2 Cf. Jeffrey A. Vogel's definition of sloth as "distress caused by the evident slowness of God's activity, impatience with having to inhabit the condition of the *viator*, revulsion, even, at having to wait on God." See Vogel, "The Speed of Sloth: Reconsidering the Sin of *Acedia*," *Pro Ecclesia* 18 (2009): 50–68, at 57. Sloth arises when one finds the difficulties of waiting for God's consummation to be too much to bear.

3 Immanuel Kant, *Critique of Practical Reason*, ed. Mary Gregor (Cambridge: Cambridge University Press, 1997), 128.

4 Kant, *Critique of Practical Reason*, 129.

5 See Kant, *Critique of Practical Reason*, 102.

6   Ludwig Feuerbach, *The Essence of Christianity*, trans. George Eliot (Amherst, N.Y.: Prometheus, 1989), 173–74. For further development of this view, see Ernest Becker, *Escape from Evil* (New York: Macmillan, 1975), discussed in Ted Peters, *Sin: Radical Evil in Soul and Society* (Grand Rapids: Eerdmans, 1994), chap. 2.

7   Jackson, *Love Disconsoled*, 153.

8   Jackson, *Love Disconsoled*, 155.

9   Jackson, *Love Disconsoled*, 156.

10 Jackson, *Love Disconsoled*, 158.

11 Jackson, *Love Disconsoled*, 159.

12 Jackson, *Love Disconsoled*, 159.

13 Jackson, *Love Disconsoled*, 160.

14 Jackson, *Love Disconsoled*, 163.

15 Jackson, *Love Disconsoled*, 165.

16 Jackson, *Love Disconsoled*, 166.

17 Jackson, *Love Disconsoled*, 168.

18 Jackson, *Love Disconsoled*, 169.

19 Jackson, *Love Disconsoled*, 170.

20 Jackson, *Love Disconsoled*, 172.

21 Jackson, *Love Disconsoled*, 173.

22 Jackson, *Love Disconsoled*, 174.

23 Jackson, *Love Disconsoled*, 175.

24 Jackson, *Love Disconsoled*, 176.

25 Jackson, *Priority of Love*, 83.

26 Jackson, *Priority of Love*, 86.

27 Jackson, *Priority of Love*, 87.

28 Jackson, *Love Disconsoled*, 159.

29 See Timothy P. Jackson, "Must Job Live Forever? A Reply to Aquinas on Providence," *Thomist* 62 (1998): 1–39.

30 Jackson, *Love Disconsoled*, 159.

31 Jackson, *Love Disconsoled*, 176.

32 As Miroslav Volf puts it, "A [spiritually] rich self looks toward the future with *trust*. It gives rather than holding things back in fear of coming out too short, because it believes God's promise that God will take care of it. Finite and endangered, a rich self still gives, because its life is 'hidden with Christ' in the infinite, unassailable, and utterly generous God, the Lord of the present, the past, and the future." See Volf, *Free of Charge*, 110.

33 Dale C. Allison Jr., *The Historical Christ and the Theological Jesus* (Grand Rapids: Eerdmans, 2009), 112.

34 Allison, *Historical Christ*, 112.

35 Allison, *Historical Christ*, 113.

36 Aquinas, *Summa*, 2-2.35.3.

37 Aquinas, *Summa*, 2-2.35.3.

38 Quoted by Aquinas in *Summa*, 2-2.28.1, obj. 1 and 2, respectively.

39 As Vogel points out, therefore, Aquinas holds that sloth "grows out of a good root, namely, the desire for spiritual fruit or growth in sanctity. If a person does not care about receiving spiritual fruit, he does not sigh at being deprived of it." Vogel, "Speed of Sloth," 63.

40 Julian of Norwich, *Showings*, ed. Denise N. Baker (New York: W. W. Norton, 2005), revelation 8, chap. 21, p. 33. I have modernized the spelling and changed "chere" to "visage."

41 Aquinas, *Summa*, 2-2.28.2, obj. 3.

42 Psalm 120:5-6 reads in the RSV, "Woe is me, that I sojourn in Meshech, that I dwell among the tents of Kedar! Too long have I had my dwelling among those who hate peace."

43 Aquinas, *Summa*, 2-2.28.2.

44 Aquinas, *Summa*, 2-2.28.2, ad 3.

45 Jackson, *Love Disconsoled*, 159.

46 Jackson, *Love Disconsoled*, 158.

47 Aquinas, *Summa*, 2-2.28.2.

48 Aquinas, *Summa*, 2-2.28.3.

49 Quoted by Aquinas in *Summa*, 2-2.28.3, *sed contra*.

50 Aquinas, *Summa*, 2-2.28.3.

51 Aquinas, *Summa*, 2-2.28.3.

52 Aquinas, *Summa*, 2-2.35.1. DeYoung explains, "*Acedia's* sorrow is therefore a restless resistance to a good (perceived as evil in some respect) that is recognized to be our own. This means that we do not have an aversion to God himself in *acedia*, but rather to ourselves-as-sharing-in-God's-nature, united to him in the bond of friendship." DeYoung, "Resistance to the Demands," 183.

53 Aquinas, *Summa*, 2-2.35.3.

54 Aquinas, *Summa*, 2-2.35.3.

55 On the cause of sloth, see especially DeYoung, "Resistance to the Demands," 188–203. As she observes, sloth "may be understood more fundamentally as resistance to the transformation of the self implicated in friendship with God" (192). See also DeYoung, *Glittering Vices*, 88–96; Pieper, *Faith, Hope, Love*, 119.

56 Aquinas, *Summa*, 2-2.35.3, ad 2.

57 Aquinas, *Summa*, 2-2.35.3.

58 Aquinas, *Summa*, 2-2.35.4, ad 2, citing Aristotle, *Nicomachean Ethics*, 10.6.

59 Aquinas, *Summa*, 2-2.35.4, ad 3.

60 Aquinas, *Summa*, 2-2.35.1, obj. 4.

61 Aquinas, *Summa*, 2-2.35.1.
62 See Aquinas, *Summa*, 2-2.35.1.
63 Jackson, *Love Disconsoled*, 158, 159.
64 Aquinas, *Summa*, 2-2.23.1.
65 Aquinas, *Summa*, 2-2.28.2.
66 Aquinas, *Summa*, 2-2.24.7, ad 2.
67 Aquinas, *Summa*, 2-2.24.7, ad 1.
68 Aquinas, *Summa*, 2-2.24.7.
69 Aquinas, *Summa*, 2-2.35.3.
70 Aquinas, *Summa*, 2-2.35.3, ad 2.

Chapter 4

1   Ralph Waldo Emerson, "History," in *The Essential Writings of Ralph Waldo Emerson*, ed. Brooks Atkinson (New York: Random House, 2000), 115.
2   Emerson, "Self-Reliance," in *Essential Writings*, 133.
3   Emerson, "Self-Reliance," 148.
4   Telushkin, *Code of Jewish Ethics*, 1:300–11.
5   Telushkin, *Code of Jewish Ethics*, 310. See also Emerson's warning against boasting in his essay "Culture" in *Essential Writings*, 651–52.
6   R. W. L. Moberly, *The Theology of the Book of Genesis* (Cambridge: Cambridge University Press, 2009), 96. Cf. James L. Kugel, *How to Read the Bible: A Guide to Scripture, Then and Now* (New York: Free Press, 2007), 65–68.
7   Moberly, *Theology of the Book of Genesis*, 242.
8   Leon R. Kass, *The Beginning of Wisdom: Reading Genesis* (New York: Free Press, 2003), 138.
9   Kass, *Beginning of Wisdom*, 429.
10 Kass, *Beginning of Wisdom*, 431.
11 Kass, *Beginning of Wisdom*, 515, 517, 518.
12 Kass, *Beginning of Wisdom*, 606–8.
13 Aquinas, *Summa*, 2-2.36.1. See also Rebecca Konyndyk DeYoung's excellent discussion of envy in her *Glittering Vices*, chap. 2. DeYoung observes, "Envy targets the internal qualities of another person, qualities that give a person worth, honor, standing, or status. If the envious do desire an external thing, it is because that object symbolizes or signifies its owner's high position or greatness" (43).
14 Aquinas, *Summa*, 2-2.36.1, ad 2. See Joseph Epstein, *Envy* (New York: Oxford University Press, 2003), 32, drawing upon Helmut Schoeck, *Envy: A Theory of Social Behavior* (Indianapolis, Ind.: Liberty Fund,

1987), in which Schoeck argues that envy has a positive social function in addition to negative ones.

15 Aquinas, *Summa*, 2-2.36.1.

16 See Aquinas, *Summa*, 2-2.36.1, ad 3. For discussion, see Epstein, *Envy*, 45–50. Epstein distinguishes between envy and jealousy; on this point see also DeYoung, *Glittering Vices*, 44: "The jealous are those who 'have' something they love which they might lose. The envious, by contrast, are the 'have-nots'—they do not have the good their rival does, and they do not have self-love. Thus, they have nothing to lose and everything to gain from another's loss."

17 Aquinas, *Summa*, 2-2.36.1, ad 4.

18 Quoted by Aquinas in *Summa*, 2-2.36.2, obj. 3.

19 Quoted by Aquinas in *Summa*, 2-2.36.2. On zeal, see DeYoung, *Glittering Vices*, 56–57: "Envy seeks to bring another down; zeal seeks to be lifted up and made better. As always, seeking improvement in virtue is grace-empowered effort: it is an earnest desire to be all that God wants us to be, not a self-help program driven by willpower and a self-made conception of a new and improved self. Whereas envy isolates us, zeal brings us into mentoring relationships within the communion of saints. . . . From a secure sense of God's love and life-giving power, untainted by the envier's conditional and comparative lens, we can see the right way to follow Paul's admonition to 'in humility regard others as better than yourselves' (Phil. 2:3)."

20 Aquinas, *Summa*, 2-2.36.2.

21 Quoted by Aquinas in *Summa*, 2-2.36.3.

22 David Bentley Hart, *The Doors of the Sea: Where Was God in the Tsunami?* (Grand Rapids: Eerdmans, 2005), 60–61.

23 Aquinas, *Summa*, 2-2.36.3.

24 Aristotle, *Rhetoric*, trans. W. Rhys Roberts, in *The Basic Works of Aristotle*, ed. Richard McKeon (New York: Random House, 1941), 2.9.1386b18–21 (p. 1398).

25 Aristotle, *Rhetoric*, 2.9.1386b30 (p. 1399).

26 William T. Cavanaugh, *Being Consumed: Economics and Christian Desire* (Grand Rapids: Eerdmans, 2008), 90.

27 Cavanaugh, *Being Consumed*, 95. Cavanaugh goes on to reference the Economy of Communion Project, founded in 1991, of the Focolare Movement. See also his valuable and appreciative engagement with Hans Urs von Balthasar in *Being Consumed*, 75–85. Cavanaugh's approach bears comparison with that of the Methodist environmentalist Bill McKibben, who argues that we have to choose between a sustainable environment and having more than one child: see McKibben, *The End of Nature* (New York: Random House, 1989); idem, *Maybe*

One: A Case for Smaller Families (New York: Simon & Schuster, 1998); idem, *Deep Economy: The Wealth of Communities and the Durable Future* (New York: Times Books, 2007). Cavanaugh's eucharistic "larger body" allows for prioritizing human beings in a way that McKibben's view of the trade-off between nature and human beings does not allow. Can we rejoice in God's gifting in our neighbor if we think that the very existence of neighbors is bringing about catastrophe?

28 Kass, *Beginning of Wisdom*, 662.

29 Gregory the Great, *Moralia in Job*, 31.45, quoted in Aquinas, *Summa*, 2-2.36.4, obj. 3 and *sed contra*.

30 See Aquinas, *Summa*, 2-2.36.4, ad 1; see also DeYoung, *Glittering Vices*, chap. 3. Following Aquinas, DeYoung treats vainglory as "the excessive and disordered desire for recognition and approval from others" (60) and differentiates vainglory from pride on the grounds that pride seeks to be greater than others (including God) whereas vainglory seeks not greatness but applause.

31 Aquinas, *Summa*, 2-2.36.4, ad 2.

32 See Gregory the Great's *Moralia in Job* as cited in Aquinas, *Summa*, 2-2.36.4, ad 1.

33 Aquinas, *Summa*, 2-2.36.4, ad 2.

34 Dante Alighieri, *The Divine Comedy*, vol. 2, *Purgatory*, trans. Mark Musa (New York: Penguin, 1985), 8.70–72 (p. 140).

35 For discussion of these "daughters" of envy, see Aquinas, *Summa*, 2-2.36.4, ad 3.

36 Telushkin, *Code of Jewish Ethics*, 1:306.

37 DeYoung, *Glittering Vices*, 54.

38 See Thomas Hobbes, *Leviathan*, ed. Edwin Curley (Indianapolis, Ind.: Hackett, 1994), 67.

39 Hobbes, *Leviathan*, 58.

40 Hobbes, *Leviathan*, 58.

41 Hobbes, *Leviathan*, 75–76; cf. 106.

42 Hobbes, *Leviathan*, 78; cf. 80 and 89.

43 Hobbes, *Leviathan*, 82. Compare DeYoung's description of true magnanimity in her *Glittering Vices*, 65.

44 Quoted by Aquinas in *Summa*, 2-2.36.2, ad 3, and 2-2.36.3, *sed contra*.

45 Aquinas, *Summa*, 3.79.1, and 3.79.1, ad 2.

46 Aquinas, *Summa*, 3.60.3, *sed contra*. For discussion, see Gilles Emery, "The Ecclesial Fruit of the Eucharist in St. Thomas Aquinas," chap. 5 in *Trinity, Church, and the Human Person* (Naples, Fla.: Sapientia, 2007). See also my "The Eucharist and the Communion of Charity," chap. 3 in *Sacrifice and Community: Jewish Offering and Christian Eucharist* (Oxford: Blackwell, 2005).

47 Emerson, "The Lord's Supper," in *The Essential Writings of Ralph Waldo Emerson*, 104.

48 Emerson, "Lord's Supper," 104.

Chapter 5

1 See Aquinas, *Summa*, 2-2.37.1, esp. ad 2 and ad 3.

2 Quoted by Aquinas in *Summa*, 2-2.37.2, obj. 3, and 2-2.37.1, *sed contra*, respectively.

3 Aquinas, *Summa*, 2-2.37.1; cf. 2-2.37.2.

4 See Aquinas, *Summa*, 2-2.38.1–2.

5 Karl Rahner, "Towards a Fundamental Theological Interpretation of Vatican II," *Theological Studies* 40 (1979): 717.

6 Rahner, "Theological Interpretation," 725.

7 Rahner, "Theological Interpretation," 726. Rahner argues that "the coming-to-be of a world Church precisely as such does not mean just a quantitative increase in the previous Church, but rather contains a theological break in Church history that still lacks conceptual clarity and can scarcely be compared with anything except the transition from Jewish to Gentile Christianity" (726–27).

8 Joseph P. Chinnici, "Reception of Vatican II in the United States," *Theological Studies* 64 (2003): 469.

9 Chinnici, "Reception of Vatican II," 481. Such pastoral engagement in quest of agreement continues "as long as the issue is seen to exist within the total complex of Church life, dialogue proceeds, and the contested practice does not migrate outside of communion through the fracturing of parties and the isolation of the part from the whole" (482).

10 Chinnici, "Reception of Vatican II," 494.

11 Note Pope Benedict XVI's remark that the council aimed to engage the modern world more positively than had earlier papal teaching "in order to present to our world the requirement of the Gospel in its full greatness and purity." Pope Benedict XVI, "A Proper Hermeneutic for the Second Vatican Council," reprinted in *Vatican II: Renewal within Tradition*, ed. Matthew L. Lamb and Matthew Levering (Oxford: Oxford University Press, 2008), xiv. See also Matthew L. Lamb's clarion call for a theological reception of the council, which as he says requires from theologians "the linguistic skills, philosophical and theological habits of mind, and scholarly judgment . . . needed to appropriate the primary patristic, monastic, scholastic, and counterreformation sources." Matthew Lamb and Matthew Levering, "Introduction," in Lamb and Levering, *Vatican II: Renewal within Tradition*, 7.

12 John W. O'Malley, *What Happened at Vatican II* (Cambridge, Mass.: Harvard University Press, 2008), 298. In an earlier essay that anticipates much of *What Happened at Vatican II*, O'Malley interprets the council's uniqueness by means of an opposition between "historical" and "classicist" thinkers: the council was uniquely "historical" in its perspective, but later church leaders attempted to reinsert the council's documents into a "classicist" framework. See John W. O'Malley, "Vatican II: Historical Perspectives on Its Uniqueness and Interpretation," in *Vatican II: The Unfinished Agenda; A Look to the Future,* ed. Lucien Richard, Daniel T. Harrington, and John W. O'Malley (New York: Paulist Press, 1987), 22–32. See also O'Malley, "Reform, Historical Consciousness, and Vatican II's Aggiornamento," *Theological Studies* 32 (1971): 573–601; idem, "Developments, Reforms, and Two Great Reformations: Towards an Historical Assessment of Vatican II," *Theological Studies* 44 (1983): 373–406; idem, "Vatican II: Did Anything Happen?" *Theological Studies* 67 (2006): 3–33. For a response to O'Malley, focused on ecclesiology, see Avery Dulles, "Nature, Mission, and Structure of the Church," in Lamb and Levering, *Vatican II: Renewal within Tradition,* 25–36. See also John M. McDermott, "Did That Really Happen at Vatican II? Reflections on John O'Malley's Recent Book," *Nova et Vetera* 8 (2010): 425–66.

13 O'Malley, *What Happened at Vatican II,* 299. Somewhat similarly, Jerome H. Neyrey proposes that the significance of *Dei Verbum* consists not primarily in what the Dogmatic Constitution teaches, but rather in what the "document did *not* say or what it said *guardedly,* for herein lies the agenda for conversation with the contemporary church." Neyrey, "Interpretation of Scripture in the Life of the Church," in Richard, Harrington, and O'Malley, *Vatican II: The Unfinished Agenda,* 43.

14 O'Malley, *What Happened at Vatican II,* 299.

15 O'Malley, *What Happened at Vatican II,* 298; cf. 310.

16 O'Malley, *What Happened at Vatican II,* 311.

17 O'Malley, *What Happened at Vatican II,* 305, cf. 41, where O'Malley associates this "biblical and patristic" style with Erasmus and the *nouvelle théologie.*

18 O'Malley, *What Happened at Vatican II,* 46.

19 O'Malley, *What Happened at Vatican II,* 295.

20 O'Malley, *What Happened at Vatican II,* 48.

21 O'Malley, *What Happened at Vatican II,* 48.

22 O'Malley, *What Happened at Vatican II,* 43.

23 O'Malley, *What Happened at Vatican II,* 48.

24 O'Malley, *What Happened at Vatican II,* 36, 37.

25 O'Malley, *What Happened at Vatican II,* 51.

26 O'Malley, *What Happened at Vatican II,* 50.

27 O'Malley, *What Happened at Vatican II*, 45, 46.

28 See O'Malley, *What Happened at Vatican II*, 35.

29 O'Malley, *What Happened at Vatican II*, 51.

30 On "people of God" in *Lumen Gentium*, see Daniel J. Harrington, "Why Is the Church the People of God?" in Richard, Harrington, and O'Malley, *Vatican II: The Unfinished Agenda*, 47–56.

31 Aquinas, *Summa*, 2-2.29.1, obj. 1 and ad 1. For discussion, see Carol Harrison, *Augustine: Christian Truth and Fractured Humanity* (Oxford: Oxford University Press, 2000), 207–8.

32 Aquinas, *Summa*, 2-2.29.1, obj. 3.

33 Aquinas, *Summa*, 2-2.29.1.

34 Cf. Amartya Sen, *Identity and Violence: The Illusion of Destiny* (New York: W. W. Norton, 2006). Describing certain excesses of multiculturalism, Sen warns against supposing "that a person's identity must be defined by his or her community or religion, overlooking all the other affiliations a person has (varying from language, class, and social relations to political views and civil roles), and through giving automatic priority to inherited religion or tradition over reflection and choice" (160; cf. 180 and elsewhere). While Sen is certainly right to insist upon the complexity of identity, he leaves unanswered the question of whether religious identity can be compartmentalized vis-à-vis "all the other affiliations" and still remain itself. Perhaps the issue instead is how the particular religion pedagogically shapes how one embodies one's various other "affiliations," and in this regard the sins against charity would be an important topic of study. For an emphasis on mutual toleration, see also Paul J. Roy, "The Developing Sense of Community (Gaudium et Spes)," in Richard, Harrington, and O'Malley, *Vatican II: The Unfinished Agenda*, 190–202.

35 Aquinas, *Summa*, 2-2.29.2.

36 Aquinas, *Summa*, 2-2.29.2, ad 3.

37 Aquinas, *Summa*, 2-2.29.2, ad 3.

38 Aquinas, *Summa*, 2-2.29.2, ad 4.

39 Aquinas, *Summa*, 2-2.29.2, ad 4.

40 Aquinas, *Summa*, 2-2.29.3, obj. 1.

41 Aquinas, *Summa*, 2-2.29.3, obj. 2.

42 Aquinas, *Summa*, 2-2.29.3, ad 3.

43 Aquinas, *Summa*, 2-2.29.3, *sed contra*.

44 Aquinas, *Summa*, 2-2.29.3, ad 2.

45 Aquinas, *Summa*, 2-2.29.4, obj. 1.

46 Aquinas, *Summa*, 2-2.29.4, obj. 2.

47 Aquinas, *Summa*, 2-2.29.4, obj. 3.

Chapter 6

1 Richard Elliott Friedman, *Who Wrote the Bible?* (New York: HarperCollins, 1997), 196–97.
2 Friedman, *Who Wrote the Bible,* 197.
3 Friedman, *Who Wrote the Bible,* 197. Friedman goes on to observe that "this author was not in the business of making up totally new stories out of thin air. . . . He was rather fashioning his own version of a sequence of known stories. He was engaged in something that was art, but not exactly fiction. It was also history. He had to be concerned with successful promulgation; that is, with his audience's willingness to accept this work as a believable account of their past. His art involved a constant balance between tradition and creativity" (198). For this reason, P does not criticize Moses quite as much as he otherwise would have, in Friedman's view.
4 Friedman, *Who Wrote the Bible,* 219.
5 Friedman, *Who Wrote the Bible,* 225. Friedman explains, "This redactor was an Aaronid priest like the person who produced P. But, ironically, his task was the exact opposite of that earlier person's. The person who produced P was fashioning a work that was an alternative to earlier sources (JE). The redactor was fashioning a work that *reconciled* opposing sources" (231).
6 Walter Brueggemann, *Theology of the Old Testament: Testimony, Dispute, Advocacy* (Minneapolis: Fortress, 1997), 578.
7 Brueggemann, *Theology,* 579.
8 Brueggemann, *Theology,* 579.
9 Brueggemann, *Theology,* 579.
10 For Augustine and the Donatist schism, see Carol Harrison, *Augustine: Christian Truth and Fractured Humanity* (Oxford: Oxford University Press, 2000), 145–57; Schlabach, *For the Joy,* 128–39.
11 Aquinas, *Summa,* 2-2.39.1.
12 Aquinas, *Summa,* 2-2.39.1.
13 Aquinas, *Summa,* 2-2.39.1. The Latin reads, *in connexione membrorum Ecclesiae ad invicem, seu communicatione.*
14 Aquinas, *Summa,* 2-2.39.1.
15 Aquinas, *Summa,* 2-2.39.1.
16 Aquinas, *Summa,* 2-2.39.1.
17 Aquinas, *Summa,* 2-2.39.1. The Second Vatican Council's Decree on Ecumenism, *Unitatis Redintegratio,* observes in a similar fashion: "In order to establish this his holy church everywhere in the world till the end of time, Christ entrusted to the college of the twelve the task of teaching, ruling and sanctifying. Among their number he selected

Peter, and after his confession of faith determined that on him he would build his church. To Peter also he promised the keys of the kingdom of heaven, and after his profession of love, entrusted all his sheep to him to be confirmed in faith and shepherded in perfect unity. Christ Jesus himself was forever to remain the chief cornerstone and shepherd of our souls. . . . Even in the beginnings of this one and only church of God there arose certain rifts, which the apostle strongly condemned. But in subsequent centuries much more extensive dissensions made their appearance and large communities came to be separated from the full communion of the Catholic Church—for which, often enough, people of both sides were to blame. Those who are now born into these communities and who are brought up in the faith of Christ cannot be accused of the sin involved in the separation, and the Catholic Church looks upon them as sisters and brothers, with respect and love" (§§2–3; translation in Norman P. Tanner, ed., *Decrees of the Ecumenical Councils*, vol. 2, *Trent to Vatican II* [Washington, D.C.: Georgetown University Press, 1990], 909–10). The *Catechism of the Catholic Church* (2nd ed. Vatican City: Libreria Editrice Vaticana, 1997) differentiates "heresy, apostasy, and schism" among the "wounds to unity" (§817). Following canon 751 of the Codex Iuris Canonici, the *Catechism*, like Aquinas, defines "schism" as "the refusal of submission to the Roman Pontiff or of communion with the members of the Church subject to him" (§2089).

18 Aquinas, *Summa*, 2-2.39.2.

19 Aquinas, *Summa*, 2-2.39.2, ad 3.

20 Aquinas, *Summa*, 2-2.39.4, *sed contra*.

21 Cf. Dennis T. Olson, *Numbers* (Louisville, Ky.: John Knox, 1996), 101–10, although Olson does not use the word "schism." Referring to Gregory of Nyssa's *Life of Moses* as well as Martin Luther, Olson, from a Protestant perspective, concludes that "the total witness of Numbers suggests communities of faith ought to honor their leaders and respect certain divisions of functions between lay people and ordained clergy. But community leaders also need to be open to their own sinfulness and to listen to voices of potential wisdom and guidance. Problems in either case, whether among leaders or followers, arise when envy, self-exaltation and personal attack take over from a genuine concern for obedience to God's will and the well-being of the entire community" (108).

22 Aquinas, *Summa*, 2-2.39.4, ad 3; see Gratian, *Decretum*, 2.23.5.44.

23 Aquinas, *Summa*, 2-2.39.1.

24 Aquinas, *Summa*, 3.61.1, *sed contra*, citing Augustine, *Contra Faustum*, 19.11.

25 Aquinas, *Summa*, 3.60.4.

26 Aquinas, *Summa*, 3.82.1.

27 Aquinas, *Summa*, 3.60.2, *sed contra*.

28 Aquinas, *Summa*, 3.79.1, citing Augustine, *In Ioan. Evang.*, 26.17. Aquinas notes that Augustine, praising the aptness of the sign of bread and wine, calls the Eucharist the "sign of unity" and "bond of charity" (3.79.1, citing Augustine, *In Ioan. Evang.*, 26.13).

29 See Aquinas, *Summa*, 3.79.4.

30 Aquinas, *Summa*, 3.82.1, ad 2.

31 Aquinas, *Summa*, 3.82.1; cf. 3.83.1, ad 3: "The priest also bears Christ's image, in whose person and by whose power he pronounces the words of consecration."

32 Aquinas, *Summa*, 3.83.1. For further discussion, see Levering, *Christ and the Catholic Priesthood*.

33 Aquinas, *Summa*, 3.83.4.

34 Aquinas, *Summa*, 3.8.6.

35 Aquinas, *Summa*, 3.8.6.

36 Aquinas, *Summa*, 3.83.3, ad 8.

37 Aquinas observes that all human beings belong to Christ's body at least potentially, because Christ died for all: "Those who are unbaptized though not actually in the Church, are in the Church potentially. And this potentiality is rooted in two things—first and principally, in the power of Christ, which is sufficient for the salvation of the whole human race; secondly, in free-will." *Summa*, 3.8.3, ad 1.

38 Henri de Lubac, *Corpus Mysticum: The Eucharist and the Church in the Middle Ages; Historical Survey*, trans. Gemma Simmonds with Richard Price and Christopher Stephens, ed. Laurence Paul Hemming and Susan Frank Parsons (Notre Dame, Ind.: University of Notre Dame Press, 2006), 260. See also John Paul II's encyclical *Ecclesia de Eucharistia*, chap. 2, as well as the Second Vatican Council's Dogmatic Constitution on the Church, *Lumen Gentium*, §3, in Norman P. Tanner, ed., *Decrees of the Ecumenical Councils*, vol. 2, *Trent to Vatican II* (Washington, D.C.: Georgetown University Press, 1990), 850.

Chapter 7

1 Aquinas, *Summa*, 2-2.41.1; cf. 2-2.41.2. Discussing the culpability attached to strife, Aquinas observes, "It is a venial sin, if a slight movement of hatred or vengeance obtrude itself, or if he does not much exceed moderation in defending himself: but it is a mortal sin if he makes for his assailant with the fixed intention of killing him, or inflicting grievous harm on him" (2-2.41.1). Strife differs from hatred in that

> strife intends a public quarrel, whereas hatred can be satisfied with secretly inflicting harm.

2 Quoted by Aquinas in *Summa*, 2-2.41.2, obj. 2–4.

3 See Aquinas, *Summa*, 2-2.42.1.

4 Second Vatican Council, *Gaudium et Spes*, in *Decrees of the Ecumenical Councils*, vol. 2, *Trent to Vatican II*, ed. Norman P. Tanner (Washington, D.C.: Georgetown University Press, 1990), 78§5 (p. 1126).

5 Second Vatican Council, *Gaudium et Spes*, 79§4 (p. 1127).

6 Second Vatican Council, *Gaudium et Spes*, 79§4 (p. 1127).

7 See *Catechism of the Catholic Church*, §§2306–17.

8 Second Vatican Council, *Gaudium et Spes*, 78§3 (pp. 1125–26).

9 Hannah Arendt, *The Promise of Politics*, ed. Jerome Kohn (New York: Schocken, 2005), 137–38.

10 Arendt, *Promise of Politics*, 50. Regarding Constantine's influence, Stanley Hauerwas argues that "with Constantinianism the true church becomes invisible because now it is assumed that God is governing the world through Constantine. As a result, peace is turned into an ideal rather than a practice constitutive of the church. Correlatively, Christians now look for sources of moral knowledge other than the Scriptures and, in particular, the teachings of Jesus. Christians begin to think the primary moral question is 'What would happen if everyone acted like that?' no longer remembering that Christians should ask, 'How must we act as disciples of Christ?'" Hauerwas, "Explaining Christian Nonviolence: Notes for a Conversation with John Milbank," in *Must Christianity Be Violent*, 175. A more nuanced perspective, showing how the church remained critically distinct from the empire and addressing the medieval situation as well, is provided by Rémi Brague, *The Law of God: The Philosophical History of an Idea*, trans. Lydia G. Cochrane (Chicago: University of Chicago Press, 2007), 128–45.

1 For a careful reading of Yoder's work (as well as of Hauerwas' work in relation to Yoder's), see Hays, *Moral Vision of the New Testament*, 239–66. Hays' chapter on "Violence in Defense of Justice" (316–46) treats many of the same biblical texts canvassed by Yoder and by Aquinas, and concludes that "Yoder and Hauerwas are . . . on firm ground in their normative arguments against violence" (340). In a recent essay, Allen Verhey defends a doctrine of just war in response to Hays: see Verhey, "Neither Devils nor Angels: Peace, Justice, and Defending the Innocent; A Response to Richard Hays," in *The Word Leaps the Gap: Essays on Scripture and Theology in Honor of Richard B. Hays*, ed. J. Ross Wagner, C. Kavin Rowe, and A. Katherine Grieb (Grand Rapids: Eerdmans, 2008), 599–625.

12 For a contemporary theology of just war that largely accords with my perspective here, see Bell, *Just War*. Although Bell does not undertake exegesis of the relevant biblical passages, his book offers a profound analysis of just war as an act of charity, of how the traditional criteria of just war can be met today, and of the particular communal practices that are necessary to engage in a just war.

13 I focus on their interpretation of Scripture because, as Hauerwas says, "pacifists cannot let their understanding of Christian nonviolence be determined by what we are against. . . . The very phrase 'Christian nonviolence' cannot help but suggest that peace is 'not violence.' Yet a peace that is no more than 'not violence' surely cannot be the peace that is ours in Christ" (Hauerwas, "Explaining Christian Nonviolence," 173). In this vein Hauerwas explains Yoder's contribution: "What made, and continues to make, Yoder's work so significant for me was his refusal to make 'pacifism' a position, an implication, derived from more determinative theological claims. You simply cannot find in Yoder any account of 'pacifism' that can be abstracted from his Christology, eschatology, ecclesiology, or understanding of the Christian life" (174).

14 See John Howard Yoder, *The Politics of Jesus: Vicit Agnus Noster*, 2nd ed. (Grand Rapids: Eerdmans, 1994). Cf. Yoder, "See How They Go with Their Face to the Sun," in *For the Nations: Essays Evangelical and Public* (Grand Rapids: Eerdmans, 1997), 51–78; this essay is found also in his posthumous collection *The Jewish-Christian Schism Revisited*, ed. Michael G. Cartwright and Peter Ochs (Grand Rapids: Eerdmans, 2003), 183–202, with valuable commentary by Peter Ochs (203–4). See also John Howard Yoder, *Christian Attitudes to War, Peace, and Revolution*, ed. Theodore J. Koontz and Andy Alexis-Baker (Grand Rapids: Brazos, 2009). I critique Yoder's approach to Ezra and Nehemiah in my introduction to Levering, *Ezra and Nehemiah* (Grand Rapids: Brazos, 2007).

15 Yoder, "See How They Go," 53.

16 Yoder, "See How They Go," 76–77.

17 See Yoder, "See How They Go," 71. See also Yoder, *Politics of Jesus*, 76–88, as well as James Turner Johnson's discussion of Gerhard von Rad's *Holy War in Ancient Israel* (German 1958; Grand Rapids: Eerdmans, 1991), in Johnson, *The Holy War Idea in Western and Islamic Traditions* (University Park: Pennsylvania State University Press, 1997), 34. For an argument that the wars in the book of Joshua fit with just war doctrine, see Richard S. Hess, "War in the Hebrew Bible: An Overview," in *War in the Bible and Terrorism in the Twenty-First Century*, ed. Richard S. Hess and Elmer A. Martens (Winona Lake, Ind.: Eisenbrauns, 2008), 28–30.

18 Yoder, "Jesus the Jewish Pacifist," in *The Jewish-Christian Schism Revisited*, 69-89, at 71. Regarding the later Jews, Yoder states, "Jews expect and accept minority status. They deny ultimate loyalty to any local nation or regime, which is what war presupposes, while they provisionally accept its administration. They look on past and present righteous violence and religious nationalism, including that in their own ancient history, as mistaken. . . . In sum: for over a millennium the Jews of the diaspora were the closest thing to the ethic of Jesus existing on any significant scale anywhere in Christendom" ("Jesus the Jewish Pacifist," 81–82). For analysis of biblical texts, especially Old Testament texts, from a Mennonite/pacifist perspective, see Elmer A. Martens, "Toward Shalom: Absorbing the Violence," in Hess and Martens, *War in the Bible*, 33–57; Ben C. Ollenburger, "The Concept of 'Warrior God' in Peace Theology," in *Essays on Peace Theology and Witness*, ed. Willard Swartley (Elkhart, Ind.: Institute of Mennonite Studies, 1988), 112–27. For specific engagement with Isaiah, especially as regards the relationship of Israel's kings to the Messiah, see M. Daniel Carroll R., "Impulses toward Peace in a Country at War: The Book of Isaiah between Realism and Hope," in Hess and Martens, *War in the Bible*, 59–78. Carroll argues for a largely realized eschatology that rules out violence (cf. 78). Jin Hee Han argues that the prophets and the wisdom literature undercut the Old Testament's otherwise terrifying portrait of God and violence: see Han, "Dethroning Violence and Terror: An Undercurrent in the Hebrew Bible," in *Surviving Terror: Hope and Justice in a World of Violence*, ed. Victoria Lee Erickson and Michelle Lim Jones (Grand Rapids: Brazos Press, 2002), 66–86.

19 Yoder, "Jesus the Jewish Pacifist," 72.

20 Cf. Stanley Hauerwas, "McInerny Did It, or Should a Pacifist Read Murder Mysteries?" in *Recovering Nature: Essays in Natural Philosophy, Ethics, and Metaphysics in Honor of Ralph McInerny*, ed. Thomas Hibbs and John O'Callaghan (Notre Dame, Ind.: University of Notre Dame Press, 1999), 170–71.

21 Yoder, "Jesus the Jewish Pacifist," 73.

22 Yoder, "Jesus the Jewish Pacifist," 74. For discussion of Constantinianism and its defenders see also Yoder, *Politics of Jesus*, 135–36, 149–58; Yoder, *Christian Attitudes*, 42–74. Following Hendrikus Berkhof's *Christ and the Powers* (Scottdale, Pa.: Herald, 1962), Yoder observes that for Paul "the very existence of the church is its primary task. It is in itself a proclamation of the lordship of Christ to the powers from whose dominion the church has begun to be liberated. The church does not attack the powers; this Christ has done. The church concentrates upon not being

seduced by them. By existing the church demonstrates that their rebellion has been vanquished." *Politics of Jesus*, 150.

23 For discussion, see the commentary by Peter Ochs and Michael Cartwright in Yoder, *Jewish-Christian Schism Revisited*. See also Arne Rasmusson, "The Politics of Diaspora: The Post-Christendom Theologies of Karl Barth and John Howard Yoder," in Jones, Hütter, and Ewell, *God, Truth, and Witness*, 103–11; Daniel Boyarin, *A Radical Jew: Paul and the Politics of Identity* (Berkeley: University of California Press, 1994); Jonathan Boyarin and Daniel Boyarin, *Powers of Diaspora: Two Essays on the Relevance of Jewish Culture* (Minneapolis: University of Minnesota Press, 2002).

24 Yoder, "Jesus the Jewish Pacifist," 74. Yoder takes seriously just-war doctrine, but he argues at length that it is not practicable. The irony, in Yoder's view, is that whereas just-war doctrine seems to be a more realistic and practical option than is pacifism, in fact just-war doctrine turns out to be impossible to put into practice. For Yoder on just-war doctrine, see his *When War Is Unjust: Being Honest in Just-War Thinking*, 2nd ed. (Maryknoll, N.Y.: Orbis, 1996), with a foreword by the Lutheran theologian Charles P. Lutz and an afterword by Drew Christiansen.

25 Yoder, *Politics of Jesus*, 2.

26 See Yoder, *Politics of Jesus*, 32. For Jesus on the jubilee year, see Yoder, *Politics of Jesus*, 60–75, largely following André Trocmé, *Jesus and the Nonviolent Revolution* (Scottdale, Pa.: Herald, 1973).

27 Yoder, *Politics of Jesus*, 38–39. As Yoder puts it, interpreting Luke 6:32-36 and Matthew 5:43-48, "Because God does not discriminate, his disciples are called upon likewise not to discriminate in choosing the objects of their love." *Politics of Jesus*, 117.

28 Yoder, *Politics of Jesus*, 46.

29 Yoder, *Politics of Jesus*, 51. The task of Christians is to live out this realized eschatology in the still-fallen world. With somewhat less nuance, John Dear sets forth this vocation: "Jesus was the greatest practitioner of nonviolence in the history of the world. In our times of total violence, global warming, and perpetual war, he offers good news at every level—personally, communally, socially, economically, spiritually, and politically. He points to a way out, a way forward, a way toward a new world of peace." Dear, *Put Down Your Sword: Answering the Gospel Call to Creative Nonviolence* (Grand Rapids: Eerdmans, 2008), ix.

30 Yoder, *Politics of Jesus*, 52. Yoder points out that in at least two cases, other Jews in Jesus' time adopted the "nonviolent resistance" that Jesus modeled: see *Politics of Jesus*, 89–92, following Josephus.

31 Yoder, *Politics of Jesus*, 96. Yoder notes that one needs to examine both Jesus' "one-on-one forgiving relationships" and "the social-institutional

community-creating aspect of Jesus' ministry" (*Politics of Jesus*, 108n16). See also Yoder, *Politics of Jesus*, 120–28, for discussion of the participation of Jesus' followers in his suffering. As Hauerwas puts it, "If the church is not peace, then the world does not have an alternative to violence. But if the church is not such an alternative, then what we believe as Christians is clearly false. For when all is said and done, the question of peace is the question of truth and why the truth that is ours in Christ makes possible a joyfulness otherwise unobtainable." Hauerwas, "Explaining Christian Nonviolence," 176.

32 Yoder, *Politics of Jesus*, 194.

33 Yoder, *Politics of Jesus*, 198.

34 Yoder, *Politics of Jesus*, 209. Regarding Romans 13, Yoder notes that "predominant traditions of interpretation seek to find support in this text for a view of government and of the Christian's obligation to it which can include the obligation to participate in war. In this mainstream tradition, which has prevailed in the churches since Constantine, Romans 13 and other texts like it stand in tension with Matthew 5. This is said alike by Protestants and Catholics, by conservative and liberal theologies. They then conclude that in the tension between these two kinds of obligations or two kinds of statements, the duties of Romans 13 take precedence in the social realm and the duties of Matthew 5 in the personal one. Then it is easy to turn the interpretation back on one's interlocutor and to say that the pacifist is one who gives precedence to the personal realm over social obligation, preferring Jesus to Paul or eschatology to responsibility" (*Politics of Jesus*, 210). As we have seen, Yoder denies that "the imperatives of Matthew 5 and Romans 13 are actually contradictory" (*Politics of Jesus*, 210). Richard Hays argues briefly in favor of Yoder's interpretation of Romans 13 in *Moral Vision of the New Testament*, 248, 330–31. For an interpretation that diverges from Yoder's by emphasizing Paul's appreciation for temporal government, see Seyoon Kim, *Christ and Caesar: The Gospel and the Roman Empire in the Writings of Paul and Luke* (Grand Rapids: Eerdmans, 2008), 40–43.

35 Yoder, *Politics of Jesus*, 210. See also John Howard Yoder, *The War of the Lamb: The Ethics of Nonviolence and Peacemaking*, ed. Glen Stassen, Mark Thiessen Nation, and Matt Hamsher (Grand Rapids: Brazos, 2010).

36 With regard to the placement of this question on war within the discussion of the sins against charity, Gregory M. Reichberg observes that of the great medieval theologians, only Aquinas and Alexander of Hales devote a special question to the topic of war. In contrast to Aquinas, Alexander of Hales discusses war among the laws of punishment. While

Aquinas places war among the sins against charity, however, Reichberg finds that "Thomas seems to exhibit much less worry about the spiritual dangers of war than does, for example, St. Augustine." Reichberg, "Is There a 'Presumption against War' in Aquinas's Ethics?" *Thomist* 66 (2002), 366. See also Frederick Russell, *The Just War in the Middle Ages* (Cambridge: Cambridge University Press, 1975); Reichberg, "Aquinas on Defensive Killing: A Case of Double Effect?" *Thomist* 69 (2005): 367–68.

37 In "Thomas Aquinas between Just War and Pacifism," *Journal of Religious Ethics* 38 (2010): 219–41, Gregory Reichberg points out that Gratian's *Decretum*, which Aquinas knew well, takes up many of the same biblical passages in part 2, causa 23. Among the biblical texts cited by Aquinas, Gratian discusses (with commentary from Augustine) Matthew 5:39, 7:12, and 26:52; Exodus 20:8; 2 Corinthians 10:4; and Joshua 8:2. See the English translation (by Peter Haggenmacher and Robert Andrews) of causa 23 in *The Ethics of War: Classic and Contemporary Readings*, ed. Gregory M. Reichberg, Henrik Syse, and Endre Begby (Oxford: Blackwell, 2006), 109–24. For further discussion of Gratian's contribution, see Russell, *Just War*, 55–85. Reichberg's article ably critiques Richard Miller's "Aquinas and the Presumption against Killing and War," *Journal of Religion* 82 (2002): 173–204.

38 In "Thomas Aquinas between Just War and Pacifism," Reichberg makes a helpful distinction between the permissibility of just war and just war as a virtue in the *secunda-secundae* of the *Summa Theologiae*. Reichberg explains that "while he [Aquinas] had good reason to discuss the *permissibility* of just war in the *quaestiones* on charity (in order, specifically, to show how waging war is not *per se* inconsistent with charity, in contradistinction to schism, brawling, sedition, etc.), the positive account of just war as a *virtue* was taken up only later, apropos of two natural dispositions: military prudence (q. 50, a. 4) and battlefield courage (q. 123, a. 5)" (225). For Aquinas' familiarity with knighthood, both as regards its ideals and its reality, see Edward A. Synan, "St. Thomas Aquinas and the Profession of Arms," *Medieval Studies* 50 (1988): 404–37.

39 Aquinas, *Summa*, 2-2.40.4. Here one might consider John Milbank's claim that pacifism goes against an intuition embedded in human nature as created: "For the impulse to protect the innocent is rooted in our animality, embodiment, and finitude. There is an analogy here to Bernard Williams' insistence that ethics should not be so counterintuitive or counternaturalistic as to challenge our natural impulse always to save our own nearest and dearest first in the event of a common catastrophe." See Milbank, "Violence: Double Passivity," in *Must Christianity Be Violent*, 196.

40 For discussion of how Aquinas augments Augustine's theology of just war by means of the notion of the common good, see Bell, *Just War*, 47. On Aquinas' theology of the common good and political theory, see Mary M. Keys, *Aquinas, Aristotle, and the Promise of the Common Good* (Cambridge: Cambridge University Press, 2006); and Richard A. Crofts, "The Common Good in the Political Theory of Thomas Aquinas," *Thomist* 37 (1973): 155–73.

41 Aquinas, *Summa*, 2-2.40.4.

42 Aquinas, *Summa*, 2-2.40.2, ad 2.

43 Aquinas, *Summa*, 2-2.40.2, ad 3. For an exploration of the meaning of warfare for secular nation-states, from a pacifist perspective, see William T. Cavanaugh, "'Killing in the Name of God,'" *New Blackfriars* 85 (2004): 510–26. Cavanaugh argues that God alone can take life, and that in Christ Jesus God takes on himself the punishment due in retributive justice. As he says, "If the killing of Christ does not put an end to killing, then it is difficult to see how the cross could be construed as a victory" (523). For a similar viewpoint, indebted to Yoder, see Michael Hanby, "War on Ash Wednesday: A Brief Christological Reflection," *New Blackfriars* 84 (2003): 168–78.

44 Aquinas, *Summa*, 2-2.40.3, obj. 3.

45 Aquinas, *Summa*, 2-2.40.3, obj. 1.

46 Aquinas, *Summa*, 2-2.40.3.

47 Aquinas, *Summa*, 2-2.40.3.

48 Aquinas, *Summa*, 2-2.40.3.

49 Aquinas, *Summa*, 2-2.40.3, citing Ambrose, *De Offic.* 1.29. On the just soldier, see also *Summa*, 2-2.44.6, ad 2. See also Bell, *Just War*, 162–63, 166–67, 175–82, 203–7.

50 Aquinas, *Summa*, 2-2.40.1. Aquinas' *Commentary on the Psalms* breaks off at Psalm 54, but it is worth noting that, as Thomas Ryan says, "Thomas conceives of the Psalms as a sort of map that charts out the human journey to salvation that begins with penance, continues with progress, and concludes with praise." Ryan, *Thomas Aquinas as Reader of the Psalms* (Notre Dame, Ind.: University of Notre Dame Press, 2000), 21. Aquinas accepts the division of the Psalms into three sets of fifty, with Psalm 82 belonging to the set devoted to justice.

51 Yoder, "Jesus the Jewish Pacifist," 74.

52 Aquinas, *Summa*, 2-2.40.1.

53 Aquinas, *Summa*, 2-2.40.1.

54 Aquinas, *Summa*, 2-2.40.1. As Verhey puts the same point, "Those who are charged with protecting the innocent should not, on the pretext of either piety or pity, renege on their political obligations, under God, to do justice. Love for enemies is not inconsistent with a concern for—or

participation in—maintaining stability and justice in the land. The violence involved in maintaining justice is indeed a mark of the 'not yet' character of our world, but it is not exercised to 'avenge yourselves' but to protect the innocent, and it is not a reason for either rulers or Christians—whether rulers or subjects—to renege on their political vocations." Verhey, "Neither Devils nor Angels," 615. See also Bell, *Just War*, 240–43.

55 Responding to Hays, Verhey argues that Augustine "was right . . . to resist reading Matthew 5:39 as an unexceptionable moral rule" (Verhey, "Neither Devils nor Angels," 605). Verhey points out Jesus' own resistance of evildoers (John 2:13-16, John 18:23) as well as the fact that Jesus' antitheses generally do not serve for Jesus as unexceptionable moral rules. He also notes that against the Manichean Faustus, "Augustine emphasized that the Old Testament law had not been discarded or contradicted by Christ's teaching," so that Matthew 5:39 rejects not violent resistance per se but rather "an interpretation of the law that was satisfied with a vengeful spirit as long as revenge stopped at the boundary of 'an eye for an eye'" (607, cf. 613). Augustine only allows defense of others, whereas Aquinas affirms self-defense so long as the intention is to defend oneself rather than to harm another. See also C. S. Lewis, "Why I Am Not a Pacifist," in *The Weight of Glory and Other Addresses*, ed. Walter Hooper (New York: Macmillan, 1980), 49–50; and Timothy P. Jackson, *The Priority of Love: Christian Charity and Social Justice* (Princeton, N.J.: Princeton University Press, 2003), 123–26, 152.

56 Thus John Milbank comments, "Standing aloof, not intervening when you might . . . is *also* an act: it *opposes* the violent person by violently leaving him to his violence and not trying to stop him in his tracks. Contrariwise, it *is* important actively and chivalrously to oppose violence: for example, to stop someone from going as far as murder, even if one thereby kills him." Milbank, "Violence," 199.

57 Aquinas, *Summa*, 2-2.40.1, ad 3.

58 Aquinas, *Summa*, 2-2.40.2, *sed contra*.

59 Aquinas, *Summa*, 2-2.40.1, obj. 2. For analysis of Romans 12–13 as focused on the rejection of vengeance and the promotion of justice for the vulnerable, see Verhey, "Neither Devils nor Angels," 615.

60 Brendan Byrne comments that in Paul's view, peace "may not always be possible, since peace requires the cooperation of both parties involved. Hence a double qualification brings a note of realism into the high ideal: 'If possible, so far as it depends upon you.'" Byrne, *Romans* (Collegeville, Minn.: Liturgical Press, 1996), 381.

61 For exegetical discussion of Romans 12 from a pacifist perspective, see Gordon Zerbe, "Paul's Ethic of Nonretaliation and Peace," in *The Love of*

Enemy and Nonretaliation in the New Testament, ed. Willard M. Swartley (Louisville, Ky.: Westminster/John Knox, 1992), 177–222.

62 Aquinas, *Summa*, 2-2.40.1, ad 2. Aquinas discusses self-defense in 2-2.64.7; for the difficulties that commentators have had in interpreting this text, see Jose Rojas, "St. Thomas' Treatise on Self-Defense Revisited," in *Recherches de Théologie Ancienne et Médiévale, Supplementa* 1, *Thomistica*, ed. E. Manning (Leuven: Peeters, 1995), 89–123.

63 Aquinas, *Summa*, 2-2.40.1, ad 2.

64 Aquinas, *Summa*, 2-2.40.1, ad 3. On just intention in just-war doctrine in light of the common good, see also Joseph E. Capizzi, "War and International Order," *Communio* 31 (2004): 280–301.

65 Augustine, *De Civ. Dei*, 19.12, quoted in Aquinas, *Summa*, 2-2.40.1.

66 Aquinas, *Summa*, 2-2.40.2, obj. 3.

67 Aquinas, *Summa*, 2-2.40.2.

68 Aquinas, *Summa*, 2-2.40.2. For discussion from a just-war perspective, see Darrell Cole, "Just War, Penance, and the Church," *Pro Ecclesia* 11 (2002): 315.

69 Aquinas, *Summa*, 2-2.40.2, ad 4.

70 Aquinas, *Summa*, 2-2.40.2, ad 1. As Verhey rightly remarks, "Jesus consistently rejected violence as a messianic strategy, as a means to achieve the good future of God. . . . In memory of Jesus and in hope, the church will be suspicious of violence." Verhey, "Neither Devils nor Angels," 619.

71 Aquinas, *Summa*, 2-2.124.2, and 2-2.124.2, ad 2.

72 See Aquinas, *Summa*, 1-2.94.2: "Man has a natural inclination to know the truth about God, and to live in society: and in this respect, whatever pertains to this inclination belongs to the natural law." See also *Summa*, 2-2.59.1, ad 1, where Aquinas distinguishes between "legal justice" and "divine justice" so as to make the point that while all sin is against God, nonetheless injustice includes the ways in which sins violate the common good or violate the good of a neighbor; as well as 2-2.26.4: "God is loved as the principle of good, on which the love of charity is founded; while man, out of charity, loves himself by reason of his being a partaker of the aforesaid good, and loves his neighbor by reason of his fellowship in that good." For discussion see Bell, *Just War*; Keys, *Aquinas, Aristotle*; Michael Sherwin, "St. Thomas and the Common Good," 307–28.

73 Aquinas, *Summa*, 2-2.40.2, and 2-2.40.2, ad 4.

74 Aquinas, *Summa*, 2-2.40.2. Here Aquinas has in view the distinction between the church on earth and the church in heaven. For the argument that Christian pacifism conflates the two by means of "an extremely non-activist sense of the inauguration of the Kingdom," see Christopher J. Insole, *The Politics of Human Frailty: A Theological Defense of Political Liberalism* (Notre Dame, Ind.: University of Notre Dame

Press, 2004), 121–22. See also Verhey's observation that the cross is both an image "of Christ's suffering and of his nonresistance to his own suffering" and "an image of his solidarity with those who suffer, his identification with those who are least, with the poor and oppressed, with other victims of injustice and violence and those who remain vulnerable in this sad world." Verhey, "Neither Devils nor Angels," 617.

75 Yoder, *The Politics of Jesus*, 210.

76 In arguing against revenge and in urging Christians to "costly acts of nonretaliation," Miroslav Volf distances himself from nonviolence but holds nonetheless that particular military conflicts must not receive Christian legitimation. He states, "Tyrants may need to be taken down from their thrones and the madmen stopped from sowing desolation. . . . It may also be that measures which involve preparation for the use of violent means will have to be taken to prevent tyrants and madmen from ascending to power in the first place or to keep the plethora of ordinary kinds of perpetrators that walk our streets from doing their violent work. . . . But if one decides to put on soldier's gear instead of carrying one's cross, one should not seek legitimation in the religion that worships the crucified Messiah. For there, the blessing is given not to the violent but to the meek (Matt 5:5). There are Christians who have a hard time resisting the temptation to seek religious legitimation for their (understandable) need to take up the sword. If they give in to this temptation, they should forego all attempts to exonerate their version of Christian faith from complicity in fomenting violence." Volf, *Exclusion and Embrace: A Theological Exploration of Identity, Otherness, and Reconciliation* (Nashville: Abingdon, 1996), 306. If tyrants and other criminals should be opposed by violent means, can Christians undertake such opposition with "religious legitimation" in any sense, or have such Christians abandoned the blessing that "is given not to the violent but to the meek"? What is needed is a more differentiated understanding of "religious legitimation" and of what is being legitimized. Bradley Lewis observes in this regard that "the notion of the common good seems just the sort of idea one needs to explain the need for and legitimacy of state institutions without investing them with exaggerated 'meaning,'" and he finds that modern states continue to be intelligible by reference to the common good. Lewis, "Can a Christian Be a Democrat? A (Devoted) Member of the *Polis*? Or, The Common Good and the Modern State," in *Love Alone Is Credible: Hans Urs von Balthasar as Interpreter of the Catholic Tradition*, ed. David L. Schindler (Grand Rapids: Eerdmans, 2008), 1:345–48. See also Russell Hittinger, "The Problem of the State in *Centesimus Annus*," *Fordham International Law Journal* 15 (1991–1992): 952–96. For examination of the distinction

between the body politic and the body of Christ, see Pope Benedict XVI, *Deus Caritas Est*, esp. §§26–29.

77 See Bell's concluding section, "Just War as Witness," in Bell, *Just War*, 242–43; as well as Bell's reflections on just war as discipleship on 27–36.

78 See Aquinas, *Summa*, 3.62.5.

79 For further reflection along these lines, see especially G. E. M. Anscombe, "War and Murder: The Use of Violence by Rulers," in *Ethics, Religion and Politics* (Oxford: Blackwell, 1981), 51–61. See also Keys' reflections on the distinction between the acquired and infused moral virtues, in Keys, *Aquinas, Aristotle*, 234–35. See also Josef Pieper, *The Four Cardinal Virtues*, trans. Daniel F. Coogan (Notre Dame, Ind.: University of Notre Dame Press, 1966), 117–21.

80 See, most recently, Pontifical Council for Justice and Peace, *Compendium of the Social Doctrine of the Church* (Washington, D.C.: USCCB Publishing, 2005), chap. 11, esp. §§500–505 (pp. 217–19).

Chapter 8

1 See Aquinas, *Summa*, 2-2.31.2, *sed contra*.

2 See Aquinas, *Summa*, 2-2.31.3; cf. *Summa*, 2-2.26, on the order of charity.

3 Aquinas, *Summa*, 2-2.31.3. In this vein Aquinas interprets Luke 14:12-14, where Jesus says to his host at a banquet, "When you give a dinner or a banquet, do not invite your friends or your brothers or your kinsmen or rich neighbors, lest they also invite you in return, and you be repaid. But when you give a feast, invite the poor, the maimed, the lame, the blind, and you will be blessed, because they cannot repay you. You will be repaid at the resurrection of the just." In Aquinas' view, Jesus is here warning against cupidity and insisting upon beneficence toward all, rather than ruling out our duties to our family. See *Summa*, 2-2.31.3, ad 1.

4 Hans Urs von Balthasar, *Theo-Drama: Theological Dramatic Theory*, vol. 4: *The Action*, trans. Graham Harrison (San Francisco: Ignatius, 1994; originally published in German in 1980), 299. Von Balthasar discusses Girard's *Violence and the Sacred*, trans. Patrick Gregory (Baltimore, Md.: The Johns Hopkins University Press, 1979; originally published in French in 1972), and his *Things Hidden Since the Foundation of the World*, trans. Stephen Bann and Michael Metteer (Stanford, Calif.: Stanford University Press, 1987; originally published in French in 1978). For a recent theology of the cross that ably follows Girard, see S. Mark Heim, *Saved from Sacrifice: A Theology of the Cross* (Grand Rapids: Eerdmans, 2006).

5   See René Girard, *I See Satan Fall Like Lightning*, trans. James G. Williams (Maryknoll, N.Y.: Orbis, 2001; originally published in French in 1999), 172–74.

6   Von Balthasar, *Theo-Drama*, 4:301–2.

7   Girard, *I See Satan*, 13.

8   Girard, *I See Satan*, 16.

9   Girard, *I See Satan*, 19.

10 Girard, *I See Satan*, 19.

11 Girard, *I See Satan*, 23.

12 Girard, *I See Satan*, 23.

13 Girard, *I See Satan*, 23.

14 Girard, *I See Satan*, 26.

15 Girard, *I See Satan*, 30.

16 By "Satan" Girard does not mean a distinct personal being or fallen angel; he instead means "rivalistic contagion and its consequences." Girard mistakenly thinks that traditional Christian theology affirms that "Satan has no actual being." See *I See Satan*, 45. As Girard goes on to explain, "But why doesn't Satan present himself as an impersonal principle in the same way as the scandals? Because he designates the principal consequence of the single victim mechanism, the emergence of a false transcendence and the numerous deities that represent it, Satan is always *someone*" (46; cf. 149).

17 Girard, *I See Satan*, 34, 36.

18 Girard, *I See Satan*, 41.

19 Girard, *I See Satan*, 42.

20 Girard, *I See Satan*, 142; cf. 147–50. Girard sums up his criticism of medieval and Reformation theologies of the cross: "Medieval and modern theories of redemption all look in the direction of God for the causes of the Crucifixion: God's honor, God's justice, even God's anger, must be satisfied. These theories don't succeed because they don't seriously look in the direction where the answer must lie: sinful humanity, human relations, mimetic contagion, which is the same thing as Satan. They speak much of original sin, but they fail to make the idea concrete. That is why they give an impression of being arbitrary and unjust to human beings, even if they are theologically sound" (150).

21 Girard, *I See Satan*, 191.

22 Aquinas, *Summa*, 2-2.43.1.

23 Aquinas, *Summa*, 2-2.43.1.

24 Aquinas, *Summa*, 2-2.43.1, ad 4.

25 Aquinas, *Summa*, 2-2.43.2, ad 1.

26 Aquinas, *Summa*, 2-2.43.2, ad 1.

27 Quoted by Aquinas in *Summa*, 2-2.43.4, obj. 2.

28 Quoted by Aquinas in *Summa*, 2-2.43.4, obj. 2.
29 Aquinas, *Summa*, 2-2.43.3, obj. 1.
30 See Aquinas, *Summa*, 2-2.43.3.
31 Aquinas, *Summa*, 2-2.43.3, ad 2.
32 See Augustine, *Contra Epistolam Parmen.*, 3.2, cited in Aquinas, *Summa*, 2-2.43.7.obj 1, and Augustine, *De Civ. Dei*, 1.9, in Aquinas, *Summa*, 2-2.43.7. obj. 1 and 3.
33 Quoted by Aquinas in *Summa*, 2-2.43.7, obj. 2.
34 Aquinas, *Summa*, 2-2.43.8, obj. 3.
35 Aquinas, *Summa*, 2-2.43.8.
36 Aquinas, *Summa*, 2-2.43.8, *sed contra*.
37 Aquinas, *Summa*, 2-2.43.8, ad 2.
38 Aquinas, *Summa*, 2-2.43.8, ad 2. For Aquinas' understanding of property, see, most recently, Christopher A. Franks, *He Became Poor: The Poverty of Christ and Aquinas's Economic Teachings* (Grand Rapids: Eerdmans, 2009).
39 Quoted by Aquinas in *Summa*, 2-2.43.7.
40 Aquinas, *Summa*, 2-2.43.7, ad 2.
41 Aquinas, *Summa*, 2-2.43.4, obj. 2 and 3.
42 Quoted by Aquinas in *Summa*, 2-2.43.6, obj. 1.
43 See Aquinas, *Summa*, 2-2.43.6, ad 1.
44 Aquinas, *Summa*, 2-2.43.6, ad 3.
45 Aquinas, *Summa*, 2-2.43.5, ad 2. See Edgardo A. Colón-Emeric, *Wesley, Aquinas, and Christian Perfection: An Ecumenical Dialogue* (Waco, Tex.: Baylor University Press, 2009), 108–11, 166–72.
46 Aquinas, *Summa*, 2-2.43.6, ad 2.
47 See Aquinas, *Summa*, 2-2.43.5, obj. 1 and ad 1.
48 Girard, *I See Satan*, 33.
49 Aquinas, *Summa*, 2-2.43.5, ad 1.
50 Von Balthasar, *Theo-Drama*, 4:309.
51 Von Balthasar, *Theo-Drama*, 4:309.

Conclusion

1 Pieper, *Faith, Hope, Love*, 170; Gilson's remark is from his *History of Christian Philosophy in the Middle Ages* (London: Sheed & Ward, 1955), 83.
2 See Miroslav Volf's eloquent *Free of Charge*, 61–71, 107–10.
3 Aquinas, *Summa*, 2-2.32.2. See also Hart, *Atheist Delusions*, 29–31.
4 The feminist philosopher Eva Feder Kittay argues that it is from the experience of dependence that we come to recognize "independence" as *inter*dependence. By exploring dependence, we learn that we are not

"essentially independent," but rather are essentially interdependent. This interdependence has its sustaining source, Aquinas would add, in God's gifting. See Eva Feder Kittay, *Love's Labor: Essays on Women, Equality, and Dependency* (New York: Routledge, 1999), xii; cf. Alasdair MacIntyre, *Dependent Rational Animals: Why Human Beings Need the Virtues* (Chicago: Open Court, 1999).

5   Peter Bamm, *Die Unsichtbare Flagge* (Munich: Kösel, 1952), quoted in Hannah Arendt, *Eichmann in Jerusalem: A Report on the Banality of Evil*, 2nd ed. (New York: Penguin, 1994), 232.

6   See John Chrysostom, "On Repentance and Prayer," in *On Repentance and Almsgiving*, trans. Gus George Christo (Washington, D.C.: Catholic University of America Press, 1998), 50–53. In his homily "On Repentance and Compunction" in the same volume (86–110), Chrysostom connects repentance with almsgiving.

7   Walter Brueggemann, *David's Truth in Israel's Imagination and Memory*, 2nd ed. (Minneapolis: Fortress, 2002), 60.

8   Brueggemann, *David's Truth*, 61.

9   Paul Wadell, *The Primacy of Love: An Introduction to the Ethics of Thomas Aquinas* (New York: Paulist Press, 1992), 148.

10 Hart, *Atheist Delusions*, 45.

11 Hart, *Atheist Delusions*, 237.

12 Hart, *Atheist Delusions*, 166–67, drawing upon Erich Auerbach's *Mimesis: The Representation of Reality in Western Literature*, trans. Willard R. Trask (Princeton, N.J.: Princeton University Press, 1953), 41.

13 Hart, *Atheist Delusions*, 166 (title of chap. 13). One thinks here also of C. S. Lewis' *Till We Have Faces: A Myth Retold* (New York: Harcourt Brace, 1956).

Works Cited

Abelard, Peter. *Exposition of the Epistle to the Romans*. Translated by Gerald E. Moffatt. In *A Scholastic Miscellany: Anselm to Ockham*, edited by Eugene R. Fairweather. Philadelphia: Westminster, 1956.

Alighieri, Dante. *The Divine Comedy*. Vol. 2, *Purgatory*. Translated by Mark Musa. New York: Penguin, 1985.

Allison, Dale C., Jr. *The Historical Christ and the Theological Jesus*. Grand Rapids: Eerdmans, 2009.

Anscombe, G. E. M. "War and Murder: The Use of Violence by Rulers." Chap. 6 in *Ethics, Religion and Politics*. Oxford: Blackwell, 1981.

Aquinas, Thomas. *On Charity (De Caritate)*. Translated by Lottie H. Kendzierski. Milwaukee, Wis.: Marquette University Press, 1984.

———. *On Love and Charity: Readings from the "Commentary on the Sentences of Peter Lombard."* Translated by Peter A. Kwasniewski, Thomas Bolin, and Joseph Bolin. Washington, D.C.: Catholic University of America Press, 2008.

———. *Summa Theologiae*. Translated by the Fathers of the English Dominican Province. Westminster, Md.: Christian Classics, 1981.

Arendt, Hannah. *Eichmann in Jerusalem: A Report on the Banality of Evil*. 2nd ed. New York: Penguin, 1994.

———. *The Promise of Politics*. Edited by Jerome Kohn. New York: Schocken, 2005.

Aristotle. *Nicomachean Ethics.* Translated by H. Rackham. Loeb Classical Library, vol. 73. Cambridge, Mass.: Harvard University Press, 1934.

————. *Rhetoric.* Translated by W. Rhys Roberts. In *The Basic Works of Aristotle,* edited by Richard McKeon, 1325–1451. New York: Random House, 1941.

Assmann, Jan. *Moses the Egyptian: The Memory of Egypt in Western Monotheism.* Cambridge, Mass.: Harvard University Press, 1997.

Auerbach, Erich. *Mimesis: The Representation of Reality in Western Literature.* Translated by Willard R. Trask. Princeton, N.J.: Princeton University Press, 1953.

Augustine. *City of God.* Translated by Henry Bettenson. New York: Penguin, 1984.

Ayres, Lewis. *Nicaea and Its Legacy: An Approach to Fourth-Century Trinitarian Theology.* Oxford: Oxford University Press, 2004.

————. "'Remember That You Are Catholic' (*serm.* 52.2): Augustine on the Unity of the Triune God." *Journal of Early Christian Studies* 8 (2000): 39–82.

Balthasar, Hans Urs von. *Theo-Drama: Theological Dramatic Theory.* Vol. 4, *The Action.* Translated by Graham Harrison. San Francisco: Ignatius, 1994; originally published in German in 1980.

Bamm, Peter. *Die Unsichtbare Flagge.* Munich: Kösel, 1952.

Barnes, Michel. "Augustine in Contemporary Trinitarian Theology." *Theological Studies* 56 (1995): 237–50.

Becker, Ernest. *Escape from Evil.* New York: Macmillan, 1975.

Bell, Daniel M. Jr. *Just War as Christian Discipleship: Recentering the Tradition in the Church Rather than the State.* Grand Rapids: Brazos, 2009.

Bernard of Clairvaux. *Life and Works of Saint Bernard.* Vol. 2. Edited by John Mabillon. Translated and edited by Samuel J. Eales. 4 vols. London: Burns & Oates, 1896.

Blackburn, Simon. *Being Good.* Oxford: Oxford University Press, 2001.

Bloom, Harold. *Jesus and Yahweh: The Names Divine.* New York: Riverhead, 2005.

Bobik, Joseph. "Aquinas on *Communicatio*: The Foundation of Friendship and Caritas." *Modern Schoolman* 64 (1986): 1–18.

————. "Aquinas on Friendship with God." *New Scholasticism* 60 (1986): 257–71.

Bockmuehl, Markus. *Jewish Law in Gentile Churches: Halakhah and the Beginning of Christian Public Ethics.* Grand Rapids: Baker Academic, 2000.

Boersma, Hans. *Violence, Hospitality, and the Cross: Reappropriating the Atonement Tradition.* Grand Rapids: Baker Academic, 2004.

Boyarin, Daniel. *A Radical Jew: Paul and the Politics of Identity.* Berkeley: University of California Press, 1994.

Boyarin, Jonathan, and Daniel Boyarin. *Powers of Diaspora: Two Essays on the Relevance of Jewish Culture.* Minneapolis: University of Minnesota Press, 2002.

Boyle, Leonard. *The Setting of the "Summa Theologiae" of Saint Thomas.* Toronto: Pontifical Institute of Mediaeval Studies, 1982.

Bradley, Denis J. M. "Thomas Aquinas on Weakness of the Will." In *Weakness of Will from Plato to the Present,* edited by Tobias Hoffman, 82–114. Washington, D.C.: Catholic University of America Press, 2008.

Brague, Rémi. *The Law of God: The Philosophical History of an Idea.* Translated by Lydia G. Cochrane. Chicago: University of Chicago Press, 2007.

Brown, Peter. *Authority and the Sacred: Aspects of the Christianisation of the Roman World.* Cambridge: Cambridge University Press, 1995.

Brueggemann, Walter. *David's Truth in Israel's Imagination and Memory.* 2nd ed. Minneapolis: Fortress, 2002.

———. *Theology of the Old Testament: Testimony, Dispute, Advocacy.* Minneapolis: Fortress, 1997.

Brustein, William I. *Roots of Hate: Anti-Semitism in Europe before the Holocaust.* Cambridge: Cambridge University Press, 2003.

Byrne, Brendan. *Romans.* Collegeville, Minn. Liturgical Press, 1996.

Capizzi, Joseph E. "War and International Order." *Communio* 31 (2004): 280–301.

Carroll R., M. Daniel. "Impulses toward Peace in a Country at War: The Book of Isaiah between Realism and Hope." In Hess and Martens, *War in the Bible,* 59–78.

Cartwright, Michael G. "Afterword: 'If Abraham Is Our Father . . .': The Problem of Christian Supersessionism *after* Yoder." In Yoder, *Jewish-Christian Schism Revisited,* 205–40.

Catechism of the Catholic Church. 2nd ed. Vatican City: Libreria Editrice Vaticana, 1997.

Cavanaugh , William T. *Being Consumed: Economics and Christian Desire.* Grand Rapids: Eerdmans, 2008.

―――. " 'Killing in the Name of God.' " *New Blackfriars* 85 (2004): 510–26.

―――. *The Myth of Religious Violence: Secular Ideology and the Roots of Modern Conflict.* Oxford: Oxford University Press, 2009.

―――. *Theopolitical Imagination: Discovering the Liturgy as a Political Act in an Age of Global Consumerism.* New York: T&T Clark, 2002.

Cessario, Romanus. *Christian Faith and the Theological Life.* Washington, D.C.: Catholic University of America Press, 1996.

―――. *The Godly Image: Christ and Salvation in Catholic Thought from Anselm to Aquinas.* Petersham, Mass.: St. Bede's, 1990.

―――. *Introduction to Moral Theology.* Washington, D.C.: Catholic University of America Press, 2001.

―――. *The Moral Virtues and Theological Ethics.* Notre Dame, Ind.: University of Notre Dame Press, 1991.

Chase, Kenneth R., and Alan Jacobs, eds. *Must Christianity Be Violent? Reflections on History, Practice, and Theology.* Grand Rapids: Brazos, 2003.

Chinnici, Joseph. "Reception of Vatican II in the United States." *Theological Studies* 64 (2003): 461–94.

Chrysostom, John. "On Repentance and Prayer." In *On Repentance and Almsgiving,* translated by Gus George Christo, 43–55. Washington, D.C.: Catholic University of America Press, 1998.

Clarke, W. Norris. *The Creative Retrieval of St. Thomas Aquinas: Essays in Thomistic Philosophy, New and Old.* New York: Fordham University Press, 2009.

Cole, Darrell. "Just War, Penance, and the Church." *Pro Ecclesia* 11 (2002): 313–28.

Collins Vacek, Edward. *Love, Human and Divine: The Heart of Christian Ethics.* Washington, D.C.: Georgetown University Press, 1994.

Colón-Emeric, Edgardo A. *Wesley, Aquinas, and Christian Perfection: An Ecumenical Dialogue.* Waco, Tex.: Baylor University Press, 2009.

Corrigan, Kevin. "Love of God, Love of Self, and Love of Neighbor: Augustine's Critical Dialogue with Platonism." *Augustinian Studies* 34 (2003): 97–106.

Costa, Mario, Catherine Keller, and Anne Mercedes. "Love in Times of Empire: Theopolitics Today." In *Evangelicals and Empire: Christian*

Alternatives to the Political Status Quo, edited by Bruce Ellis Benson and Peter Goodwin Heltzel, 291–305. Grand Rapids: Brazos, 2008.

Crofts, Richard A. "The Common Good in the Political Theory of Thomas Aquinas." *Thomist* 37 (1973): 155–73.

D'Arcy, Martin. *The Mind and Heart of Love.* New York: Henry Holt, 1947.

Dawkins, Richard. *The God Delusion.* Boston: Houghton Mifflin, 2006.

de Lubac, Henri. *Catholicism: Christ and the Common Destiny of Man.* Translated by Lancelot C. Sheppard and Elizabeth Englund. San Francisco: Ignatius, 1988.

———. *Corpus Mysticum: The Eucharist and the Church in the Middle Ages; Historical Survey.* Translated by Gemma Simmonds with Richard Price and Christopher Stephens. Edited by Laurence Paul Hemming and Susan Frank Parsons. Notre Dame, Ind.: University of Notre Dame Press, 2006.

Dear, John. *Put Down Your Sword: Answering the Gospel Call to Creative Nonviolence.* Grand Rapids: Eerdmans, 2008.

Dewan, Lawrence. *Wisdom, Law, and Virtue: Essays in Thomistic Ethics.* New York: Fordham University Press, 2007.

DeYoung, Rebecca Konyndyk. *Glittering Vices: A New Look at the Seven Deadly Sins and Their Remedies.* Grand Rapids: Brazos, 2009.

———. "Resistance to the Demands of Love: Aquinas on the Vice of Acedia." *Thomist* 68 (2004): 173–204.

Drake, H. A. *Constantine and the Bishops: The Politics of Intolerance.* Baltimore, Md.: The Johns Hopkins University Press, 2000.

Dulles, Avery. "Nature, Mission, and Structure of the Church." In Lamb and Levering, *Vatican II: Renewal within Tradition*, 25–36.

Emerson, Ralph Waldo. *The Essential Writings of Ralph Waldo Emerson.* Edited by Brooks Atkinson. New York: Random House, 2000.

Emery, Gilles. *Trinity, Church, and the Human Person.* Naples, Fla.: Sapientia, 2007.

Epstein, Joseph. *Envy.* New York: Oxford University Press, 2003.

Ferreira, M. Jamie. *Love's Grateful Striving.* Oxford: Oxford University Press, 2001.

Feuerbach, Ludwig. *The Essence of Christianity.* Translated by George Eliot. Amherst, N.Y.: Prometheus, 1989.

Franks, Christopher A. *He Became Poor: The Poverty of Christ and Aquinas's Economic Teachings.* Grand Rapids: Eerdmans, 2009.

Friedman, Richard Elliott. *Who Wrote the Bible?* New York: HarperCollins, 1997.

Gibbon, Edward. *The Decline and Fall of the Roman Empire.* 6 vols. New York: Random House, 1994.

Gilson, Étienne. *History of Christian Philosophy in the Middle Ages.* London: Sheed & Ward, 1955.

Girard, René. *I See Satan Fall Like Lightning.* Translated by James G. Williams. Maryknoll, N.Y.: Orbis, 2001; originally published in French in 1999.

———. *Things Hidden Since the Foundation of the World.* Translated by Stephen Bann and Michael Metteer. Stanford, Calif.: Stanford University Press, 1987; originally published in French in 1978.

———. *Violence and the Sacred.* Translated by Patrick Gregory. Baltimore, Md.: The Johns Hopkins University Press, 1979; originally published in French in 1972.

Gratian. *Decretum.* English translation by Peter Haggenmacher and Robert Andrews in *The Ethics of War: Classic and Contemporary Readings,* edited by Gregory M. Reichberg, Henrik Syse, and Endre Begby, 109–24. Oxford: Blackwell, 2006.

Green, Joel B. *Body, Soul, and Human Life: The Nature of Humanity in the Bible.* Grand Rapids: Baker Academic, 2008.

Griffiths, Paul J. *Intellectual Appetite: A Theological Grammar.* Washington, D.C.: Catholic University of America Press, 2009.

Hall, Amy Laura. *Kierkegaard and the Treachery of Love.* Cambridge: Cambridge University Press, 2002.

Han, Jin Hee. "Dethroning Violence and Terror: An Undercurrent in the Hebrew Bible." In *Surviving Terror: Hope and Justice in a World of Violence,* edited by Victoria Lee Erickson and Michelle Lim Jones, 66–86. Grand Rapids: Brazos, 2002.

Hanby, Michael. "War on Ash Wednesday: A Brief Christological Reflection." *New Blackfriars* 84 (2003): 168–78.

Harrington, Daniel J. "Why Is the Church the People of God?" In Richard, Harrington, and O'Malley, *Vatican II: The Unfinished Agenda,* 47–56.

Harrison, Carol. *Augustine: Christian Truth and Fractured Humanity.* Oxford: Oxford University Press, 2000.

Hart, David Bentley. *Atheist Delusions: The Christian Revolution and Its Fashionable Enemies.* New Haven, Conn.: Yale University Press, 2009.

————. *The Beauty of the Infinite: The Aesthetics of Christian Truth.* Grand Rapids: Eerdmans, 2003.

————. *The Doors of the Sea: Where Was God in the Tsunami?* Grand Rapids: Eerdmans, 2005.

Hauerwas, Stanley. "Explaining Christian Nonviolence: Notes for a Conversation with John Milbank." In Chase and Jacobs, *Must Christianity Be Violent,* 169–83.

————. "McInerny Did It, or Should a Pacifist Read Murder Mysteries?" In *Recovering Nature: Essays in Natural Philosophy, Ethics, and Metaphysics in Honor of Ralph McInerny,* edited by Thomas Hibbs and John O'Callaghan, 163–75. Notre Dame, Ind.: University of Notre Dame Press, 1999.

Hays, Richard B. *First Corinthians.* Louisville, Ky.: John Knox, 1997.

————. *The Moral Vision of the New Testament: Community, Cross, New Creation; A Contemporary Introduction to New Testament Ethics.* New York: HarperCollins, 1996.

Heim, S. Mark. *Saved from Sacrifice: A Theology of the Cross.* Grand Rapids: Eerdmans, 2006.

Hess, Jonathan M. *Germans, Jews and the Claims of Modernity.* New Haven, Conn.: Yale University Press, 2002.

Hess, Richard S. "War in the Hebrew Bible: An Overview." In Hess and Martens, *War in the Bible,* 19–32.

Hess, Richard S., and Elmer A. Martens, eds. *War in the Bible and Terrorism in the Twenty-First Century.* Winona Lake, Ind.: Eisenbrauns, 2008.

Hittinger, F. Russell. "The Problem of the State in *Centesimus Annus.*" *Fordham International Law Journal* 15 (1991–1992): 952–96.

————. "When It Is More Excellent to Love than to Know: The Other Side of Thomistic 'Realism.'" *Proceedings of the American Catholic Philosophical Association* 57 (1983): 171–79.

Hobbes, Thomas. *Leviathan.* Edited by Edwin Curley. Indianapolis, Ind.: Hackett, 1994.

Insole, Christopher J. *The Politics of Human Frailty: A Theological Defense of Political Liberalism.* Notre Dame, Ind.: University of Notre Dame Press, 2004.

Jackson, Timothy P. *Love Disconsoled: Meditations on Christian Charity.* Cambridge: Cambridge University Press, 1999.

————. "Must Job Live Forever? A Reply to Aquinas on Providence." *Thomist* 62 (1998): 1–39.

————. The Priority of Love: Christian Charity and Social Justice. Princeton, N.J.: Princeton University Press, 2003.

Jacobs, Alan. "Afterword." In Chase and Jacobs, Must Christianity Be Violent, 224–35.

Johnson, James Turner. The Holy War Idea in Western and Islamic Traditions. University Park: Pennsylvania State University Press, 1997.

Johnson, Kelly. The Fear of Beggars: Stewardship and Poverty in Christian Ethics. Grand Rapids: Eerdmans, 2007.

Jones, L. Gregory. "The Theological Transformation of Aristotelian Friendship in the Thought of St. Thomas Aquinas." New Scholasticism 61 (1987): 373–99.

Jones, L. Gregory, Reinhard Hütter, and C. Rosalee Velloso Ewell, eds. God, Truth, and Witness: Engaging Stanley Hauerwas. Grand Rapids: Brazos, 2005.

Julian of Norwich. Showings. Edited by Denise N. Baker. New York: W. W. Norton, 2005.

Kant, Immanuel. Critique of Practical Reason. Edited by Mary Gregor. Cambridge: Cambridge University Press, 1997.

Kass, Leon R. The Beginning of Wisdom: Reading Genesis. New York: Free Press, 2003.

Keaty, Anthony W. "Thomas's Authority for Identifying Charity as Friendship: Aristotle or John 15?" Thomist 62 (1998): 581–601.

Keenan, James. Goodness and Rightness in Thomas Aquinas's "Summa Theologiae." Washington, D.C.: Georgetown University Press, 1992.

Keller, Catherine. Face of the Deep: A Theology of Becoming. New York: Routledge, 2003.

Keys, Mary M. Aquinas, Aristotle, and the Promise of the Common Good. Cambridge: Cambridge University Press, 2006.

Kierkegaard, Søren. Works of Love: Some Christian Reflections in the Form of Discourses. Translated by Howard Hong and Edna Hong. New York: Harper & Row, 1962.

Kim, Seyoon. Christ and Caesar: The Gospel and the Roman Empire in the Writings of Paul and Luke. Grand Rapids: Eerdmans, 2008.

Kittay, Eva Feder. Love's Labor: Essays on Women, Equality, and Dependency. New York: Routledge, 1999.

Komter, Aafke E. Social Solidarity and the Gift. Cambridge: Cambridge University Press, 2005.

Kosman, L. A. "Platonic Love." In Eros, Agape, and Philia, edited by Alan Soble, 149–64. St. Paul, Minn.: Paragon House, 1989.

Kugel, James L. *The God of Old: Inside the Lost World of the Bible.* New York: Free Press, 2003.

———. *How to Read the Bible: A Guide to Scripture, Then and Now.* New York: Free Press, 2007.

Kwasniewski, Peter A. "St. Thomas, *Extasis* and Union with the Beloved." *Thomist* 61 (1997): 587–603.

Lamb, Matthew, and Matthew Levering, eds. *Vatican II: Renewal within Tradition.* Oxford: Oxford University Press, 2008.

Levenson, Jon D. *The Death and Resurrection of the Beloved Son: The Transformation of Child Sacrifice in Judaism and Christianity.* New Haven, Conn.: Yale University Press, 1993.

Levering, Matthew. *Christ and the Catholic Priesthood: Ecclesial Hierarchy and the Pattern of the Trinity.* Chicago: Hillenbrand, 2010.

———. *Christ's Fulfillment of Torah and Temple: Salvation according to Thomas Aquinas.* Notre Dame, Ind.: University of Notre Dame Press, 2002.

———. *Jewish-Christian Dialogue and the Life of Wisdom: Engagements with the Theology of David Novak.* London: Continuum, 2010.

———. Review of *Face of the Deep: A Theology of Becoming. Theological Studies* 66 (2005): 905–7.

———. *Sacrifice and Community: Jewish Offering and Christian Eucharist.* Oxford: Blackwell, 2005.

Lewis, Bradley. "Can a Christian Be a Democrat? A (Devoted) Member of the *Polis*? Or, The Common Good and the Modern State." In *Love Alone Is Credible: Hans Urs von Balthasar as Interpreter of the Catholic Tradition,* vol. 1, edited by David L. Schindler, 339–48. Grand Rapids: Eerdmans, 2008.

Lewis, C. S. *The Four Loves.* New York: Harcourt, Brace, 1960.

———. "Why I Am Not a Pacifist." In *The Weight of Glory and Other Addresses,* edited by Walter Hooper, 33–53. New York: Macmillan, 1980.

Lewis, Thomas, Fari Amini, and Richard Lannon. *A General Theory of Love.* New York: Random House, 2000.

Lütz, Manfred. "The Church, Love, and Power." In *Where Are the Helpers? Charity and Spirituality,* edited by Paul Josef Cordes, translated by Anthony J. Figueiredo and James D. Mixson. Notre Dame, Ind.: University of Notre Dame Press, 2010.

Machuga, Ric. *In Defense of the Soul: What It Means to Be Human.* Grand Rapids: Brazos, 2002.

MacIntyre, Alasdair. "Conflicts of Desire." In *Weakness of Will from Plato to the Present*, edited by Tobias Hoffman. Washington, D.C.: Catholic University of America Press, 2008.

———. *Dependent Rational Animals: Why Human Beings Need the Virtues*. Chicago: Open Court, 1999.

———. *Three Rival Versions of Moral Enquiry: Encyclopaedia, Genealogy, and Tradition*. Notre Dame, Ind.: University of Notre Dame Press, 1990.

Mack, Michael. *German Idealism and the Jew: The Inner Anti-Semitism of Philosophy and German Jewish Responses*. Chicago: University of Chicago Press, 2003.

Malloy, Christopher J. "Thomas on the Order of Love and Desire: A Development of Doctrine." *Thomist* 71 (2007): 65–87.

———. *Love of God for His Own Sake and Love of Beatitude: Heavenly Charity According to Thomas Aquinas*. Ph.D. dissertation, Catholic University of America, 2001.

Mansini, Guy. "Aristotle on Needing Friends." *American Catholic Philosophical Quarterly* 72 (1998): 405–17.

———. "Mercy 'Twice Blest.'" In *John Paul II and St. Thomas Aquinas*, edited by Michael Dauphinais and Matthew Levering. Naples, Fla.: Sapientia, 2006.

———. "*Similitudo, Communicatio*, and the Friendship of Charity in Aquinas." In *Recherches de théologie ancienne et médiévale. Supplementa* vol. 1, *Thomistica*, edited by E. Manning, 1–26. Leuven: Peeters, 1995.

Marion, Jean-Luc. *Prolegomena to Charity*. Translated by Stephen Lewis. New York: Fordham University Press, 2002; originally published in French in 1986.

Martens, Elmer A. "Toward Shalom: Absorbing the Violence." In Hess and Martens, *War in the Bible*, 33–57.

McAleer, Graham J. *Ecstatic Morality and Sexual Politics: A Catholic and Antitotalitarian Theory of the Body*. New York: Fordham University Press, 2005.

McDermott, John. "Did That Really Happen at Vatican II? Reflections on John O'Malley's Recent Book." *Nova et Vetera* 8 (2010): 425–66.

McKibben, Bill. *Deep Economy: The Wealth of Communities and the Durable Future*. New York: Times Books, 2007.

———. *The End of Nature*. New York: Random House, 1989.

————. *Maybe One: A Case for Smaller Families.* New York: Simon & Schuster, 1998.

Milbank, John. "Violence: Double Passivity." In Chase and Jacobs, *Must Christianity Be Violent,* 183–200.

Miller, Richard. "Aquinas and the Presumption against Killing and War." *Journal of Religion* 82 (2002): 173–204.

Moberly, R. W. L. "Is Monotheism Bad for You? Some Reflections on God, the Bible, and Life in the Light of Regina Schwartz's *The Curse of Cain.*" In *The God of Israel,* edited by Robert P. Gordon, 94–112. Cambridge: Cambridge University Press, 2007.

————. *The Theology of the Book of Genesis.* Cambridge: Cambridge University Press, 2009.

Murphy, Nancey. *Bodies and Souls, or Spirited Bodies?* Cambridge: Cambridge University Press, 2006.

Nussbaum, Martha C. *Upheavals of Thought: The Intelligence of Emotions.* Cambridge: Cambridge University Press, 2001.

Nygren, Anders. *Agape and Eros.* Translated by Philip S. Watson. Philadelphia: Westminster, 1953.

O'Donovan, Oliver. *The Problem of Self-Love in St. Augustine.* New Haven, Conn.: Yale University Press, 1980.

Ogbonnaya, A. O. *On Communitarian Divinity: An African Interpretation of the Trinity.* New York: Paragon House, 1994.

Ollenburger, Ben C. "The Concept of 'Warrior God' in Peace Theology." In *Essays on Peace Theology and Witness,* edited by Willard Swartley, 112–27. Elkhart, Ind.: Institute of Mennonite Studies, 1988.

Olson, Dennis T. *Numbers.* Louisville, Ky.: John Knox, 1996.

O'Malley, John. "Developments, Reforms, and Two Great Reformations: Towards an Historical Assessment of Vatican II." *Theological Studies* 44 (1983): 373–406.

————. "Reform, Historical Consciousness, and Vatican II's Aggiornamento." *Theological Studies* 32 (1971): 573–601.

————. "Vatican II: Did Anything Happen?" *Theological Studies* 67 (2006): 3–33.

————. "Vatican II: Historical Perspectives on Its Uniqueness and Interpretation." In Richard, Harrington, and O'Malley, *Vatican II: The Unfinished Agenda,* 22–32.

————. *What Happened at Vatican II.* Cambridge, Mass.: Harvard University Press, 2008.

Osborne, Thomas M. "The Augustinianism of Thomas Aquinas's Moral Theory." *Thomist* 67 (2003): 279–305.

———. *Love of Self and Love of God in Thirteenth-Century Ethics.* Notre Dame, Ind.: University of Notre Dame Press, 2005.

———. "Perfect and Imperfect Virtues in Aquinas." *Thomist* 71 (2007): 39–64.

Outka, Gene. *Agape: An Ethical Analysis.* New Haven, Conn.: Yale University Press, 1972.

Pangle, Lorraine Smith. *Aristotle and the Philosophy of Friendship.* Cambridge: Cambridge University Press, 2003.

Peters, Ted. *Sin: Radical Evil in Soul and Society.* Grand Rapids: Eerdmans, 1994.

Peterson, Erik. *Der Monotheismus als politische Problem. Ein Beitrag zur Geschichte der politischen Theologie im Imperium Romanum.* Leipzig: Jacob Hegner, 1935.

Pieper, Josef. *Faith, Hope, Love.* Translated by Richard Winston and Clara Winston. San Francisco: Ignatius, 1997.

———. *The Four Cardinal Virtues.* Translated by Daniel F. Coogan, Richard Winston, Clara Winston, and Lawrence E. Lynch. Notre Dame, Ind.: University of Notre Dame Press, 1966.

Pinckaers, Servais. "The Body of Christ: The Eucharistic and Ecclesial Context of Aquinas's Ethics." In *The Pinckaers Reader: Renewing Thomistic Moral Theology*, edited by John Berkman and Craig Steven Titus, translated by Mary Thomas Noble, Craig Steven Titus, Michael Sherwin, and Hugh Connolly, 26–45. Washington, D.C.: Catholic University of America Press, 2005.

———. *The Sources of Christian Ethics.* Translated by Mary Thomas Noble. Washington, D.C.: Catholic University of America Press, 1995.

Plato. *Symposium.* In *The Collected Dialogues of Plato including the Letters*, edited by Edith Hamilton and Huntington Cairns, translated by Michael Joyce, 527–74. Princeton, N.J.: Princeton University Press, 1961.

Pontifical Council for Justice and Peace. *Compendium of the Social Doctrine of the Church.* Washington, D.C.: USCCB Publishing, 2005.

Pope, Stephen J. *The Evolution of Altruism and the Ordering of Love.* Washington, D.C.: Georgetown University Press, 1994.

Pope Benedict XVI. *Caritas in Veritate* (encyclical). Vatican translation. Vatican City: Libreria Editrice Vaticana, 2009.

————. *Deus Caritas Est* (encyclical). Vatican translation. Boston: Pauline, 2006.

————. "A Proper Hermeneutic for the Second Vatican Council." Reprinted in Lamb and Levering, *Vatican II: Renewal within Tradition*, ix–xv.

Pope John Paul II. *Ecclesia de Eucharistia* (encyclical). Vatican translation. Boston: Pauline, 2003.

Rad, Gerhard von. *Holy War in Ancient Israel*. Grand Rapids: Eerdmans, 1991; originally published in German in 1958.

Rahner, Karl. "Towards a Fundamental Theological Interpretation of Vatican II." *Theological Studies* 40 (1979): 716–27.

Rasmusson, Arne. "The Politics of Diaspora: The Post-Christendom Theologies of Karl Barth and John Howard Yoder." In Jones, Hütter, and Ewell, *God, Truth, and Witness*, 88–111.

Ratzinger, Joseph. *Faith and the Future*. San Francisco: Ignatius, 2009; originally published in German in 1970.

Reichberg, Gregory M. "Aquinas on Defensive Killing: A Case of Double Effect?" *Thomist* 69 (2005): 341–70.

————. "Is There a 'Presumption against War' in Aquinas's Ethics?" *Thomist* 66 (2002): 337–67.

————. "Thomas Aquinas between Just War and Pacifism." *Journal of Religious Ethics* 38 (2010): 219–41.

Reinders, Hans. *Receiving the Gift of Friendship: Profound Disability, Theological Anthropology, and Ethics*. Grand Rapids: Eerdmans, 2008.

Richard, Lucien, Daniel T. Harrington, and John W. O'Malley, eds. *Vatican II: The Unfinished Agenda; A Look to the Future*. New York: Paulist Press, 1987.

Rojas, Jose. "St. Thomas' Treatise on Self-Defense Revisited." In *Recherches de théologie ancienne et medieval. Supplementa* 1, edited by E. Manning, 89–123. Leuven: Peeters, 1995.

Roy, Paul. "The Developing Sense of Community (Gaudium et Spes)." In Richard, Harrington, and O'Malley, *Vatican II: The Unfinished Agenda*, 190–202.

Russell, Frederick. *The Just War in the Middle Ages*. Cambridge: Cambridge University Press, 1975.

Ryan, Thomas. *Thomas Aquinas as Reader of the Psalms*. Notre Dame, Ind.: University of Notre Dame Press, 2000.

Rziha, John. *Perfecting Human Actions: St. Thomas Aquinas on Human Participation in Eternal Law.* Washington, D.C.: Catholic University of America Press, 2009.

Scheler, Max. *Ressentiment.* Translated by Lewis B. Coser and William W. Holdheim. Milwaukee, Wis.: Marquette University Press, 2003.

Schindler, Jeanne Heffernan. "A Companionship of *Caritas*: Friendship in St. Thomas Aquinas." In *Friendship and Politics: Essays in Political Thought,* edited by John von Heyking and Richard Avramenko, 139–62. Notre Dame, Ind.: University of Notre Dame Press, 2008.

Schlabach, Gerald W. *For the Joy Set before Us: Augustine and Self-Denying Love.* Notre Dame, Ind.: University of Notre Dame Press, 2001.

Schneider, Laurel C. *Beyond Monotheism: A Theology of Multiplicity.* London: Routledge, 2008.

———. *Re-imagining the Divine: Confronting the Backlash against Feminist Theology.* Cleveland, Ohio: Pilgrim, 1999.

Schoeck, Helmut. *Envy: A Theory of Social Behavior.* Indianapolis, Ind.: Liberty Fund, 1987.

Schwartz, Regina M. *The Curse of Cain: The Violent Legacy of Monotheism.* Chicago: University of Chicago Press, 1997.

Sen, Amartya. *Identity and Violence: The Illusion of Destiny.* New York: W. W. Norton, 2006.

Sherwin, Michael. "Aquinas, Augustine, and the Medieval Scholastic Crisis concerning Charity." In *Aquinas the Augustinian,* edited by Michael Dauphinais and Matthew Levering, 181–204. Washington, D.C.: Catholic University of America Press, 2007.

———. *By Knowledge and By Love: Charity and Knowledge in the Moral Theology of St. Thomas Aquinas.* Washington, D.C.: Catholic University of America Press, 2005.

———. "St. Thomas and the Common Good: The Theological Perspective; An Invitation to Dialogue." *Angelicum* 70 (1993): 307–28.

Silverman, Eric J. *The Prudence of Love: How Possessing the Virtue of Love Benefits the Lover.* Lanham, Md.: Lexington, 2010.

Spicq, Ceslaus. *Agape in the New Testament.* 3 vols. St. Louis, Mo.: B. Herder, 1963.

Stroumsa, Guy G. *The End of Sacrifice: Religious Transformations in Late Antiquity.* Translated by Susan Emanuel. Chicago: University of Chicago Press, 2009.

Stump, Eleonore. *Aquinas.* London: Routledge, 2003.

Synan, Edward A. "St. Thomas Aquinas and the Profession of Arms." *Medieval Studies* 50 (1988): 404–37.

Tanner, Norman P., ed. *Decrees of the Ecumenical Councils*. Vol. 2, *Trent to Vatican II*. Washington, D.C.: Georgetown University Press, 1990.

Telushkin, Joseph. *A Code of Jewish Ethics*. Vol. 1, *You Shall Be Holy*. New York: Random House, 2006.

———. *A Code of Jewish Ethics*. Vol. 2, *Love Your Neighbor as Yourself*. New York: Random House, 2009.

Tillich, Paul. *Love, Power, and Justice: Ontological Analyses and Ethical Applications*. Oxford: Oxford University Press, 1954.

Torrell, Jean-Pierre. "La charité comme amitié chez saint Thomas d'Aquin." *La Vie Spirituelle* 155 (2001): 265–83.

Trocmé, André. *Jesus and the Nonviolent Revolution*. Scottdale, Pa.: Herald, 1973.

Verhey, Allen. "Neither Devils nor Angels: Peace, Justice, and Defending the Innocent; A Response to Richard Hays." In *The Word Leaps the Gap: Essays on Scripture and Theology in Honor of Richard B. Hays*, edited by J. Ross Wagner, C. Kavin Rowe, and A. Katherine Grieb, 599–625. Grand Rapids: Eerdmans, 2008.

Vogel, Jeffrey A. "The Speed of Sloth: Reconsidering the Sin of *Acedia*." *Pro Ecclesia* 18 (2009): 50–68.

Volf, Miroslav. "Christianity and Violence." In Hess and Martens, *War in the Bible*, 1–17.

———. *The End of Memory: Remembering Rightly in a Violent World*. Grand Rapids: Eerdmans, 2006.

———. *Exclusion and Embrace: A Theological Exploration of Identity, Otherness, and Reconciliation*. Nashville: Abingdon, 1996.

———. *Free of Charge: Giving and Forgiving in a Culture Stripped of Grace*. Grand Rapids: Zondervan, 2005.

Wadell, Paul J. *Friendship and the Moral Life*. Notre Dame, Ind.: University of Notre Dame Press, 1989.

———. *The Primacy of Love: An Introduction to the Ethics of Thomas Aquinas*. New York: Paulist Press, 1992.

Wagoner, Robert E. *The Meanings of Love: An Introduction to Philosophy of Love*. Westport, Conn.: Praeger, 1997.

Wasserstein, Wendy. *Sloth*. New York: Oxford University Press, 2005.

Wenzel, S. *The Sin of Sloth: Acedia in Medieval Thought and Literature*. Chapel Hill: University of North Carolina Press, 1967.

Wielockx, Robert. *La discussion scholastique sur l'amour d'Anselme de Laon à Pierre Lombard d'après les imprimés et les inédits.* Ph.D. dissertation, Catholic University of Louvain, 1981.

Wilken, Robert Louis. "A Constantinian Bishop: St. Ambrose of Milan." In Jones, Hütter, and Ewell, *God, Truth, and Witness,* 73–87.

————. *The Spirit of Early Christian Thought: Seeking the Face of God.* New Haven, Conn.: Yale University Press, 2003.

William of St. Thierry. *The Nature and Dignity of Love.* Translated by Thomas X. Davis. Kalamazoo, Mich.: Cistercian, 1981.

Yoder, John Howard. *Christian Attitudes to War, Peace, and Revolution.* Edited by Theodore J. Koontz and Andy Alexis-Baker. Grand Rapids: Brazos, 2009.

————. *The Jewish-Christian Schism Revisited.* Edited by Michael G. Cartwright and Peter Ochs. Grand Rapids: Eerdmans, 2003.

————. *The Politics of Jesus: Vicit Agnus Noster.* 2nd ed. Grand Rapids: Eerdmans, 1994.

————. "See How They Go with Their Face to the Sun." In *For the Nations: Essays Evangelical and Public,* 51–78. Grand Rapids: Eerdmans, 1997.

————. *The War of the Lamb: The Ethics of Nonviolence and Peacemaking.* Edited by Glen Stassen, Mark Thiessen Nation, and Matt Hamsher. Grand Rapids: Brazos, 2010.

————. *When War Is Unjust: Being Honest in Just-War Thinking.* 2nd ed. Maryknoll, N.Y.: Orbis, 1996.

Zerbe, Gordon. "Paul's Ethic of Nonretaliation and Peace." In *The Love of Enemy and Nonretaliation in the New Testament,* edited by Willard M. Swartley, 177–222. Louisville, Ky.: Westminster/John Knox, 1992.

Scripture Index

General Index

Aaron, 93, 95–99, 103–4, 115, 175
Abelard, Peter, 160, 165
Abraham, 35, 49, 164
Acts of the Apostles, 2, 79, 88, 89
agape, 5, 10, 44
Akiva, Rabbi, 10
Alighieri, Dante, 73–74, 171
Allah, 34–37
Allison, Dale C., 49, 53, 167
almsdeeds, 9–10
almsgiving, 2, 22, 191
ambition, 19, 63, 67, 68, 140–41
Amini, Fari, 154
amor, 5–6
annihilation, 47–49, 56–59, 61
Anscombe, G.E.M., 188
appetite, 85–87, 89, 90, 143
Aquinas, St. Thomas: contrasted
    with Harold Bloom on hatred
    of God, 36–39; on beneficence,
    127; on discord between Paul
    and Barnabas, 79; on earthly
    and eschatological joy, 50–55,
60–62; on ecclesial peace,
83–84, 91; on envy, 67–76;
on excommunication, 101; on
hatred and rebellion against
God, 29–32; on interior and
exterior peace, 84–85, 91; on
Jesus and Pharisees on scandal,
137–39, 142; on Jesus' teaching
on peace, 87–88, 91; on peace
with God, 85–87, 91; on peacemaking, 90–91; on perfect and
imperfect peace, 88–89, 91; on
saints and scandal, 139–42; on
scandal and spiritual downfall,
127, 131–32, 142; on scandal
and the weak (passive vs. active
scandal), 135–37, 141–42; on
scandal as contagion, 133–34,
142; on schism and the liturgy,
99–101, 105; on sedition, 107;
on sloth as spiritual sorrow,
55–62; on strife, 107; on the
act of charity, 19–25; on the